Life with Father

GENDER RELATIONS
IN THE AMERICAN EXPERIENCE

Joan E. Cashin and Ronald G. Walters,
Series Editors

Margaret Creighton and Lisa Norling, eds., *Iron Men, Wooden Women:
Gender and Seafaring in the Atlantic World, 1700–1920*

Stephen M. Frank, *Life with Father: Parenthood and Masculinity
in the Nineteenth-Century American North*

Anya Jabour, *Marriage in the Early Republic:
Elizabeth and William Wirt and the Companionate Ideal*

Life with Father

PARENTHOOD AND MASCULINITY
IN THE NINETEENTH-CENTURY
AMERICAN NORTH

Stephen M. Frank

The Johns Hopkins University Press

Baltimore and London

© 1998 The Johns Hopkins University Press
All rights reserved. Published 1998
Printed in the United States of America on acid-free paper
9 8 7 6 5 4 3 2 1

The Johns Hopkins University Press
2715 North Charles Street
Baltimore, Maryland 21218-4363
The Johns Hopkins Press Ltd., London
www.press.jhu.edu

Library of Congress Cataloging-in-Publication Data
will be found at the end of this book.

A catalog record for this book is available from the British Library.

ISBN 0-8018-5855-0

For Laura and our children,
Anna and Ethan,
and
in memory of Benjamin,
who opened the window
into fatherhood

Contents

Acknowledgments

This is a study about family relationships. Although I owe much to many scholars, my first debt is to my immediate family—to Laura, Anna, and Ethan. By teaching me the meaning of fatherhood, they have helped to write this book in ways that I can only begin to acknowledge. For the warm light of their love, and for Laura's strength and friendship, I am grateful beyond measure.

My investigation of fatherhood began as a dissertation in the history department at the University of Michigan. Maris A. Vinovskis first suggested the possibility of writing about fatherhood and saw me through the various stages of researching and writing my dissertation, for which I thank him. I am grateful as well for the guidance of the other teachers at Michigan with whom I studied and worked: W. Andrew Achenbaum; Todd M. Endelman; Terrence J. McDonald; and J. Mills Thornton III. Achenbaum and McDonald, who served as members of my dissertation committee, offered useful comments and suggestions.

The close reading and critical comments of Robert L. Griswold on a penultimate draft of this work contributed significantly to its final form. I am grateful to him for his generosity of spirit and keen insights. E. Anthony Rotundo, who read an early version of portions of the text, offered valuable comments and directed me to significant source material, for which I am deeply obliged.

I owe a great deal to the staffs of the various archives and libraries with whom I consulted. I would especially like to thank the staff of the Bentley Historical Library at the University of Michigan, from which much valuable source material was drawn.

At the Johns Hopkins University Press, I am grateful to Celestia N. Ward for her careful editing of the manuscript and to Robert J. Brugger for his valuable editorial suggestions. I am indebted to Joan E. Cashin and Ronald G. Walters for their helpful comments.

On a more personal note, my parents, Morton and Bernice Frank, have patiently encouraged me to finish this book, which, I know, will be an enormous source of pride for them.

Life with Father

A Father's Care

In March 1864, Louisa Hughes of New Haven, Connecticut, and her husband, Enos, traveled to Louisville, Kentucky, to attend the birth of a grandchild. Their daughter Mary, the fifth of eight children, all grown but some still living at home, gave birth to a daughter on March 16. Toward the end of that month, the time arrived to return to New Haven. Louisa had fallen ill, however, and was not well enough to travel. Unable or unwilling to delay his departure, Enos left for New Haven without her. "Oh how I grieved to let him go from me," Louisa recorded in her diary, "but I am glad my children at home will have their Fathers care."[1]

At the age of thirteen, Edwin M. Stanton, who grew up to become Lincoln's Secretary of War, lost his father. Writing in the 1870s, Stanton's cousin, a man named Nathan Thomas, marveled at his famous relation's success in life. Stanton, Thomas said, had scaled the heights of American politics even though he was left at a tender age to "battle his way through life unaided by a father's care."[2]

A "father's care"; the phrase rings through nineteenth-century letters and diaries, and yet historians have not heard it clearly. Because of the priority given to mothers and children whenever inquiry turns to nineteenth-century domestic life, fathers have been, until quite recently, forgotten family members. There are many reasons for this inattention to fathers, not least of which is the reality of women's and children's rising status in nineteenth-century American homes. More to the point, scholarly fascination with the social and cultural construction of difference between the sexes has obscured the extent to which nineteenth-century Americans thought of parenting as a shared commitment and mutual endeavor. The tendency to overlook this common domestic ground is owed in part to an overly literal understanding of the so-called separate spheres, the ideology by which nineteenth-century Americans understood relations between the sexes. By imagining that the spheres metaphor physically divided nineteenth-century life into two arenas—a public realm for men and a private one for women—historians have tended to impose an inordinate segregation on the sexes. We have misjudged, in turn, the salience of private life in the formation of masculine identity. Fortunately, the "spheres" paradigm is in the process of being revised, with more attention being paid to the interdependence of men and women. Accordingly, we have begun to recapture the importance of men's domestic commitments, and not incidentally, an understanding of parenting in the past as an experience shared by the sexes.[3]

This study shows that throughout the last century fatherhood remained a vital component in the social definition of manhood. Precisely because of its centrality to men's lives and to the functioning of their families in the past, fatherhood opens a window on significant and heretofore little-explored parts of nineteenth-century masculine experience. My findings are stated quite simply: Notwithstanding an expanded role for mothers, fathers participated actively in child rearing, both when their children were young and as they grew older. Men and women alike were influenced by nineteenth-century domestic ideals, which placed a high premium on devotion to family life. The exercise of what contemporaries called "parental solicitude" was a social norm highly prized by both sexes. Men were repeatedly urged to combine the drive toward competitive achievement with intense love of home. I maintain that, by undertaking a "father's care," men attempted, with varying degrees of success, to reconcile these potentially conflicting gender ideals.

Not all nineteenth-century men parented in the same way, of course. Men do not now, and did not then, balance their work and family commitments identically or exercise equal authority in the family. Varying material and cultural circumstances shaped the nature and extent of paternal involvement in the nineteenth century, and in the final analysis no single model of fatherhood fit all men. The letters, diaries, and personal narratives on which this study is based document a wide range of paternal behavior and beliefs. Fathers emerge from their pages who valued, and managed at times to maintain, relations with their wives and children that were both affectionate and harmonious. Other fathers were self-centered and aloof, and still others, stiflingly overbearing. Nor did one emotional posture preclude men from adopting other modes of parenting as circumstances changed or experience warranted. Beyond the idiosyncrasies of particular families and events, however, enough fathers occupied places toward the affectionate cnd of the emotional spectrum to refute stereotypes of the starched Victorian patriarch, self-contained and presiding remotely over his family.[4] The long reassessment of patriarchal family relations that began in the eighteenth century, if not earlier, and gained momentum in the era of the American Revolution, had produced by the nineteenth century a distinctively modern form of fatherhood, one based more on spousal partnership than on patriarchal hierarchy.[5]

A number of large historical developments influenced this reconfiguration of family roles. As men were drawn toward income-producing work, the separation of home and workplace imposed real constraints on nineteenth-century fathers. To varying degrees, new modes of earning a living distanced fathers from home, imposing new responsibilities and conferring more power on mothers. Equally important, work absorbed more of men's emotional energy, thereby transforming their domestic experience. As growing numbers of men adjusted to market relations in a commercialized society, however, they did not necessarily ascribe less importance to domestic life. On the contrary, business activity often fostered the conviction that, outside of the family, the social world was a selfish and hostile arena, shot through with hypocrisy.[6] Accordingly, market-oriented work often had the ironic effect of intensifying domestic feeling. Relations with family—what men sometimes referred to as the circle of "friends" at home—came to stand in stark and often appealing contrast to business relations abroad, in the world of "strangers." Within the bounds of sentimental middle-class culture, distance did in fact make some hearts grow fonder.

However immersed men became in the world of commerce, breadwinning and "paying the bills" never encompassed all that it meant to be a father. Countervailing pressures urged men to maintain other sorts of domestic commitments even as they entered offices, workshops, and factories. The lingering weight of earlier styles of fatherhood continued to engage men in children's education and guidance. For some men, a religiously grounded ideal of Christian fatherhood retained its importance. For others, so-called companionate family ideals mediated the separation of work and domestic life. No secular norm for fatherhood prescribed a single set of duties governing the actual behavior of all men all the time, but a distinctive social type—the "family man"—emerged in the nineteenth century as a standard against which behavior was judged. This new male identity was a cultural invention of the middle class. Many attributes defined the nineteenth century's family men, including intense anxiety about the moral and material welfare of children in a rapidly changing society and the belief that mothers alone could not secure a child's future prospects.

A number of studies concur that what today we speak of as the modern American middle-class family emerged first in the years between the American Revolution and about 1830. Historians disagree, however, on whether ethnic and working-class families embraced white, Protestant, middle-class values. Similarly controversial is the extent to which actual middle-class family life adhered to or diverged from newly emergent domestic ideals.[7] Given such uncertainty, it should come as no surprise that current understandings of the status of nineteenth-century American fathers are also riddled with inconsistency. Interpretations come full circle: For the historian Mary P. Ryan, fatherhood "lost its meaning" in feminized middle-class households; according to Steven Mintz, fathers dominated Victorian homes; in Richard Sennett's late-nineteenth-century Chicago—as in Ryan's Utica, New York, several decades earlier—fathers were unable or unwilling to exercise authority.[8] Such inconsistencies suggest that the entire question of fatherhood's status in the nineteenth century needs to be rethought.

This study takes as its central problem the reconstruction of the white middle-class father's child-rearing role in the nineteenth-century American North. Variations by race, class, ethnicity, and region complicate the story told here. While detailed analysis of these differences is beyond the scope of this book, a number of observations can usefully be sketched here.

Long after the collective family economy was displaced by the domestic, child-centered, middle-class household, working-class parents and children continued to think of themselves as a work unit. Labor force participation by women and children posed a critical dilemma for working-class and immigrant fathers, who were confronted with middle-class ideals at odds with collective family effort. By embracing the sentimental, rather than economic, value of children, middle-class fathers distanced themselves from those below them on the social scale, who continued to send their children to work. In addition, the employment of women outside the home could create a struggle for power within working-class households, especially when men clung to the sole-provider role, a masculine responsibility taken for granted by middle-class fathers. Children in immigrant families who brought language skills learned in school, new perceptions of American behavior, new work habits, and new leisure interests into the home also challenged traditional paternal authority. Confronted by these multiple challenges, fathers and their families in different ethnic groups adapted Old World values to fashion distinctive economic strategies and new paternal roles.[9]

The experience of black fathers both under slavery and in freedom was also different from that of white, middle-class men. Most scholars agree that the conditions of bondage made gender relations among slaves different from those of whites, but they disagree on exactly how different. Although most slave children lived in stable two-parent households, the roles played by their parents were shaped by the harsh conditions of slavery. Recent scholarship dispels the myth of weak ties between slave fathers and their families and the corresponding stereotype of a prevalent slave "matriarchy." As the historian Peter Kolchin points out, however, slave families were typically less male-dominated than nineteenth-century free families. This was so for at least two reasons: First, because slave unions had no legal status, slave fathers had no more property rights than did mothers. Slave fathers consequently lacked the authority over mothers of their children that the legal system bestowed on free men. Second, slave fathers were more likely than mothers to be separated from their children. Men were hired out, were sold off, and ran away more often than women. When parents lived on separate plantations, fathers, rather than mothers, typically traveled to visit their families on weekends. Accordingly, mother-headed households, while not the norm, were relatively common.[10]

The impact of slavery on children undermined paternal authority as well. Children who saw their parents verbally or physically abused knew where ultimate power lay and soon learned to conform to the wishes of both their parents and their owners. These and other indignities prevented black men from adhering to white middle-class conventions, but the constraints did not prevent them from feeling outraged at their inability to exercise fully the rights and responsibilities of fatherhood. By all accounts, most black men believed that masculinity rested on a foundation of family duty and struggled against the subversion of their paternal authority. Fathers and mothers alike strove to afford their children a basic refuge from the horrors of slavery, providing them with love and attention, imparting family customs and religious values, and teaching them the caution needed to survive in a hostile white society.

In the years following slavery, the vast majority of black children continued to live in two-parent households. As blacks adapted to the vagaries of urban life, the family remained a vibrant institution, with parents rendering vital assistance to children. Cities, however, were especially hard on black fathers. The proportion of African American families headed by females in the late nineteenth and early twentieth centuries exceeded that of native-born and immigrant whites. Persistent discrimination and under- or unemployment in Northern and Southern cities undermined the ability of black fathers to support their children. As a result, black fathers left their families more often than did whites.[11]

The particular experiences of black and working-class fathers affirm that there are other stories to tell about nineteenth-century American fatherhood than the one told in the chapters that follow. This book is a point of departure, investigating the experience of a single (though hardly uniform) class of men in one region of the country. To establish a historical context, the first chapter explores the vital role played by fathers in colonial New England. It also sketches some of the demographic and economic trends that affected fatherhood in colonial times and throughout the nineteenth century. Analyzing family advice literature, Chapter 2 identifies a shift in social-role prescriptions for fathers. Over the course of the nineteenth century, a naturalistic perspective on fatherhood displaced a moral one. While this shift limited the scope of paternal responsibility, it reaffirmed the importance of domestic involvement for men.

Subsequent chapters assess how prescribed norms and values were translated into (or contradicted by) the behavior of actual fathers. Chapter 3 analyzes the time available to fathers. It shows that the amount of time men actually spent with their families changed less dramatically than did their subjective experience of domestic life. Chapters 4 through 6 are loosely informed by a life-course perspective, which recognizes that family roles change both across historical time and over the individual life span. Chapter 4 investigates the transition to fatherhood. In the nineteenth-century, many fathers were present when their children were born. The chapter assesses the meaning that marrying and becoming a father had for men. Exploring paternal relations with young children, Chapter 5 identifies a newly important role for nineteenth-century fathers as their children's playmates. Fatherly play provided men with access to tender feeling and the softer side of their masculinity, but also downgraded the father's child-rearing responsibility.

Chapter 6 examines relations with older children. As children grew up, the obligation to secure a place for them in society came to the fore. This task became more complicated over time. In a changing economy, sons were less likely to follow a father's occupation. Pressure mounted to provide sons with the means to get ahead, adding to a father's care a decidedly modern burden of anxiety about what was needed to ensure a child's life chances. These and other concerns that lent domesticity a masculine face throughout the nineteenth century were especially pronounced during the Civil War era. The conflict itself dramatized the nineteenth-century father's importance to his family, a theme explored in the study's Conclusion.

The evidence in this study is drawn from the reminiscences, diaries, and letters of nearly two hundred American families. Only by a focused reading of such material can we hope to unearth what actual fathers did and thought. Unfortunately, while this approach has the power to illuminate intimate details of family life that would otherwise be lost to us, it reflects primarily (though not exclusively) the experience of the white, native-born, Protestant middle and upper classes. These are the families whose personal papers are most likely to have been preserved by local historical societies and in archives, and they are disproportionately represented in this study. Characteristics of the universe of primary documents that provide the book's empirical basis are described in a note on sources at the end of the text.

The locale of this study is the towns and villages of the American North, particularly New England and the Midwest. I had hoped that by focusing on two geographic areas I might detect regional variability in the father's role. Region, however, did not emerge as a significant factor. Almost certainly this was because of the study's concentration on two regions of the country that shared a common heritage. New Englanders played a large role in the nineteenth-century migration to the new lands of the "Old Northwest." Twentieth-century historians have referred to the population movement as a "Yankee Exodus" into what many contemporary emigrants called the "second New England."[12] As New Englanders moved west in search of fresh farm lands, they brought their family cultures with them. Consequently, different styles of fatherhood attributable to region were not apparent in the source material that I consulted. Where residence mattered most was in the difference between rural and urban homes. Social transformation swept the countryside in the nineteenth century, but new styles of fatherhood were pioneered primarily in urban middle-class households.

While I can offer no definitive conclusions about variations between North and South, much current scholarship suggests that fathers in Southern planter families resembled their elite Northern counterparts more than they differed from them. Family duty was an important source of masculine identity for Southern planters and Northern businessmen alike. Moreover, while Southern paternal styles ranged from patriarchal to egalitarian, growing numbers of planters in the nineteenth century became more affectionate with their wives and children. Like their Northern middle-class counterparts, Southern men increasingly expected to find great happiness in their domestic relations.[13]

The nineteenth century was a period of change for fathers, a time when fatherhood became more closely identified with breadwinning and with activities men engaged in away from home. The overall trajectory that fatherhood followed had been established earlier, however, and exploring the father's role in colonial America and the early republic is the appropriate place to begin.

Chapter 1

Fatherhood in Colonial New England and the Early Republic

All masters of families doe once a week (at the least) catechize their children and servants in the grounds and principles of Religion.

Massachusetts Laws of 1648

A vast chasm of change separates men's experience of domestic life in early America from what it became in the nineteenth century.[1] In colonial times fathers, not mothers, were chiefly responsible for the moral education of the young. Several factors explain the colonial father's central position in the family, but his authority rested primarily on religious belief.

Almost all English settlers in America were Protestants, whose beliefs emphasized paternal moral guidance and called for an intensely responsible father. Not all Protestant fathers raised their children in the same way, of course. Denominational differences made for different styles of fatherhood in the colonies. Puritans and Quakers both placed great emphasis on child rearing, for instance. But whereas Puritans emphasized breaking a child's will, Quakers adopted a more nurturant approach. Quaker society exhibited greater maternal emphasis, with the mother, not the father, providing the key link between church and family. In the Southern colonies, Anglican parents took a more relaxed approach to child rearing than did either their Puritan or Quaker counterparts.[2]

In the North, ethnic and racial differences added to the mix, distinguishing the experience of, say, Dutch or Mohawk fathers in New York from that of Scotch-Irish fathers in Pennsylvania or West African fathers in Massachusetts. Amid this diversity, white English settlers soon established a weighty role for fathers in New England. Although the physical care of young children was a mother's duty, fathers in early New England quickly assumed responsibility not only for their children's material support but also for their spiritual and intellectual instruction. Accordingly, the father acted as moral preceptor and chief family educator. As household head, he exercised ultimate authority over other family members, including his servants. He was responsible for their behavior, and he represented his family in the community.

Much of this understanding of the New England father's prerogatives and responsibilities is owed to historian Edmund S. Morgan's classic study of Puritan family life.[3] Morgan outlined a series of paternal responsibilities on the part of New England men that subsequent scholarship has largely confirmed and supplemented. Among other tasks assigned to fathers, paternal education was considered paramount by Puritans. Childhood literacy was considered necessary not principally to advance a child's material welfare (the notion that education was an instrument of economic advancement did not arrive until the nineteenth century),[4] but because salvation was impossible without it. Accordingly, the main business of education was to prepare children for conversion by teaching them to read the Bible and catechizing them in the doctrines and moral precepts of Christianity. This task, which ensured both the religious welfare of the children and the stability of society, was much too important to be left to weekly lessons learned in church. Nor could mothers alone be trusted to undertake instruction at home.

General cultural assumptions about women's moral and intellectual inferiority, and suspicion that mothers were prone to indulgence, made them less suitable parents in the Puritan mind. A woman's more pliant and emotional temperament made her an unequal match for children, whose willful natures needed to be governed rigorously for the sake of their own salvation.[5] Fathers, considered more able to control their emotions, could be counted on to administer regular discipline. The fact that female literacy rates were substantially lower than men's throughout most of the seventeenth century compounded these prejudices. Mothers were initially less equipped than fathers to catechize and educate their children.[6] For all these reasons, Protestant family advisers insisted that fathers should take the predominant role in child rearing and should exercise moral leadership of the family. It fell to the father in his capacity as moral preceptor to enforce good behavior. When children erred, the father was held chiefly accountable.

Fathers enacted this moral leadership through the rituals of everyday life. Upon rising in the morning, upon retiring at night, and at meals in between, a responsible Puritan father led his household in prayer, the singing of psalms, and Bible reading. Home worship fulfilled not only a moral function, it symbolically reinforced the father's role as head of the household by reminding other family members who was in charge.

In addition to social custom and daily ritual, the law recognized and reinforced the father's moral authority. In New England, local governments insisted that fathers train their children to be literate, religious, and economically productive citizens. After 1648, for instance, Massachusetts fathers were legally required to teach their children and apprentices the principles of religion from a catechism once a week and to provide them "so much learning as may inable them perfectly to read the English tongue, and knowledge of the Capital lawes: upon penaltie of twentie shillings for each neglect therein."[7]

Such education, and consequently a father's direct involvement with his children, began when they were very young and largely in their mother's care. Fathers probably began to tutor boys and girls in moral values from about age three, which was considered the age of comprehension. Puritan parents viewed children and childhood much differently than do parents today. They had a higher estimation both of small children's intellectual abilities and of their capacity for self-control. For the sake of the child, the work of salvation, including early lessons in the reality of death and damnation, could not begin too soon.[8]

A father's duty to issue instructions and reproofs and his need to exercise emotional restraint in order to enforce discipline circumscribed the amount of affection that he might display. The historian E. Anthony Rotundo maintains that early American fathers tended to express approval and disapproval, rather than affection and anger, in relation to their children. Similarly, historian Laurel Thatcher Ulrich observes that paternal government in early New England served to balance maternal love. In a society that valued stability and order more than sentiment, tender nurturing and open expressions of affection were viewed with misgiving. Too much affection on the

part of mothers risked raising spoiled, disrespectful children. Fathers, therefore, were called upon to exercise the firm discipline and pious rule-making
needed to forestall the potentially troublesome consequences of maternal
love. This is not to suggest that fathers were necessarily severe parents. Although some fathers undoubtedly employed harsh methods, most exercised
discipline and guidance rather than acting as punitive authoritarians.[9]

While fathers, rather than mothers, were chiefly responsible for catechizing both boys and girls, other aspects of children's socialization soon sorted
themselves out by gender. Daughters, who would follow their mothers in
the career of housewife, could begin their vocational training at a very
young age at their mothers' sides. Sons, too, could begin working alongside their fathers while still quite young. At a time when farming engaged
the vast majority of men and when artisanal production centered on the
home, boys often learned vocational skills by watching their fathers work.
As John Demos and other historians have observed, the home-based economy made fathering in the preindustrial past an extension of routine domestic activity.[10]

The first function of a father's work was not to afford vocational guidance,
of course, but to provide for his family's subsistence. In colonial Massachusetts, a father who shirked his economic responsibility could be indicted for
idleness and neglect. The provider role, however, incorporated an unmistakable educational dimension. For just as fathers were supposed to teach
their children from a catechism once a week, they were legally obliged to instruct them "in some honest lawful calling, labour or imployment, either
in husbandry, or some other trade profitable for themselves, and the Com-
mon-wealth if they will not or cannot train them up in learning to fit them
for higher imployments." Fathers who defaulted on any of these responsibilities might have their children removed from their households and placed
in foster families.[11]

While sons anticipated following in their fathers' footsteps, many children—both boys and girls—received training away from home, though not
in schools. Schools played only a minor role in childhood education throughout the seventeenth century and for part of the eighteenth century. The few
schools established in early America, particularly in New England, were intended to educate future clergymen rather than to teach children the basics
of reading and writing. Although some New England parents sent their

youngest children to dame-schools or their older children to private elementary schools, until the latter part of the eighteenth century the family was considered the primary institution for educating children.

By the end of the eighteenth century, however, private schools were a significant supplement to, and in some cases replaced, education in the home. In Massachusetts, for instance, by the mid-eighteenth century children began to go to school rather than stay at home to be taught. By 1800 school attendance in Massachusetts was nearly universal. Elsewhere as well the importance of schools expanded rapidly. As the nineteenth century progressed, parents increasingly turned their children over to schools to learn the basics of reading and writing. Although parents were reluctant to keep children in school longer than necessary to obtain a basic common-school education, by mid-century most children in the United States received at least some training in school.[12]

From the colonial era to about the time of the Civil War, the institutions of apprenticeship and servanthood supplemented training at home and in school. A boy's choice of calling was usually decided between the ages of 10 and 14. Training in a trade generally involved an apprenticeship to a master of the trade, which lasted seven years and ended by age 21. Girls ended their servitude somewhat younger, generally by age 18. Fathers were expected to guide their sons' vocational choice, but an analysis of the written agreements governing placement indicates that both parents participated in the decision to settle their children with other persons' families.[13]

While children who had gone to live with a master could not leave the master's household without his permission, servitude and apprenticeship in early America did not necessarily involve the severing of ties to parents and home. John Demos has pointed out that children were frequently placed not with strangers but in the homes of kin, and Edmund Morgan suggests that children were frequently able to return home to visit their families, especially when their parents lived in the same town.[14] Thus, servanthood did not signal indifference in fathers toward the children they sent away. In some cases these arrangements were matters of economic necessity; in others, they reflected belief in the value of the training the children would receive.

The presence of servants in a household extended a father's care to children other than his own. Prevalent assumptions about family life made little distinction between a father's biological children and the servants and apprentices living under his roof. For purposes of everyday care and supervision, all were under his charge, and he was responsible for providing children and servants alike with food, clothing, shelter, and instruction. The legal obligations and responsibilities incorporated in the master-servant relationship thereby reflected and helped to constitute the meaning of fatherhood in the colonial era. Fatherhood conferred the legal right to the services and labor of the children in a man's household. At the same time, a father was obliged to support and educate the children in his care in exchange for their labor.[15] The instrumental quality of this reciprocal relationship would reverberate in father-child relations well into the nineteenth century.

The similarity between the father-child and master-servant relationship did not imply that fathers had the same emotional attachment to servants as to their biological children. Several factors, including the Puritan belief that transmission of grace followed family lines, distinguished children from unrelated household members. Children were more likely to be church members, and, unlike servants, they had expectations of inheriting property. A father's responsibility to his biological children, therefore, did not end until they were settled in marriage. By approving or disapproving of a proposed match and by allotting portions of the family property to the new couple, the colonial father played a central role in the courtship and marriage of his sons and daughters. As with placing children as servants, however, these were decisions that involved both parents, not the father alone.[16]

The father in early New England, then, shouldered a heavy burden of moral leadership and family education. In a hierarchically ordered society, wherein the subordination of wives to husbands, children to parents, and servants to masters was assumed, New Englanders considered the father's duty to enforce good behavior to be the foundation of all political and religious authority in the community. This family leadership role was considered compatible with the father's obligation to provide for his family and to educate his children. To the extent that his literacy allowed, the father taught his children and servants to read and write; to the extent that his religiosity permitted, he catechized them and led family devotions. The father performed a wide variety of other duties as well: He helped select marital partners and supplied property to children about to establish independent households; he arranged apprenticeships for, and corresponded with, teenage children living as servants or apprentices away from home; and he provided everyday care, supervision, instruction, and material support for the children and servants living under his roof.

Large as the father loomed in the family, his role was unstable even in the colonial era. His primacy in educating the child, for instance, did not last long. As many New England men stopped joining the Puritan church after the mid-seventeenth century, communal authorities cast about for someone religiously equipped and willing to catechize the children and servants in the household. They explored various alternatives, such as using primary school teachers or hiring a second clergyman. Eventually, and somewhat reluctantly, clergymen turned to wives, who continued to join the church in larger numbers than their husbands. Gradually, therefore, the education of young children at home became identified with mothers.[17] Books of parenting advice, which had depicted the father as the important parent in the seventeenth century, began in the eighteenth century to address themselves to mothers. Other signs as well point to instability in the father's role in early America. The historian Daniel Scott Smith takes several demographic developments— including rising premarital pregnancy rates, increased outmigration from settled communities, and the increasing tendency of daughters to marry out of birth order—to mean that eighteenth-century fathers were unable to maintain their control over children on the old seventeenth-century model.[18]

A wide array of economic and cultural forces further elevated the mother's role as the eighteenth century gave way to the nineteenth. Under the heading of cultural influence, republican political ideology and softened Christian theology (particularly the growing acceptance among evangelical denominations of childhood conversion) were perhaps the most important vehicles for new modes of parenting.

In the social ferment of the revolutionary era, an outpouring of advice books, philosophical tracts, and novels popularized new ideas about children and the family. Eighteenth-century writers, who habitually dramatized issues of political authority in terms of family relationships, came to view patriarchal dominance as a threat not only to the emergent republican social order, but to the well-being of particular families. Unyielding patriarchs, according to the republican view, imperiled the happiness of wives and children as surely as tyrants threatened political liberty.[19]

All was not lost, however. Through their capacity for goodness, women in the early republic came to be seen as uplifting influences on their husbands and children, a source of religious values in the home and a counterforce to the unbridled commercialism and self-interest of the public sphere. This reappraisal of women's moral worth gained force under the influence of the Romantic Movement. Traits associated with the female character that were once disparaged, such as affection and susceptibility to emotion, now were cast in a more favorable light. These changes are often summarized under the rubric of "republican motherhood." It is more accurate, however, to speak of the "republican wife," since eighteenth-century moralists focused more on the influence a woman could (and should) have on her husband than on her power to shape her children's lives.[20]

More favorable assessments of womanhood went hand in hand with new ideas about children and how they should be raised. Romantic descriptions of children as naturally innocent, social, and affectionate reshaped parental attitudes by calling for more loving and tender methods of child nurturing. Equally important, many Protestant ministers began to question strict Calvinist notions of infant depravity, stressing instead the child's redeemability. Belief in the redeemable child's susceptibility to maternal influence linked the antipatriarchalism of the eighteenth century to the domesticity of the nineteenth, preparing the way for the exaltation of motherhood and the child-centered private home.[21]

In terms of demographic change, a dramatically declining birth rate distinguished nineteenth-century fatherhood from fatherhood in early America. Other demographic trends affecting family formation ensured, however, that the overwhelming majority of nineteenth-century men would occupy the role of father throughout their adult lives, as their predecessors had.[22] In the past, nearly all men expected to wed and become fathers, and very firm marital-age norms and fertility patterns governed family formation. In the seventeenth and eighteenth centuries, men tended to marry later, at about age twenty-seven during the early years of New England settlement. As the seventeenth and eighteenth centuries progressed, age at first marriage ranged gradually downward. By the second half of the eighteenth century, men were marrying at about age twenty-five in Massachusetts.

Women initially married quite young, just over age twenty in the early years of settlement. As men's average age at first marriage fell, women's rose, to about twenty-two or twenty-three over the same time span. This pattern, which reflected an evening-out of the sex ratio in the seventeenth and eighteenth centuries as the proportion of women in the population increased, remained remarkably stable during the nineteenth century.

One study of Massachusetts communities places the mean age at first marriage in the period 1845–60 at about twenty-six for males and twenty-four for females. Small variations (less than a year) have been found for the years between 1850 and 1890.[23] Table 1 abstracts the marriage experience of successive birth cohorts dating from the mid-nineteenth century. Overall, the data present a picture of surprising stability in age at marriage and proportion of the population ever marrying. The enormous economic and social transformations of the late nineteenth century—massive immigration, westward population movement, and both urban and industrial growth—had little effect on the age at which men and women married during this period.

In colonial times, a first child typically was born about a year after a couple had married. Thereafter, a child arrived roughly every two years for up

Table 1. Median Age at Marriage and Estimated Proportion
Ever Married for Cohorts Born 1865–1874 to 1895–1904

Birth Cohort	Median Marriage Age	% Ever Married
Males		
1865–74	26.2	90.2
1875–84	25.9	91.6
1885–94	25.5	92.3
1895–1904	25.0	92.5
Females		
1865–74	23.8	91.1
1875–84	23.6	91.1
1885–94	22.9	92.1
1895–1904	22.6	92.2

Source: John Modell, Frank F. Furstenberg Jr., and Douglas Strong, "The Timing of Marriage in the Transition to Adulthood: Continuity and Change, 1860–1975," *American Journal of Sociology* 84, suppl. (1978): S123.

to twenty years, although as the mother aged the interval between births increased slightly. In all, as many as eight or nine children were born to a colonial couple during the span of their married lives. Not all those children lived under the paternal roof at the same time, of course. Household size swelled and contracted at various stages in a family's life. John Demos's analysis of the Bristol, Rhode Island, census of 1689 suggests an average household size of six persons, with households of four, five, and six persons being the most common.[24]

Given the roughly two-year spacing of births, it was only as a father neared middle age that his household began to include a large number of children of various ages. The family of a forty-five-year-old man, for instance, could contain a grown son or daughter about to marry and form an independent household, an infant, and all the children in-between. After middle age the size of a father's household contracted, as children began leaving home to set up households of their own. However, a father who was forty-five when his last child was born would have neared the end of his natural life by the time that child reached maturity.

Relatively modest divorce rates also reinforced fatherhood's tenure. While premature death sometimes separated a father from his family, divorce remained uncommon throughout the colonial period and for much of the nineteenth century. A slow secular rise in divorce rates began in the decades after the Civil War. By 1890, demographers estimate, one marriage in ten ended in divorce, compared to approximately half of all marriages contracted in 1990.[25]

In contrast to relatively stable marriage and divorce patterns, fertility declined dramatically beginning in the second half of the eighteenth century. In the nineteenth century, the average number of children born to white women who survived to menopause was halved. As Table 2 shows, the birthrate fell steadily during the antebellum period, from 7.04 in 1800 to 5.21 in 1860, the year before the Civil War began. From 1865, when the war ended, until the late 1870s, there was little overall decline. Thereafter, the general pattern resumed, and the total fertility rate fell to 3.56 in 1900.[26]

Table 3 shows that although fertility fell sharply as the century progressed, for most of the period families remained large by modern standards. An average household size of between five and six persons in 1790 was reduced to

Table 2. Total Fertility Rates (TFR) for White Females 1800-1900

Year	TFR	Year	TFR
1800	7.04	1860	5.21
1810	6.92	1870	4.55
1820	6.73	1880	4.24
1830	6.55	1890	3.87
1840	6.14	1900	3.56
1850	5.42		

Source: Daniel Scott Smith, "Family Limitation, Sexual Control, and Domestic Feminism in Victorian America," *Feminist Studies* 1 (1973): 44.

between four and five persons in 1900. Just who lived in these households is a source of some controversy. Although a small population of elderly people limited the proportion of extended households in the nineteenth century, recent demographic research demonstrates that co-residence by an elderly parent with the younger generation was the social norm.[27]

Throughout the period households remained larger in rural than in urban areas. The drop in birthrates occurred everywhere, but the impact was greatest in urban middle-class homes. Beginning at a lower base in 1800, fertility ratios in the cities remained lower throughout the century. Living in cities by itself, however, did not have an immediate, simple impact on fertility behavior. Within the same city, different population groups behaved differently in different neighborhoods. In terms of ethnicity, most studies have found that the overall fertility of immigrants was higher than that of native-born whites. Class also played a role: generally speaking, the higher the father's occupational status, the fewer his children. Thus the size of business- and professional men's families contracted more rapidly than did those of other occupational groups. By 1890 business- and professional men had significantly fewer children than either skilled or unskilled workers or farm owners: almost half the professional men had no more than two children; 60 percent had no more than three; and less than a quarter had five or more offspring.[28]

Table 3. Distribution of Households by Size, 1790 and 1900

Household Size	1790	1900
1	3.7	5.1
2	7.8	15.0
3–4	25.5	34.4
5–6	27.1	25.1
7 or more	35.9	20.4
Total	100.0	100.0
Average	5.8	4.8

Source: Frances E. Kobrin, "The Fall in Household Size and the Rise of the Primary Individual in the United States," *Demography* 13 (February 1976): 129.

While the inner dynamics of the fertility transition are controversial, understanding the role played by fathers helps to clarify some of the conflicting explanations offered by historians. According to some scholars, changing gender relations led to the fertility decline. In this view, the rise in women's moral status and the enhanced power over domestic affairs conferred on wives by the ideology of separate spheres early in the nineteenth century equipped women to exercise greater control over sexual relations. By granting or refusing sex to their husbands, the argument goes, women sought to limit their childbearing in order to preserve their health, ease the burden of constantly caring for young children, and enhance their autonomy. Certainly, those were all powerful incentives. Men, however, were hardly indifferent to at least the most immediate concern—the health risks associated with childbirth. Ample evidence, some of it adduced later in this study, attests to men's empathizing deeply with women's fears about the perils of childbirth. This suggests, in turn, that the decision to limit sexual relations was not a woman's alone, but rather was based on a mutual understanding between husband and wife.[29]

A second school of thought grounds the decline of fertility in changing economics, not in new gender relations. Richard Easterlin, a leading proponent of the economic school, links the fertility transition to a father's intention to provide his sons with a start in life equivalent to his own. For

Easterlin, the declining availability of land and rising capital costs of farming encouraged farmers to limit the size of their families. Others in the economic school maintain that parents were less concerned with guaranteeing sons an adequate portion than with assuring that at least one child remain in the community to care for them when they could no longer live by themselves.

In fact, both sorts of economic concerns motivated parents as they devised strategies to serve themselves and their children. As we discover in the course of this study, however, anxiety about providing children with an adequate start in life became a hallmark of the nineteenth century's new style of fatherhood, especially in urban middle-class households, where fertility rates were lowest. From this perspective, the parents' mutual concern about their children's future prospects was a strong inducement for family limitation.[30]

Such motivation has a decidedly modern ring, but another factor, high infant mortality, likened the demography of nineteenth-century fatherhood to conditions that prevailed in early America, rather than to demographic trends today. Between 10 and 30 percent of children in the colonial era did not survive their first year of life; this is roughly ten times the infant mortality rate in the United States today. At such levels, most fathers in the seventeenth and eighteenth centuries could expect to lose one or more children. High mortality levels persisted in most areas of the country throughout the nineteenth century, though working-class, immigrant, and African American parents were likelier to lose children than were their counterparts among the native-born middle class. Rapid progress resulting from public health initiatives in the largest cities in the 1880s and 1890s, especially among the foreign-born, and the decline in fertility rates moderated the impact of infant mortality. In most population groups, however, many nineteenth-century fathers continued to know by personal or proximate experience what it meant to lose a child.[31]

The psychological meaning of high child mortality rates is controversial. Some scholars, notably Lawrence Stone and Edward Shorter, believe that the prospect of loss caused parents to hedge their emotional involvement with children who might not survive the perils of infancy. This view, however, has been subjected to a fundamental critique. Linda Pollock and others have argued convincingly that such an interpretation of the demographic facts is psychologically implausible: grief over the death of a child is as likely to evoke heightened feelings of concern and care for surviving children as it is to lead to parental disengagement. This study corroborates that view by showing that the illness and death of children were occasions for outpourings of paternal solicitude.[32]

The foregoing discussion underscores two points. First, fathers in old New England and the early republic shouldered a heavy burden of care for the rising generation. In addition to providing for their families, fathers were expected to play a large role in the moral and intellectual development of their children. Demographic trends, which showed that most men were saddled with fathering responsibilities for most of their lives, reinforced this obligation and the saliency of the father's role. Second, the early American father's role was in transition. Over the course of the eighteenth century, the education of young children at home gradually became identified with mothers, so that by the nineteenth century they were seen as natural caretakers.

From this perspective, the nineteenth century was a time when families worked out the implications of expanded maternal responsibility and a diminished role for fathers. The advent of moral motherhood and breadwinning fatherhood, however, did not deny men a domestic role. Rather, it encouraged fathers to redefine paternalism in ways that balanced breadwinning with their customary duty to see to it that their children received a proper upbringing. The male list of priorities now included a shrunken set of paternal requirements but still associated manliness with being a good father and husband. Honoring domestic commitments was a measure of manhood. That at least was the message directed at middle-class men in the nineteenth century's outpouring of family advice.

Chapter 2

"Their Own Proper Task"

Nineteenth-Century Advice to Fathers

Although so large a share of the care of children devolves upon
the mother, let the father be careful not to underrate his own
duties or influence.

Theodore Dwight Jr., 1834

Few features of Victorian family advice have attracted more scholarly attention than its flag-waving for motherhood. Although the nineteenth century's reevaluation and magnification of motherhood was foreshadowed by
ideals of maternal tenderness current in the seventeenth and eighteenth
centuries, a new and insistently maternal note entered the social conversation about parenting when American women, educators, social reformers,
clerics, and physicians turned their pens to issues of family governance and
child rearing in the opening decades of the nineteenth century.[1] Domestic
advice writers were clamoring—sometimes anxiously, often hopefully, and
always in tones of moral urgency—to enthrone wives and mothers as the
natural and primary parents of children, especially young children. By the
1840s, when literature written to aid fathers and mothers in the education
of their children reached a peak of popularity, a new, more powerful form
of motherhood had taken shape for American women.[2] In important ways,
fathers and fatherhood have become a lost chord in the antebellum fanfare
for mothers and the power of mothers' love.

Historians have long recognized the celebration of motherhood inscribed in American writing on domesticity.[3] Distracted perhaps by the undeniable importance that Victorian Americans placed on maternal care for the proper nurture of their children and for the stability of their society, few historians considered what the prescriptive writers had to say about fathers and fatherhood. While nineteenth-century commentators saw mothers as taking the lead in child rearing, we have too readily assumed that the concept of fatherhood and ideas about what a good father might be were absent from popular advice literature.[4] They were not. New thinking about fathers attended the formulation of new ideas about mothers, if only because most family advisers believed that raising children was an arena of mutual responsibility in which both mothers and fathers had active roles to play. Notwithstanding their amplification of specifically maternal duty, nineteenth-century moralists insisted that both sexes assume parental obligations, not only for the sake of the children but for the parents' own spiritual well-being and for the benefit of society.[5]

Intense concern about fathers in particular emerged in the 1830s and 1840s, when commentators fashioned an ideal of Christian fatherhood.[6] The virtues of Christian fatherhood were preached to men throughout the nineteenth century and continue to find an audience today, especially among men in evangelical and fundamentalist denominations. From its inception, however, the Christian fatherhood ideal looked backward, toward modes of family organization that had prevailed in the recognizably religious culture of early New England. Later in the nineteenth century, the authors of advice to men addressed fathers less often in the name of religion, using instead moralistic medical and scientific teachings to formulate an ideal of manhood rooted in being a father.

In some respects, late-century advocates of what might be called "paternal manhood" simply recast the Christian fatherhood ideal in secular terms. Certainly one of their aims—to maintain men's involvement in family life—was the same as that of the previous era's advisers. To encourage masculine domestic engagement, later commentators translated the moral and spiritual benefits previously ascribed to fatherhood into biological traits that fit what historian E. Anthony Rotundo recently identified as the late-nineteenth-century paradigm of "passionate manhood."[7] In medical advice and popular scientific discussions, men were told that they needed to become fathers in order to achieve a complete and virile manhood.

These two ideological moments, the articulation of the ideal of Christian fatherhood early in the century and that of paternal manhood toward its close, bracketed a crucial transition in the way nineteenth-century men thought about their family roles. Increasingly, the husband's role displaced that of the father, a development reflected in the books of marital advice to young husbands produced throughout the 1830s, 1840s, and 1850s. While they addressed domestic relations, these manuals had little to say about paternal responsibility per se. Rather, the good father came to be seen as a companionate husband who provided his wife with the material means and, equally important, the warm emotional atmosphere she needed to carry out her essential role as mother. As Margaret Marsh has shown, this masculine domestic ideal was amplified later in the nineteenth century by such writers as Harriet Beecher Stowe, Abby Morton Diaz, and Margaret Sangster.[8] In modified form, it continues to reverberate in the last decades of the twentieth century, as the emotional basis of the so-called new fatherhood.

Whether in the name of religion or biology, nineteenth-century cultural commentators expended considerable energy and a small ocean of ink to win men over to domesticity. In the process, they guaranteed that paternity would remain a key component in the definition of middle-class male sex roles throughout the period. Notwithstanding historiographic fascination with moral motherhood and the masculinity of the marketplace, such a finding should not surprise us. Anthropologists have long recognized the considerable cultural work undertaken in most societies to reconcile men to paternal responsibility. At no time during the nineteenth century was American society an exception to that rule.[9]

Advice Literature in Masculine Context

Before describing these developments in greater detail, it will be useful to sketch briefly the history of family advice and its significance to men.[10] The nineteenth century's steady stream of conduct-of-life books originated in Great Britain, where a first wave of writers, active between 1780 and 1810, pioneered popular writing on domestic themes. By the 1820s a group of native-born pastors and educators, largely in New England, were compiling their lectures and sermons into practical family manuals for an avid local readership.[11]

A school of conservative New England writers, men who believed that family governance was becoming laxer than it had been when the Puritan Church exerted greater authority over social relations, gained a popular audience in the 1830s. Such writers as the educator Theodore Dwight Jr., Amherst College president Heman Humphrey, and the physician William Alcott tended to stress the father's domestic responsibility, although they did not propose a return to the patriarchalism of the past. Companionate family ideals and the mother's acknowledged importance had become so widely accepted that such backtracking was out of the question. Accordingly, fatherhood's mid-century publicists urged men to complement, not replace, the mother's influence over her children. Even so strong a proponent of men's domestic duties as Theodore Dwight Jr. saw the mother, rather than the father, taking the lead in the all-important task of forming the child's moral character.

In the 1830s and 1840s, the publications of maternal associations of evangelically oriented women and of voluntary reform associations devoted to causes such as temperance swelled the stream of domestic advice being penned by prominent New Englanders. Temperance writers especially warmed to the question of men's domestic duties, criticizing those fathers whose drunkenness dragged their families down a path toward destitution and dependence.

By midcentury, a group of best-selling female writers and editors had also joined the enterprise of domestic advice and reform. A centralized publishing industry now circulated their advocacy of a powerful form of motherhood to a national market of largely female readers. These writers, whom Hawthorne lumped together disparagingly as a "damned lot of scribbling women," were in fact ideologically diverse. Reformers such as Catharine Beecher, Catharine Maria Sedgwick, and Sarah Josepha Hale saw motherhood as the means to social salvation. Their belief, shared by many reform-minded men, was that redemption of individual souls at home would lead collectively to the creation of a virtuous society. Parenting, in this view, affected more than the well-being of children. Inwardly, it affected the moral character of the parent; outwardly, it touched the welfare of society at large. Other advisers, such as Lydia Maria Child and Eliza Farrar, invested motherhood with less moral significance but insisted that a woman's domestic duties had to be performed diligently precisely because they were her duties.[12]

Notwithstanding the commercial success of these female authors, prescriptive literature continued to be written by and for men. Between 1830 and 1860, young men who no longer lived with their employers increasingly turned to professional advice books for information on how to make their way in the world. Manuals like *The Young Man's Friend* and *The Young Man's Guide* substituted for a master's or a father's vocational guidance. These books combined moral admonitions with practical hints for the first generation of youth in industrial cities, advising them about how to succeed in business through early rising, diligence, self-denial, self-discipline, and respect for rules. Although these economic pointers had little to say about the conduct of family relations, marriage manuals and domestic fiction said a great deal.[13]

What one historian has labeled a "masculine domestic dream" filled the pages of popular fiction written between 1820 and 1860 by both male and female authors. Significantly, themes that emphasized the importance of marriage as a source of joy and fulfillment for men were featured not only in fiction written for a female audience but also in novels written by men and intended for a male readership. Such "men's authors" as the adventure writer William Gilmore Simms created narratives that incorporated the belief that "a man without a loving woman and a comfortable home was incomplete."[14]

The masculine domesticity touted by fiction writers found expression in nineteenth-century marriage manuals as well. The popularity of this advice, like that of the guidebooks on social and economic mobility, reflected the emergence of a youthful population of city dwellers. Most migrants to cities during the period 1830 to 1860 were young married couples or single youth who would soon enter marriage. As a result, mid-century cities contained a higher proportion of people in their twenties and a lower proportion of young children and old people than was found in rural areas. This population of young married couples who had left parents behind formed a ready market for marriage manuals and child-nurture books.[15]

The marriage manuals, some addressed to new husbands, were written mostly by ministers and reform-minded physicians. Sociologist Michael Gordon pointed out that the ideal husband depicted in this literature was a practicing Christian, had no immoral habits, and (reflecting belief that the body was temple of the soul) was in excellent health. Such a man valued home life and carried out his parental duties, although these were not often specified. The model husband assumed the dominant role in the marital relationship, but he was not a tyrant. Rather than frequenting taverns, he spent his evenings at home with his wife and children. He was neat and frugal, so as not to burden his wife with unnecessary labor. More than being considerate, though, he was an intensely loving man, capable of reciprocating his wife's affection. His main family responsibilities lay in his role as breadwinner. Without striving for great riches, the model husband provided for his family to the best of his ability.[16]

Clearly, then, the nineteenth century's domestic canon was relevant to men's lives. New ideas about wives and mothers encouraged writers to reformulate ideas about men and their domestic duties. Some of these ideas were addressed directly to men, both in popular fiction and in marriage manuals for new husbands. Men also received these messages secondhand, via the books and magazines read by their wives and the expectations that such reading created. For the most part, these understandings emphasized what historians have labeled companionate family ideals. These strictures helped to shape a distinctive middle-class form of masculinity grounded in steady provision and an appreciation of family life. Commentators most often considered men in their role as husbands and breadwinners, as witnessed by the outpouring of marriage manuals and guides for getting ahead, but that was not their only concern. The social role of father was put under the microscope as well. Cultural anxiety about fathers emerged with striking intensity in New England in the 1830s, when conservative family advisers identified the problem of "paternal neglect."

Paternal Neglect and the Ideal of Christian Fatherhood

New England educator Theodore Dwight Jr. was among the first to sound the alarm that fatherhood was an imperiled social institution. In *The Father's Book* (1834), Dwight asserted that men were using increased maternal care and their own work obligations as excuses to shirk parental responsibility. "Although so large a share of the care of children devolves upon the mother, let the father be careful not to underrate his own duties or influence," Dwight warned men. "There are few who do all they might for the physical, intellectual, moral and religious education of their children; and when the importance of their own proper task is considered, and the improper influences by which they are too often induced to neglect it, they must acknowledge it is their duty to make new exertions in behalf of their children."[17]

Dwight's apprehensions were echoed by conservative clergymen and educators for the next two decades. In 1842 the Rev. John S. C. Abbott, a Calvinist pastor from Worcester, Massachusetts, observed that "paternal neglect is at the present time one of the most abundant sources of domestic sorrow." Writing in *Parent's Magazine*, Abbott warned that the "responsibility of correctly rearing up a family, equally devolves upon both father and mother." Families could not be well regulated, he cautioned, "unless there be cooperation of both parents in watching over and governing the children."[18]

For advisers such as Dwight and Abbott, family governance was in uneasy, even alarming, transition as changes in the modes of men's work drew fathers out of the home. In part, these writers feared that the mother's expanded role and gentler methods of child rearing were an invitation to indulgence and social disorder. To forestall raising a generation of spoiled children, maternal care had to be balanced by paternal governance and control. As the Boston minister Artemas Muzzey put the problem in 1854: "Authority has nearly passed away from the fireside and influence and moral suasion have as yet but imperfectly supplied its place. In this state of things, the conscientious parent is troubled, and is looking anxiously for light on the means and methods of fulfilling his task."[19]

Ultimately, however, misgivings about family governance focused less on the expanded exertions of mothers (which even the most traditional advisers affirmed more than they feared) than on perceived shortcomings of men themselves. Two concerns about how men behaved in public underlay the charge of paternal neglect. The first focused on the arenas of masculine achievement, the worlds of business and politics. Proponents of an activist and engaged fatherhood chided men for devoting too much time to the scramble for wealth and political office. By immersing themselves singlemindedly in these pursuits, men were exhibiting what one minister and educator termed a "criminal indifference" to the religious education and moral development of their children.[20] Thus, moralists used paternal responsibility to condemn the aggressive ambition that many contemporaries, especially Whigs, feared had been unleashed by the market economy.

To some extent, an older elite's anxiety about new modes of success informed this criticism of an aspiring middle class. The second complaint, however, focused not on men hellbent for achievement, but rather on those flirting with failure and the loss of middle-class respectability in the male world of play and relaxation. Critics feared that men were spending too much time at their families' expense, mingling in post offices, stores, hotels, and especially in neighborhood taverns. Misgivings about masculine recreational culture found acute expression in the strong temperance theme in family advice. Family periodicals in the 1840s, notably *Mother's Assistant*, featured stories in which a happy family was reduced to misery by the drunkenness of the father. Warnings about the evils of alcohol, anxiety about drunken fathers, and admonitions to support the temperance cause were constant topics in domestic advice to parents throughout the century, so much so that one historian has described the temperance crusade as a "battle against men outside the family."[21]

In a series of articles in *Godey's Lady's Book* in 1855 the writer T. S. Arthur outlined the general temperance complaint. Arthur contrasted upright and dissolute husbands: The upright husband took delight in his family, spent his evenings at home reading with his wife and children, and generally fulfilled his domestic obligations. His dissolute counterpart was selfish and inconsiderate, had a foul temper, paid no attention to his children, and left his wife alone night after night in order to carouse in taverns with his male cronies. For better or worse, Arthur insisted, men set the tone and pace of family life; they had the power to make their wives happy or miserable.[22]

For those sounding the tocsin against paternal neglect, all was not lost, however. By reordering their priorities, men could achieve the ideal of the Christian father who shared in the religious and moral instruction of his children. Accordingly, neglectful fathers were urged time and again to elevate home duties over material ambition and business concerns. "Had not the father better be the poorer at the end of the year, by some hundreds or thousands, than thus to sacrifice to mammon the dearest interests of the little flock which God has entrusted to his care?" asked an anonymous adviser in *Parent's Magazine*. "He knows not what he loses, till he makes a fair trial of doing his duty in this particular."[23]

Similarly, physician and indefatigable family adviser William Alcott (author of more than thirty books on marriage) asserted that men for whom public influence and acclaim were top priorities had their goals exactly backwards: "Let him first exert a holy and heavenly influence on his wife and family. These are his more immediate disciples—his favored twelve, always with him. Let him enstamp on these the image of his Lord and Savior." As historian Jan Lewis recently observed, such Christlike imagery was the dominant note in nineteenth-century domestic advice to women, imposing an extraordinary burden of self-sacrifice on mothers. The same imagery was also applied, albeit less pervasively, to men. But when it was used, it echoed the teachings of St. Paul to suggest that men reassert strong household leadership by fulfilling a traditional religious role.[24]

For all their criticism of blind ambition, moralists saw little conflict between the ideal of Christian fatherhood and the role of family provider. While it was true that breadwinning was too easily used as an excuse for neglecting other child-rearing tasks, the proponents of Christian fatherhood insisted that men need not choose between earning a living and providing other forms of fatherly care. "We have time for all that is required of us," advised Artemas Muzzey. "We can do everything necessary for the subsistence and comfort of our families, and still form in ourselves and our children the Christian character."[25] The Christian father was the good provider's alter ego, rather than his foil.

Father's Proper Tasks

Fathers who undertook their proper tasks fulfilled three primary responsibilities: they provided for their families, they cooperated with mothers in molding the moral character of their children, and they equipped these children, especially sons, with qualities needed to advance in life (such habits as self-government, industry, economy, and temperance). To assist men in this work, family advisers compiled a substantial list of activities for ideal fathers.

In explicitly Christian advice, it went nearly without saying that a father should lead his family in daily devotions and use the Sabbath as an occasion for fatherly instruction and guidance. More generally, he needed to model "genuine Christian" behavior. For by exercising sound judgment, especially where moral considerations such as truthfulness or honesty in business were concerned, a father could play an essential role in the formation of his children's character. The advocates of Christian fatherhood shared with more secular advisers a vision of active paternal engagement in domestic life. Any time fathers were not at work was time that could and should be spent profitably in juvenile instruction. Even paternal illness might be turned to moral purpose. As long as fathers were laid up at home, Theodore Dwight offered, why not use their sickbeds as the backdrop for teaching object lessons in faith and endurance? Family time was precious, and the good father was someone on whom no child-rearing opportunity was lost.[26]

Meal times were also favored occasions for fathers to take charge of their families. William Alcott recommended that fathers use the morning meal to announce the plan of the day and the evening meal to lead a family review of the past day's actions. The ideal father converted the dinner table into a seminar table whose educational benefits, in Alcott's estimation, could surpass "the whole course of instruction at our common schools."[27] This glorified image of the good father training his children through edifying table talk, as well as by reading to his family in the living room after dinner, was one of the nineteenth century's most enduring paternal stereotypes. Fathers were lauded who kept dictionaries and other reference works handy in the dining room as aids to instruction, or who selected snippets from the morning newspaper to read aloud, or who planned special topics of conversation for the family circle.[28] This was part and parcel of what John Gillis has described as the nineteenth century's ritualization of family time around the father's comings and goings. Mealtime and fireside rituals that took advantage of the father's morning and evening presence reinforced his symbolic importance and influence even as his work drew him increasingly away from home.[29]

Somewhat surprisingly, given the strength of cultural beliefs that bound mothers to young children, family advisers extended fathers' duties even into the nursery. Although primary responsibility was placed upon the mother, fathers were urged to familiarize themselves with the principles of infant care because, in Dwight's words, their "forethought and exertions" could be of assistance. William P. Dewees, a leading physician from Philadelphia, considered it "both unfortunate and unjust, that the responsibility and care of early education should so exclusively devolve upon the mother." He urged fathers to come to their wives' relief in order to "command a conformity from the child which would be highly useful to its future welfare."[30]

The idea of paternal involvement in infant care should not be pushed too far. Suggestions that fathers participate in the instruction of young children were typically offered by men in advice written before 1840. In mid-century advice written by and for women, management of young children was viewed as a maternal monopoly. Characteristically, Lydia Sigourney sought to persuade women "to take charge of the entire education of their children, during the earlier years of life."[31] Sigourney believed that the mother was chiefly responsible for the nurturing of children up to age seven, when their characters were most plastic and susceptible to parental influence. This accorded with arguments by educators that instruction of younger children was best undertaken by female teachers, who were temperamentally suited to the task, but that older students required, in Horace Mann's phrase, the "more forcible, subduing power of masculine hands."[32]

Just as a father's instruction was relatively more important to older children, his advice was wanted more by sons than daughters. Fathers were regularly urged to take a particular interest in boys' development, to encourage their sons' studies, and to teach young men the lessons of sexual morality.[33] Above all, the father had an indispensable role to play as his sons' vocational guide. Theodore Dwight Jr.'s advice is illustrative. Daughters, declared Dwight, were more readily socialized to adult roles because mothers at home taught them the tasks of domestic economy. Fathers, on the other hand, had to make a concerted effort to introduce their sons to the world of work in order to instill a "respect for useful labor" and an acquaintance with "the moving springs of society."[34]

While evangelical ministers placed discipline high on the list of paternal duties, the mother was expected to teach the child its first lessons in obedience. The father involved himself as the child advanced in years, and then primarily in the most incorrigible cases.[35] With earlier will-breaking methods of child rearing in retreat, mothers were deemed capable of developing the child's own conscience, in most cases without relying on paternal intervention. Accordingly, by midcentury fathers were being urged in no uncertain terms to abandon an authoritarian posture in the family in favor of tender ties with children.

Whereas the prescripts of Christian fatherhood accorded with earlier notions of paternal responsibility, enjoining fathers to adopt a single standard of nurturant parenting departed from the father's traditional role. Laurel Thatcher Ulrich observed that, in the colonial era, the mother represented the "affectionate mode" in a dual concept of child rearing that emphasized the father's control.[36] But with friendship displacing hierarchy as the template for family relations, fathers had to reevaluate their approach to children. For, if affection was now more vital to child rearing, it followed that men should become more like their wives in their method of parenting. To act as friends and companions to their children, men had to reimagine (though not abandon) a central aspect of masculine identity: patriarchal authority over children. Anticipating masculine resistance, proponents of father-child companionship were quick to insist that friendly relations would not undermine paternal authority, but rather bolster control by creating an incentive for obedience.

The advice of Horace Bushnell, the famous Congregational minister, is a case in point. "One of the first duties of a genuinely Christian parent is a generous sympathy with the plays of his children," Bushnell asserted. He urged fathers to provide toys, arrange playtimes, and invite suitable companions for their children: "Sometimes, too, the parent having a hearty interest in the plays of his children, will drop out for the time the sense of his years, and go into the frolic of their mood with them," he advised. Not only would children enjoy such playtime best of all, but this experience would also make the father's authority stronger and more welcome by bringing him closer and offering "a more complete show of sympathy."[37]

Such warmth, said the proponents of paternal affection, represented a salutary break with the past. Earlier modes of fathering that emphasized instruction and reproof had alienated fathers from their children's deepest affections and needed to be abandoned. As Artemas Muzzey observed:

> Who is there in mid-life that has not experienced, or has not witnessed, at least, the unhappy effects of this error? To how many minds has it brought a cloud over the memory of a departed father! There was reverence, it is true, for that father; but love never entered the heart. We have the grand outlines of Christian character in the picture left of him. There are stern principle, unbending integrity, truthfulness, fidelity, and

justice; but the delicate shades and the softer tints of affectionate manners, pleasing tones, the ever-beaming countenance, that speaks of a
childlike spirit,—these we miss.[38]

By midcentury, then, a rather explicit list of responsibilities mixed fatherly
obligations based on traditional religious beliefs with new family rituals and
advice to cultivate tenderer ties to children. Like the new motherhood, the
new fatherhood was thought to benefit both children and society at large.
The champions of paternal responsibility advised men, moreover, that fatherly conduct would promote their own well-being.

Fatherhood and the Self

According to bourgeois moralists, a man's children were as necessary to
him as he was to them. Since fathers had to act as role models, having children encouraged men toward moral perfection. As Horace Bushnell urged,
men and women needed to adopt the character of a parent in order to "live
a better life into the spirits of [their] children." From the need to set a moral
example it was but a short leap to the notion that men were duty-bound to
have families in order to perfect their own characters. "You can no more reach
the highest and most harmonious development of which you are capable
without children," the pseudonymous adviser Timothy Titcomb told young
adults, "than you can develop a muscle without exercise. Without them, one
of the most beautiful regions of your nature must for ever remain without
appropriate and direct culture." Authentic manhood, like true womanhood,
partook of the character of a parent, said Artemas Muzzey, because it was
"for the moral good of the parent himself to be subject to this solemn
weight."[39]

For men, the moral imperative of parenthood stemmed from two principal psychic rewards: Fatherhood softened an otherwise callous masculine
nature. Paternal responsibility also inspired fortitude. By orienting men toward the future, having children made more bearable present-day setbacks
and travails. Fatherhood's softening effect was thought to commence with
the birth of a child. For a father's heart, like a mother's, was susceptible to
the melting influence of an infant's dependency. As Lydia Sigourney understood the effect, tenderness and generosity sprang "into the father's heart,

from the cradle of his child." Nothing was more affecting to the "noble and virtuous man, as that being which perpetually needs his help, and yet cannot call for it." The birth of an infant, said Artemas Muzzey, was like a spiritual rebirth for the father, who "feels that he is another man. He looks up toward heaven, and finds no difficulty in conceiving of a bliss of which he has had a foretaste on earth."[40]

As children grew older and as men grew into fatherhood, being a father was also thought to confer philosophical perspective. Fathers could console themselves for misfortune and find room for gratitude when troubles were seen as affording moral lessons to one's children, Theodore Dwight told men. "For while we, like the sailor, are laboring in vain among the storms, the waves will thus sometimes throw up on the beach something of value to the little ones who remain in quiet upon the shore."[41] Similarly, the young men of Westminster Church in Providence, Rhode Island, were advised by their pastor, Augustus Woodbury, that their manhood would grow into "larger and fuller proportions" upon becoming husbands and fathers. The duties of educating and molding the character of children would confer a new "solemnity and dignity" to life. Upon becoming a father, a man was "taken out of much that is mean and small and trifling, and made to feel that there is more in human life than he had ever dreamed of—that his own life has a higher character, because others' lives are bound up with it for their weal or woe," Woodbury preached. A man's "fidelity to home—its various lessons and its various duties"—was "at the bottom of all true success in life."[42]

By motivating him toward a life of manly accomplishment, a wife and children perfected a man's masculine nature. In this respect, parenthood was the linchpin of mature manhood and womanhood alike, a social position that both sexes needed to occupy in order to achieve mature gender identities. Fatherhood, however, did not complete men's nature in quite the same way that motherhood did women's. A man's labor for wife and children, after all, was bound up with a world of public meanings that defined men as workers and as citizens. Consequently, fatherhood was not imposed on men as the great object of life as motherhood was for women.

Frequently, the general guidebooks for young men addressed them in their capacity as prospective husbands but made little or no mention of fatherhood; the books for young women almost invariably included one or more chapters devoted to motherhood and the power of maternal influ-ence.[43] Whereas motherhood grew out of something intrinsic to female na-ture, fatherhood was seen more as a social role that subjected men to the salutary influence of home. Through selfless acts of paternal care, a man was aided in the development of the self-mastery and self-control so central to nineteenth-century masculine gender ideals. Nonetheless, even the staunchest proponents of paternal involvement sent fathers a mixed message by em-phasizing their duties as husbands rather than as parents per se.

Mothers and Husbands

William Alcott, who chided fathers for doing too little at home, advised sons to make mothers their guides since fathers generally were unavailable to them. Paternal involvement was desirable for optimal child rearing, he de-clared, but maternal love would compensate for any deficiency in a woman's cultivation or native talent as a parent.[44]

It followed from the increased reliance on mothers that fathers could best serve their children by cultivating maternal love and reinforcing maternal authority—in short, by becoming better husbands. Rev. John Abbott criti-cized "paternal neglect," but he counseled mothers not to rely on absent hus-bands. On one hand, he would not excuse a father "for releasing himself from a full share of the responsibility" for family government. But what was the father's share? To teach his children to obey their mother. "If the father does not do this, the difficulties of the mother will be vastly increased," Abbott reasoned.[45]

Abbott was little different in this respect from the growing number of female domestic advisers who saw fathers as but ghostly presences in family life. Writing for a female readership, Lydia Maria Child seldom considered men in relation to their children. For Child, the ideal father was a husband who acquiesced in his wife's management and training of their offspring. This conception is best illustrated by an anecdote Child relates in her widely circulated volume of advice, *The Mother's Book*. The episode concerned a mother who put her four-year-old daughter to bed without supper one evening, after the girl had refused to remove herself from the dinner table to make room for unexpected guests. The girl's father was sympathetic to his daughter's plight, but he restrained the impulse to seat her on his lap and give her some supper. Commented the husband to his wife: "I will never interfere with your management; and much as it went against my feelings, I entirely approve of what you have done." For Child, the father's decision not to challenge the mother's governance had the most salutary consequences. The family, she commented, "was the most harmonious, affectionate family I ever knew. The children were managed as easily as a flock of lambs." Accordingly, she counseled mothers "as far as possible to withdraw" their children from interfering fathers, especially those who challenged maternal authority and might exert an inappropriate influence by intemperate behavior.[46]

Besides inverting traditional expectations about paternal firmness and maternal indulgence, Child's story raises the question: Which parent predominated in nineteenth-century families? The issue is extremely vexed, in part because the didactic writers themselves sent out such contradictory messages. Writing on domesticity acknowledged that women were the principal parents in most circumstances and affirmed their leading role. In this sense, the literature written by and for women, especially, contributed to the rise of what some historians have labeled "domestic feminism." Certainly, images of dutiful or deferential husbands, such as Child depicted, constituted a masculine gender ideal that served women's interests by enhancing their domestic authority.

Frequently, however, companionate ideals were advanced in a patriarchal context. Most contemporary husbands and wives did not believe that women's centrality in the home subverted the power of the man in the family. As Tocqueville described it, the Americans he met in the 1830s still considered the husband to be the "natural head of the conjugal association," who had the right to direct his spouse. In carving out a distinct sphere for the woman in the home, Tocqueville observed, the intent of democratic family ideology was not to subvert paternal power but to regulate it.[47]

Nineteenth-century advisers of parents never completely resolved the paradox of parental power. They seldom called on fathers to manage motherhood. Not even the staunchest ideologists of Christian fatherhood proposed a wholesale return to the patriarchal order of seventeenth-century New England, in which the father bore primary responsibility for the child's spiritual growth and education. At the same time, these advisers (mostly men) believed that happy households rested on a masculine authority, which they sought to reinforce. Emphasizing the role of husband and provider distinguished male authority to govern the household from the paternal relationship to children, who were now thought to be more responsive to female nurturing. In this way, the role of husband came to be elevated over that of father on the list of masculine responsibilities. In one sense, the husband's and father's roles were simply conflated. More to the point, the emphasis on a husband's obligations reflected the extent to which the father's role had been downgraded by expanded maternal care. Increasingly, good fathers came to be seen as husbands who supported their wives' child-rearing practices. The domestic imagery in lithographs and engravings affords material evidence for this proposition.

The Iconography of Parenthood

In her classic study, *The Mother's Role in Antebellum Childhood Education*, Anne L. Kuhn asserted that the typical depiction of the ideal nineteenth-century family shows the mother sitting in one corner of a living room, attending to several young children gathered around her, while the father, seated in the other corner, reads aloud to the family group or instructs an older child. Kuhn offered the example of an illustration from Samuel G. Goodrich's *Fireside Education* (1838). In it, a mother places the arms of her small son around the neck of his little sister, while the father, standing apart by a window, textbook in hand, points out astronomical features in the night sky to an older son. The caption beneath reads: "The mother sways the dominion of the heart, the father that of the intellect."[48]

The image neatly symbolizes a number of nineteenth-century beliefs about the cultivation of domestic affection, the importance of home education, and the respective functions of parents; but to judge by prints in the Currier and Ives catalog, this scene is not typical. Currier and Ives, the most successful purveyors of lithographic prints to the middle class by midcentury, produced ten times as many images of mothers and their children as they did of fathers and their children. My analysis of the New York publishing firm's catalog uncovered eighty-one images in which parents were depicted.

"The mother sways the dominion of the heart, the father that of the
intellect."

Fig. 1. From Samuel G. Goodrich, *Fireside Education* (New York, 1838).

Of these, mothers and children were represented in fifty-three prints (65%),
fathers and children in five prints (6%), and both parents and their children
in twenty-three prints (28%).[49]

   More interesting than the predominance of maternal imagery, perhaps, is
the relative paucity of parental imagery overall. Even a casual glance at the
catalog reveals that the domestic advisers' preoccupation with parents and
parenting was not necessarily reflected in other popular media. Compared
to eighty-one images on parental themes in the Currier and Ives catalog,
there are 131 images of marriage and courtship. Of a total 7,500 prints, only
405, or 5 percent, represent scenes of children and family. (By contrast, and

doubtless reflecting a distinctive feature of the market for lithographs, there are approximately 825 prints on horse-racing themes.)

Even within this strikingly small domestic universe, few images represent parents. Most often (in 61% of the prints depicting children and family), children were portrayed by themselves.[50] In the America of Currier and Ives, the realm of children was a separate sphere, most frequently located in the world of nature. This tendency to depict children without parents is owing to the nineteenth century's celebration of childhood innocence and the romantic belief that nature acted as the child's teacher. Significantly, when children were depicted with their mother, the scenes typically moved into the house.[51]

It is hardly surprising that mothers' iconographic sphere was the home. Unfortunately, there are so few images of fathers and their children that it is impossible to generalize about the spatial location of fatherhood in the world represented by Currier and Ives. Fathers were depicted both inside the house and out. When both parents were depicted with their children, however, it was slightly more likely that the setting was outdoors, rather than the domestic interiors characteristic of images of mothers and children. Hunting and fishing scenes, some of which depicted an adult male figure with an older boy, also associated men and children with the great outdoors.

The most striking feature of images of fathers and children, though, is how little interaction was represented between them. In one print, a father reads to his daughter; in another, a widower and his son stare at a portrait on an easel; in a third, a father reads a book in his study while his sleeping daughter rests her head on his lap. In the two remaining prints, fathers are simply posed with their children, not obviously engaged in any mutual activity.

Mothers—largely due to the greater sample size of prints that feature them—were depicted in a variety of parenting activities, ranging from teaching children their ABCs to bathing and dressing them, or from playing with them to instructing them in prayer. Interestingly, though, when both parents were represented, fathers appeared as engaged as mothers in the activity at hand, whether that was going to church, participating in home worship, picnicking, or taking a summer ramble. It is as if nineteenth-century illustrators were at an imaginative loss to depict fathers alone with their children but had no difficulty engaging husbands in family scenes animated by a mother's presence.

One final image, this one the frontispiece to Artemas Muzzey's best-selling *The Fireside: An Aid to Parents* (1854), symbolizes the elevation of the husband's role. In this outdoor scene, titled "Home Joys," a mother seated in a bower attends to a small daughter in a baby carriage being pulled by an older son. The girl offers her mother a bouquet of flowers, while the father, standing beside his wife with one hand on her shoulder, settles a wreath atop her head.

HOME JOYS.

Fig. 2. From A. B. Muzzey, *The Fireside:
An Aid to Parents* (Boston, 1854).

Compared to the father pictured in Goodrich's *Fireside Education*, published sixteen years earlier, Muzzey's image of a father had lost overt parental function. Instead of interacting with children, he acted in his capacity as husband. By crowning his wife with the wreath of his devotion, he reinforced filial affection for her, thereby augmenting the force of her love. Underlying this reevaluation of masculine domestic function was a double standard of parental affection.

The Double Standard of Parental Love

In an era that prized family sentiment not only as a source of emotion but also as a socializing force, men were somewhat at a disadvantage as parents. Family thinkers considered masculine authority a less potent instrument of child nurturance than a mother's love. A mother's influence, Muzzey told his readers, is "like some concentrated perfume [that] penetrates with potent but invisible agency every nook of home, pervading where the coarser authority of the father could never reach."[52]

Commentators sometimes attributed the power of motherly love to environmental conditions in the home. Sheltered from the "passion-stirring" world in the haven of the household, women could cultivate mother-child relations in an unworldly, uniquely nurturant atmosphere. The dominant note in family advice, however, naturalized the distinction. In the words of John Todd, a rigidly orthodox Congregational minister and tireless author: "The love which the father, the brother, or the sister bears, seems to be secondary, and the result of habit and association. But that which glows early and late, that which never tires or decays in the bosom of the mother, seems innate, a part of her very being."[53] William Dewees, a physician and vigorous proponent of breast-feeding, located the source of maternal love in the intense bond experienced by a nursing mother and her child. Along similar lines, Lydia Sigourney argued that the incomparable power of mothers' love was due to women's having placed themselves in peril of death to give life to their children. "How different," she said, "must an affection thus founded, be from all others."[54]

It followed from this differential assessment that a father's affection for his children was a virtue but a mother's love was an element of nature. Fathers, accordingly, could be held to a lesser standard of parental care. A dislike of

children in men was an "unfavorable omen" for marriage, according to the
physician William Alcott, but in women it was "unsupportable" because such
a feeling would be "grossly unnatural."[55]

The idea of a double standard of parental love should not be exaggerated.
Although mothers' love was considered more instinctual, few doubted that
fathers loved their children or were capable of sacrificing personal interest
on their behalf. Some writers groped toward a concept of a distinctively paternal love. Such a "manly love" was less demonstrative than a mother's love
and more difficult for children to apprehend, but it was no less deeply felt
by the father himself and no less consequential for the family's welfare.

Much of this love was evident in the sacrifices a father made to provide
for his children and their education, but it was also apparent in the ground-
work of "good principles" and "habits of industry" that he laid for them,
particularly for his sons. "To give you such advantages, cost him labor, self-
denial, and much anxious thought," said T. S. Arthur, the temperance crusader and author of popular fiction for adults and children. "Many times,
during the struggle to sustain his family, has he been pressed down with
worldly difficulties, and almost ready to despair. . . . But still, his love for his
children has urged him on."[56]

The topic of parental love was enormously interesting to middle-class
mothers and fathers alike. Evidence for this comes from an unexpected
source—the nineteenth-century vogue of phrenology. Phrenology is best
remembered today as the strange belief that the mind consists of thirty-
seven independent faculties, which correlate with bumps on the skull. One
is tempted to dismiss such theorizing as the lunatic fringe of Jacksonian
reform, but to disregard phrenology's historical importance would be a
mistake.

Phrenology was a characteristic expression of contemporary popular culture. The nineteenth century's version of psychology, phrenological teachings were a widely accepted and much discussed explanation of human behavior. The movement consistently addressed issues central to the concerns
of the emerging bourgeoisie, and its message—taken to heart by both the
masses and the well educated—reached a large audience of Americans at
midcentury. A wide array of social reformers and opinion leaders, including Horace Mann, Henry Ward Beecher, Sarah Josepha Hale, and Horace
Greeley, embraced phrenology as a social philosophy and broadcast its message to a receptive public.[57]

By codifying popular precepts about parenthood, phrenology's publicists bridged the gap between religiously grounded family advice, prevalent in the antebellum era, and the biological and medical thinking that displaced it in the latter half of the century. Mixing science, religion, and morality, phrenology was, in the words of one historian, a "way station on the road to a secular view of life." In the popular mind, the aims of the physiologists and scientists whose child-rearing advice was growing increasingly important were not much different from those of the phrenologists.[58]

Phrenological precepts about fatherhood arrayed many of the already familiar beliefs about child rearing and domesticity in the language of science. What phrenologists called the organ of "philoprogenativeness," or parental love, was central to their description of human psychology. According to phrenological theory, love was a universal element of human nature—the mainspring of all human actions. Conjugal love, in particular, was the basis of mature manhood and womanhood, transforming boys into men and girls into women. Though necessary to the development and constitutional well-being of both sexes, love was more perfectly embodied in women than in men. It also expressed itself differently, with a larger measure of devotion and self-sacrifice being ascribed to women. This moral disparity was particularly reflected in the greater development of the organ of parental love in women.[59]

For phrenologists and their adherents, parenthood was the bedrock of domestic happiness. On the phrenological chart of brain structure, the organs of conjugal and parental love were located adjacent to one another at the base of the skull (a key position, because this was where the body's magnetic energy was said to enter the brain from the spinal cord). Orson Fowler, the movement's leading American publicist, asserted that love and parenting were reciprocally related because organs located together acted together. Parenthood, in other words, was intimately linked to sexual attraction. A man's paternal feelings—more precisely, his sympathy for his wife's maternal nature—were the firmest foundation for conjugal affection and fidelity.[60]

Significantly, phrenology's conception of marriage elevated its parental aspects over conjugal ones. "Annihilate parentage," said Fowler, "and you blot out all the tender yearnings of connubial love, all the fond delights of parental endearment, all the pleasures of infantile and juvenile provision and guardianship, and thus extinguish a cluster of the holiest and happiest emotions mortals can experience; because the latter are only the satellites of the former."[61] Sustained emotional engagement in family life, therefore, required cultivating the love of children. Only when husband and wife became mother and father, Fowler declared, "can they be completely enamored of each other; because it is her *maternal* relations which most of all endear the wife to her husband, besides making her love him inexpressibly the more for being the *father of her idolized children.*"[62]

Phrenology taught that, since principal training and care of children devolved on the mother, women were divinely endowed with a larger share of philoprogenativeness, which was correspondingly less essential in the father. In this respect, phrenological theories simply affirmed the double standard of parental love, a double standard that we know, from testimony in divorce cases, was internalized by nineteenth-century Americans.[63]

At the same time, phrenology introduced ideas that foreshadowed scientific views of fatherhood promulgated by physicians and other medically minded advisers later in the century. Fowler maintained, for instance, that "sexuo-filial" attraction between parents and children of the opposite sex attached daughters more strongly to their fathers and sons, likewise, to their mothers.[64] More to the point, Fowler's insistence that conjugal ties were rooted in parental affection served medically inspired reformers who attempted to regulate male sexuality in the century's closing decades by postulating a biological need for men to become fathers.

Biological Science and the Ideal of Paternal Manhood

Of the many cultural forms that reshaped meanings for fatherhood in the latter half of the century, few were more salient than popular medical advice. Throughout the century ministers preached the virtues of Christian fatherhood, but their published advice began to appear less often in the postbellum era. To a large extent, such pronouncements were replaced by a moralistic medical literature in which ideas about fatherhood were attached to the growing assumption that the condition of a man's body was the foundation of his character. This was especially apparent in the late-nineteenth-century movement for social purity (a campaign against prostitution, venereal diseases, and the double standard of sexual morality), which used scientific arguments to extol the personal and societal benefits of fatherhood. Using science as their guide, social hygienists formulated a paradigm of masculinity within which "true manhood" could be achieved only through paternity.[65]

The social hygienists' case rested, in part, on an eclectic body of popular science purporting to describe the hereditary influence of mothers and fathers. Although experts disagreed about the nature and extent of these contributions, each parent was thought to transmit distinctive qualities to the child. Gestation and lactation added overall weight to the mother's influence, but fathers generally were believed to contribute more toward the physical form and intellectual nature of their children, while mothers imparted more of their affections, moral sentiments, nervous temperaments, and tastes.[66]

Fathers were considered particularly powerful in determining their daughters' intellects and moral characters. George Napheys, an influential physician and author of a book of sexual advice for men that went through more than twenty printings in several editions between 1871 and 1898, maintained, for instance, that some physical qualities, such as the exterior and extremities of the child, were most influenced by the father, while the internal organs were inherited from the mother. This influence varied with the sex of the child, however, and Napheys taught that "daughters partake more frequently than sons do of the intellectual peculiarities of the father." The physician Dan Newcomb echoed Napheys's views, adding that the father also transmitted his moral qualities to his daughters, while the mother conveyed hers to her sons. During gestation, he maintained, the child's mental and physical constitution was molded by the mother, but its "vitality" was the result of the father's influence at the time of conception. A father's responsibility to his offspring, therefore, began before birth.[67]

Since all paternal endowments were impressed upon offspring at once, the condition of the father when his children were conceived was especially important. The paternal endowment needed to be conveyed with immense energy, in order to impart the greatest possible momentum to the child's mental and physical functions. Some advisers even counseled prospective fathers to have intercourse early in the day, before they were worn down and their vital powers were sapped. It went without saying that the father should be sober at the time of conception. Time and again men were warned that children conceived by a drunken father were themselves liable to intemperance—or worse.[68]

The principles of hereditary transmission made prospective fatherhood the linchpin of what G. J. Barker-Benfield aptly termed the "spermatic economy," the system of beliefs underlying the masturbation phobia in nineteenth-century medical advice to men.[69] What advocates of male sexual restraint called "seminal continence" was essential to youth in order to attain full masculine development and necessary to mature men in order to "maintain a high tone of vitality and manly vigor." The prospective father's "impregnative force," an attribute that influenced not only his capacity to beget children but his mental faculties as well, depended on his ability to refrain from masturbating and to exercise sexual self-control. The man who retained his seminal endowment charged his being with manly power, generated within himself a higher interior life, and prepared himself, in the phrases of one publicist, for "the crowning function of manhood": "the godlike purpose" of procreation.[70]

Sexual restraint was not enough, however; paternity was also required, because men could achieve mature and noble gender identities *only* as fathers. In an 1869 volume of advice, Fowler declared that the man who failed to beget healthy children failed "in all else manly. This [paternity] is the *chit* of manhood."[71] Accordingly, he designated the fathers of families honored masculine types, "aristocrats, dignitaries, privileged characters, enjoying special immunities and honor, and always ranking [above] those who are not *pater-familias*." Not only had fathers demonstrated their manliness by having children, domestic life added dignity, weight, and responsibility to masculine character, thereby elevating a man's social worth. Bachelors, by contrast, owing to the "comparative torpidity of their connubial and parental elements," experienced a "diminution of energy in all their other faculties" and ranked "far lower in the scale of being and estimation than their true sphere in other respects." Another adviser, Samuel R. Wells, termed bachelors men whose "higher nature had been stifled and suppressed."[72]

Fowler and Wells were not alone. Late-nineteenth-century physicians typically defined as "unnatural" the man who avoided fatherhood or who separated sex from reproduction. Such disparaging views accorded with earlier critiques of bachelors as men who refused to assume the manly responsibilities of marriage, fatherhood, productive labor, and political duty. Whereas sober fathers sacrificed for their families and achieved self-fulfillment, bachelors—especially young men living in cities—indulged their appetites, exposing themselves to the moral and physical dangers of masturbation and prostitution. In the end, bachelors were doomed to suffer loneliness and alienation, while fathers realized the domestic fulfillment inherent in their masculine nature.[73]

Victorian Virility and the Stages of Manhood

The risks of bachelorhood notwithstanding, a remarkably stable consensus held that men should delay marriage until at least age twenty-five. In medical literature, this recommendation was based on the presumption that the body matured in successive stages and that reproduction should take place only after the male body had acquired its full development, in a man's mid-twenties. Premature intercourse (i.e., before a man was capable of producing perfect sperm) would not only beget puny and sickly children but would also be injurious to the father himself, enfeebling his constitution, hastening physical decline, and leading ultimately to premature death.[74]

Significantly, pubescence did not coincide with the emergence of virility as Victorian scientists and physicians defined the term. While youth became sexually potent at puberty, which writers placed anywhere from age fourteen to seventeen, virility was achieved a decade or more later, when a man was biologically ready and, equally important, socially prepared for fatherhood.

It followed from setting the marriageable age at about twenty-five, some ten years after the onset of puberty, that the intervening period was a critical decade of preparation for fatherhood and adult life. By the close of the nineteenth century, these years had become increasingly circumscribed and codified into a uniform set of experiences for youth, which the psychologist G. Stanley Hall and others labeled "adolescence."[75] Medical theories stressed the need during this period for young men to establish the self-control (continence) required for continued development of their constitution and faculties, including, critically, the capacity for paternity.[76]

The influential British physician William Acton, whose treatise on reproductive disorders went through eight American editions and became established as a contemporary medical classic, maintained that the period of virility commenced when the sexual passion of youth was tempered with a desire for fatherhood.[77] Only then should the physician recommend marriage:

> At a certain period in every man's life — occurring generally somewhere between twenty-five and thirty — he is conscious, if he has lived on the whole a chaste life, of a great change in those sexual tendencies of which he has been frequently conscious before. They are no longer the fitful fancies of a boy, but are capable, he feels, of ripening at once into the steady rational passion, or rather purpose, of the full-grown man. The

natural longing is there still, but is no longer toward mere sensual indulgence only (it will be remembered that I am speaking of the *conti-
nent* man), but is deeply tinctured with the craving for wife—and
home—and children.[78]

Acton termed this mellowed but incomparably powerful sexuality "the
feeling of virility." He used the concept to replant the flag of masculinity in
the realm of parenthood, thereby reviving patriarchal ideology on a scientific basis. "This feeling of *virility*," Acton wrote, "is much more developed
in man than is that of maternity in woman. Its existence, indeed, seems necessary to give a man that consciousness of his dignity, of his character as head
and ruler, and of his importance, which is absolutely essential to the well-
being of the family, and through it, of society itself."[79]

The physician George Napheys echoed these views. "The season of virility has commenced," he wrote, when "the vague and fleeting fancies of youth
have been transformed into a well-defined yearning for home and children
and a help-meet." Only then were sexual relations permissible.[80] Other tem-
peramental changes accompanied these domestic longings. Virile men became less selfish, their relish for moral and intellectual pursuits intensified,
and they were more capable of steady and disciplined work. The causal arrow
ran in both directions. On one hand, these changes suited men for paternity.
At the same time, subjection to family responsibility compelled the father to
acquire the habits of industry, frugality, and economy needed to care for wife
and children. Accordingly, for Napheys manhood had a natural history that
achieved fruition in midlife, when the masculine nature was centered in the
family. Children born to men between twenty-five and forty-five, the period
when the physical and intellectual activities of most men were at their height
and when the impetuous sensuality of youth was tempered by paternal responsibility, were generally predicted to be more vigorous than those conceived by men younger or older.[81] Indeed, the period from roughly ages
twenty-five to forty-five came to be seen as a window of opportunity for
fatherhood, when men would produce the healthiest and most talented offspring.

For late-nineteenth-century physicians, scientists, and health reformers,
the coincidence of fatherhood and mature manhood was evidence of nature's harmonious design. Providence had decreed that only fully developed

men produced completely formed sperm, because men needed full physical growth in order to "work hard and build homes for their families, and to earn food and clothing for them," said one purity crusader. "They need to get an education, that they may teach their children. This takes time, and makes all come out right together."[82]

In this view, the first fifteen to twenty years of fatherhood were the crowning reward and prime of a man's life. Provided that seminal continence was observed, the mature male body continued to develop beyond age twenty-five, for the next twenty years or so, as conserved sperm were absorbed and assimilated. According to E. R. Shepherd, an author of advice to men, this was the prime of life—the age at which a man could endure the greatest mental and physical strains. It was, in his words, "a sort of harvest season of life," when a man's "knowledge of life and the world; his insight into human nature, gained by experience, serves to temper and guide him in the use of these ripe powers, and to make him the valued leader of younger men." Not least of life's harvest was the filial love that compensated a father for his sacrifices.[83]

In realizing virility's "appointed purpose," fatherhood was the crowning reward for the self-restraint, self-culture, and self-mastery central to Victorian conceptions of masculinity. This biological celebration of paternity had little to say about the tasks of fatherhood, but its logic was to reinvest the parental role with masculine meaning. Indeed, in the views of many scientists and physicians, the instinct for parenthood was as powerful in men as it is in women.

From Moralism to Naturalism

The advice literature examined in this chapter was a source of belief that impinged primarily upon the urban bourgeoisie. Accordingly, it is possible to exaggerate the influence of the ideal of paternal manhood in the late nineteenth century and likewise to exaggerate the power of Christian fatherhood in the previous era. Advocates of paternal manhood clustered in the social hygiene movement, although they were not exclusively purity crusaders. Moreover, their prescripts vied with alternative definitions of manhood centered on achievement at work and participation in the burgeoning realm of masculine sociability.[84] Similarly, the Protestant publicists of Christian fatherhood exhorted men at a time when males formed a minority of active church members, to say nothing of how their message was received by Catholic men and non-Christians.

The differences within each of these two paradigms ought to be obvious enough to make their juxtaposition a valuable indicator of an event in the history of nineteenth-century thinking about fatherhood: the diminution of debate about what fathers should do for their children and the enlargement of concern about what paternity could do for men. Clearly, this was a reorientation of thinking, not the introduction of a new line of thought. The advocates of Christian fatherhood had a well-developed sense of fatherhood's benefits for men as well as for children. Indeed, one of the most striking features of nineteenth-century domestic thought is how long and how loudly fatherhood's "therapeutic" benefits for men were proclaimed. Antebellum moralists saw fatherhood as a source of personal satisfaction and a reward overlooked by those who neglected their paternal responsibility. By curbing competitive aggressiveness, moreover, fatherhood called forth the self-sacrificing side of masculine nature, which also aided society. The problem was to convince men of these benefits in an era that exalted motherhood at every turn. From this perspective, the Christian fatherhood ideal was an attempt to engage men in family life by grounding the role of the father in a traditional and specifically masculine responsibility for children's moral welfare and for household leadership.

In an increasingly secular society, this backward-looking attempt to stabilize men's domestic commitments on the basis of religion was inherently problematic, and ultimately some other way had to be found to reassert the relevance of parenthood to men. This task was undertaken by the publicists of paternal manhood in the 1870s and 1880s. Insisting that paternal responsibility began before conception, these medically minded reformers replaced a moralistic (Christian) perspective on fatherhood with a naturalistic (secular) one. They asserted that being a father was as constitutive of man's nature as being a mother was of woman's—a matter of consequence in an age that naturalized motherhood and reflexively looked to women as children's guiding lights.

Like the advocates of Christian fatherhood, the ideologists of paternal manhood hoped to fortify patriarchal authority within the family. The feeling of virility, Acton wrote, was needed to give a man an awareness of his character as "head and ruler" of his household. At the same time, reform-minded physicians responded to the decline of patriarchal control within the family by attempting to wrest authority over child rearing from mothers and place it in their own (predominantly masculine) hands.[85]

Significantly, physicians were the first to question the doctrine of maternal love. "If love alone would make children strong and healthy; if love alone would train their minds aright, then children would, in mind and body, be all that could be desired," asserted the physician Pye Henry Chavasse in an 1873 volume of parent-advice. "But alas! love alone is not sufficient for such purposes." Accordingly, Chavasse urged mothers to "turn student" in order to make themselves fit as parents.[86] The result was to professionalize motherhood by equipping it with "expert" advice, without articulating a new role for fathers. This threw yet another roadblock in the path of fathers, who were hard pressed to challenge their wives' expertise. In the end, then, late-nineteenth-century fathers were left with a new rationale for involving themselves with their children (to perfect their manly nature) but with few guideposts for action and, perhaps, the sense that patriarchal power had shifted out of the home and into the hands of medical experts.

Ironically, historians have documented the existence of a significant number of nurturing family men in this period. Scholars such as Mark Carnes and Margaret Marsh suggest that, as the economic position of the middle-class family became more secure at the turn of the twentieth century, work commanded less emotional energy and men were better able to devote themselves to domestic life.[87] Recently, E. Anthony Rotundo pointed out that new, "primitive" standards of late-nineteenth-century manhood associated with the "strenuous life" rendered such masculine domesticity a contradiction in terms. "If a man was spending more time at home exercising the skills which supposedly belonged to women, what kind of man was he?" Rotundo asks rhetorically.[88] The publicists of paternal manhood had an answer, of course: he was the most virile sort of man.

In many ways, the cultural shift away from what fathers could do for their children and toward what paternity could do for men limited the scope of paternal involvement. The relocation of patriarchal authority outside the home, in social institutions such as the medical profession and the judiciary, had a similar dampening effect. The ideal of paternal manhood, however, may have provided some men with the reassurance that appreciating family life and spending more leisure time with children were compatible with masculinity.

Over the course of the nineteenth century, religious and secular moralists went to great lengths to convince men that fatherhood was the assumption of a man's highest responsibility and that family duty was a cornerstone of masculine identity. Did middle-class men take this message to heart? To what extent did their actual behavior accord with, or deviate from, this domestic ideal? How did life in a commercial, industrializing society sustain or inhibit men's ability to act as fathers? Let us turn to these and other questions.

Chapter 3

Time and Togetherness

Toward an Understanding of Paternal Availability
in the Nineteenth Century

My daily duties sometimes press hard.

Amos A. Lawrence, 1861

Between the ages of four and six, Theodore Potter seldom saw his father. Potter, who was born on a farm in Saline, Michigan, in 1832, recalled that when he was a boy about four years old his father found work as a surveyor, "which took him away from home much of the time for the next two years." The struggle for economic security compelled Potter's father to relocate his family at least twice by the time Theodore turned thirteen. From Saline, the family moved some twenty miles to Plymouth, Michigan, and then, in 1845, to a pioneer homestead in Eaton County, seventy miles farther west. What he earned surveying helped Theodore's father realize his ambition of settling his family on a productive farm of his own. Although pursuit of that goal removed him for long periods from a family that grew to include seven children, few contemporaries doubted that he was fulfilling his obligation as a father, whose first duty was to provide for his family. Notwithstanding his periodic absences, Potter was doing what was expected of a man; he was, in a favored nineteenth-century phrase, exhibiting a "father's care" for his family, as distinguished from a "mother's love" for her children.[1]

A half-century later, on Christmas Day, 1895, a middle-class mother of two young children, living near Chicago, noted in her diary that her husband, a school principal named Fulton Ormsby, had left home on a professional trip. "Papa starts for Springfield tonight at 11:30," Edna Ormsby recorded. "He has gone to the city to take the train so we are alone except for Sena up stairs. We have never slept a night in our home without him and it seems very lonely. We pray God to keep him safe and bring him back to us. He is such a good papa how could we live without him."[2]

The concept of fatherhood does not change overnight, or even over sixty years. But between the time of Potter's surveying expeditions in the 1830s, which absented him from home for the better part of two years, and Fulton Ormsby's trip to Springfield in 1895, which required his first night away from his wife and family in five years of marriage, one thing that had changed in many middle-class homes was the expectation of family togetherness. Indeed, in the nineteenth century, attitudes toward paternal absence changed more dramatically than did the amount of time that men actually had available to spend with their families.

No theme has so dominated scholarly understandings of nineteenth-century fatherhood as the impact of industrialization on paternal availability. The story historians tell is simple enough: Beginning in the first decades of the nineteenth century and increasingly thereafter, men were drawn out of their families toward income-producing work, a development that propelled fathers on a downward path toward distance and part-time involvement in family life.[3]

The trend toward "part-time" fathering over the course of the nineteenth century is easily exaggerated, however, and often misconstrued. The amount of time fathers had available to spend with children varied considerably throughout the century, depending on a man's occupation, place of residence, and class position. Contemporary testimony such as Theodore Potter's (emphasizing persistent paternal absence from a farm in rural Michigan early in the century) and Edna Ormsby's (highlighting a father's relatively uninterrupted domestic presence in a suburban Chicago home as the century drew to a close) should caution us against assuming that changes in paternal availability progressed in linear fashion or that increasingly onerous time constraints were uniformly imposed by the process of industrialization. The experience of men like Potter suggests that the formation of a commercial economy, which affected both rural and urban areas, had an earlier and a more widespread impact on fatherhood than did urban-industrial change.[4]

The consequences of men's increased involvement in a web of market relations were complex, with profound implications both for family unity and for paternal authority. We can begin to unravel some of this complexity by recognizing that the separation of work and home was a slow and uneven process and that the time constraints imposed by economic transformation varied widely. In many places—certain New England mill towns, for instance—as much or more unity of work and family existed in cities as in farming areas.[5]

It is important to specify the time constraints imposed by economic change, but it is equally crucial to recognize that time spent at home corresponds only loosely, if at all, to a father's actual influence over children or his ability to set the tone of family life. Both of these powers ultimately rest on cultural understandings of the father's role. The historian Bernard Wishy speculates that work-related absence may actually have enhanced the father's authority over children by distinguishing the infrequent occasions when this authority was exercised from the mother's more routine, day-to-day governance. Along similar lines, John Demos hints that separation of the father's place of work from home may have invested his endeavors in the alien and somewhat mysterious world of the market with an aura of heroism.[6]

Such conjectures suggest that no simple equation relates time available to fathers and their place in the family. More time spent by fathers away at work necessarily enhanced the decision making and authority of mothers at home. At the same time, family members adapted to paternal absence in the light of social understandings of the father's leadership role. Did wives, children, and fathers themselves view time spent at work as a rejection of fatherhood (as did the publicists of "paternal neglect" in the 1830s and 1840s) or as a necessary element of it? Did work-imposed distance create a new type of father? The social role expectations that helped nineteenth-century Americans answer those questions were formed in the country, around the rhythms and labor demands of an agrarian way of life, and these expectations were reformulated in the city, around new modes of work and altered understandings of family togetherness.

Family Time in Rural Homes

From early in the century, the poorest fathers in the countryside—farmers who owned little or no land—were absent from home most often. Some men were gone for weeks, months, or even years at a time, wandering about, looking for employment, and working when they found it.

Asa Sheldon, who was born in 1788 and grew to manhood in and around Wilmington, Massachusetts, recalled such a hard-pressed father: "My father owning but a few acres of land, worked much of his time stoning wells and cellars and consequently was with his family but little. Generally working in Salem, we saw but little of him, except on the Sabbath." Sheldon's situation was hardly unique. Leonard Stockwell, who was born in 1798, saw little of his wife and children for extended periods during the 1830s and 1840s. With no farm of his own, Stockwell worked land on shares and earned what he could as a day laborer. For a period of time, he worked away from his home in Millbury, Massachusetts, during the week and returned to his family only on Sunday. Even when he found jobs close enough to home to sleep in his own bed each night, long hours separated him from his wife and children during the day.[7]

Persistent absences placed sharp constraints on men's ability to act as fathers. One further example illustrates how continual leave-taking might also distress father-child relations. Emily Ward, born in 1809, recalled that her father moved his family so frequently that no two of his four children were born in the same place. Even with his family settled on a relative's farm in Vermont, Emily's father was absent from home much of the time between 1812 and 1817, when she grew from age three to age eight. Ward left home first to work as a boatman on Lake Ontario, and later as a fisherman on Lake Erie, selling his catch at various port cities in Pennsylvania, Ohio, and Kentucky. "My father was a rover," Emily recalled bitterly. "I remember that as a very young child I hated it, and I thought, when I had a home of my own, I never would move, and I never did but once."[8] Emily Ward's recollections are particularly resentful, but the mildly plaintive note with which paternal absence is often recounted in the memoir literature hints at children's glum acceptance of a father's frequent economic excursions. More pointedly, the intimations of disapproval highlight the increased premium placed on family togetherness in later decades, when the narrators wrote their stories.

Landless men were not the only fathers drawn from home by financial circumstances. In the countryside, any number of economic enterprises could
separate fathers from their families. Men who worked in distant fields might
return home only for meals. Trips to town to purchase supplies or tend to
other business were common. To supplement income, ambitious farmers
sometimes worked neighboring acres. As land grew scarce later in the century, some men planted crops on pieces of land several miles away from their
home farms. Others worked by the day, at carpentry, for instance, or helping neighbors with odd jobs.

In slack seasons, Midwestern farmers were sometimes separated from
their wives and children for months at a time, working in northern mining
and lumber camps, where they earned money for farm and family supplies
or to purchase land. A significant number of farmers had what amounted to
dual careers—as surveyors, as shopkeepers, or in petty trade. For country
shopkeepers and merchants, in particular, the commercialization of society
combined two worlds in one. Frequently, they relied on sons or hired hands
to work their farms while they minded their stores or traveled to tend business accounts.[9]

Nor were fathers the only family members recurrently separated from rural
homes. Children, too, came and went. Beginning in their teens, children
periodically left home for training, education, or employment. Especially in
the antebellum countryside, where district schools and opportunities for
work were widely scattered, children frequently lived apart from their families for months on end. Indeed, teenagers in industrial cities were more likely
to live with their families than were those in rural areas, for the simple reason that urban youth could find work in mills and factories close to home.[10]

Farms, of course, merged home and workplace, and many rural fathers
spent a good deal of time with children on a day-to-day basis, either working with sons or attending to children in the hours after work. While this
heightened availability of rural fathers did exist, it was frequently disrupted.
Farm fathers loomed large on the landscape of childhood and were exceptionally important role models for growing sons, but their accessibility is
easily exaggerated by idyllic visions of the rural past. Significant tension between work and family time existed even in rural America, where uninterrupted togetherness was seldom the rule. Many economic tasks separated
fathers from their families once agriculture moved beyond subsistence farm-

ing. Equally important, children were not expected to reside continuously at home. Accordingly, the argument that industrialization displaced fathers from their households must be tempered with the recognition that families in the commercialized countryside had grown accustomed to considerable separation. Indeed, for fathers like Leonard Stockwell, sons like Asa Sheldon and Theodore Potter, and daughters like Emily Ward, industrialization and the growth of cities might well have seemed to bring fathers and their families closer together rather than drive them apart. From this perspective, what nineteenth-century moralists lamented as the loss of fathers to the workplace was not so much a change in the amount of time men actually spent with their children as a shift in cultural emphasis, in the desire for greater family togetherness.

Family Time in Cities and Towns

Just as work and family life were less integrated in the countryside than we like to imagine, so was the impact of urban-industrial change less wrenching to fatherhood than we sometimes suppose. For much of the nineteenth century, the routines and rhythms of urban life permitted substantial involvement with family. Fathers who were employed in workshops, factories, stores, and offices had more latitude to combine work and home life than do many of their counterparts today, in part because most men continued to live only a short distance from their workplace.

The separation of home and residence was a slow process whose social meaning is still not well understood. We know, however, that distance varied sharply by occupation and class and that rates of separation differed from city to city. Urban historians have shown that, as late as 1880, many men continued to combine home and work. For those who labored outside their homes, most continued to live within a short walk of their workplaces.

In Manhattan, virtually no man separated his place of business from his place of residence by more than a mile before 1840.[11] Sam Bass Warner Jr. found that, at midcentury, many artisans in Boston kept shop and home in the same building and that factories, wharves, and offices were but a few blocks from middle-class homes. Not until the 1870s did members of Boston's middling ranks begin to reside in the "streetcar suburbs" serviced by street railways, and even then the proportion commuting increased only from roughly 20 percent in the 1870s to 50 percent by the 1890s.[12]

Theodore Hershberg and his colleagues maintain that as late as the 1880s the bulk of Philadelphia's labor force was "by necessity tied to the blocks surrounding the firms in which they earned their livelihood." A smaller, but growing, number of wealthier citizens in white-collar professions commuted to work from neighborhoods on the city's edges. Among white-collar professionals, the separation of work and home varied widely by occupation. Whereas 95 percent of Philadelphia's physicians combined home and work in 1880, only 17.6 percent of lawyers did so. Table 4, below, suggests that such variability affected shopkeepers and artisans in the middling ranks of society as well. An overwhelming proportion of confectioners (90.6%) and majorities of carpenters (53%) and cabinetmakers (54.3%) combined home and work in 1880. Indeed, the proportion of carpenters who lived and worked under the same roof increased from the earlier period, probably owing to a proliferation of small firms as the building and construction industry expanded between 1850 and 1880. Overall, the separation of home and work was apparently tied to scale of labor. Small firms in the crafts served local markets and had low profits, a trend that reinforced the combination of work and residence.[13]

It is difficult, and perhaps foolish, to apply a rule of distance to measure emotional proximity to children. Diary evidence, however, confirms that

Table 4. Percent of Professionals, Proprietors, and Artisans Combining Home and Work in Philadelphia, 1850 and 1880

	1850	1880
Physicians	100.0	95.0
Lawyers	52.6	17.6
Confectioners	91.1	90.6
Bookbinders	30.3	9.3
Blacksmiths	23.7	23.0
Cabinetmakers	64.2	54.3
Carpenters	39.0	53.0

Source: Theodore Hershberg et al., *Philadelphia: Work, Space, Family, and Group Experience in the Nineteenth Century* (New York, 1981) 136.

professional and business vocations did not normally interfere with fatherly responsibility through midcentury and, in some cases, well beyond that time. Professionals and businessmen spent much time attending to work commitments, but many children in middle-class homes spent at least some time during the week with their fathers, who, in addition to breakfast and dinner, might be home for the afternoon meal or otherwise available to their children during the workday.

Elizabeth Gurney Taylor, born in Sturgis, Michigan, in 1840, kept a diary beginning in 1854, which documents that her father, Chester Gurney, routinely combined work in town with family life. As a teenager, Elizabeth occasionally visited her father at his office, and he was often at home in the afternoon for dinner. Seldom did a month pass without several references to her father's weekday presence at home in the forenoon or afternoon on one domestic errand or another. Gurney was in and out of the house during the week for many chores: to help slaughter chickens; to take the family's "old brass" to the tin shop to exchange for new utensils; to carry home apples, coffee, and other groceries; to bring home newspapers and town gossip; to carry a pair of galoshes to Elizabeth at school; to take his wife's and daughters' bonnets to the milliner to be done over; and to transport his family to buy provisions.[14]

Similarly, when he was thirteen years old, Walter Curtis, who was born in 1874 and grew up in Detroit, frequently visited his father's office, occasionally taking him his lunch. Alice Stone Blackwell, the only child of the prominent woman suffragists Lucy Stone and Henry Blackwell, also had regular weekday contact with her father, a self-employed businessman and editor. Alice, who grew up in the Dorchester suburb of Boston in the 1860s and 1870s, sometimes accompanied her father into the city, where she visited the public library or Boston Athenaeum while he proceeded to the office. Amos A. Lawrence, an elite Boston merchant, kept the door to his counting room open to his children, who visited him there from time to time. He also regularly saw his children at home for the afternoon meal.[15]

Just as Elizabeth Gurney Taylor's diary offers a snapshot of how fathers could combine office work and domestic involvement in a small town, Lawrence's diary provides a glimpse of how a member of Boston's business elite balanced work and family commitments. Lawrence, who was born in Boston in 1814, married in 1842 at the age of twenty-seven. By 1858 his family had grown to include seven children. The year that his first child was born, 1843, Lawrence established the firm of Mason and Lawrence, which became a highly successful selling agency for several large textile mills in New England. Lawrence was a busy man. Throughout the 1850s and 1860s he devoted much time to a long list of business, philanthropic, and political interests. Independent of his firm, he was involved in textile manufacture. He was also an antislavery activist and educational philanthropist who was involved in managing the affairs of Harvard College and the Episcopal Theological School in Cambridge. In 1860 he ran unsuccessfully for governor of Massachusetts.

Lawrence clearly felt the time constraints on his family life. "My daily duties sometimes press hard," he noted in his journal on June 10, 1861. Nonetheless, he managed to combine his work and social activism with a substantial amount of family time. According to his diary, each day began in the company of his children, who joined him in his bedroom for personal prayers soon after he awoke. Formal family prayers were conducted in the library just before breakfast, which the family ate together at 7 A.M. Lawrence, who had moved his family to suburban Brookline in 1851, left for work on horseback at eight. He arrived at his counting room in Boston shortly after 9 and worked until about 3 P.M., when he began his ride back to Brookline to join his family for dinner. After dinner, Lawrence took a short nap, then attended to work on his estate and spent leisure time with his family. Generally this meant playing with his children or taking them on rides in his wagon, sometimes joined by his wife. The family assembled again at 7:45 P.M. for tea, after which Lawrence listened to the children's prayers and, at 8:30, helped put them to bed. Another nap, then a period of reading and writing until about midnight ended a typical day.[16]

While the foregoing examples cluster around white-collar professionals and office workers at the top of the social structure, fathers in a wide range of occupations were able to combine work commitments with at least some paternal involvement. Itinerant ministers, for instance, who were frequently absent from their families for months at a time, sometimes took their children with them on evangelizing missions. Physicians had their children help tend offices, often located at home. Children of shopkeepers sometimes accompanied their fathers to the store to visit, play, or work. Sundry motives lay behind these involvements, ranging from putting children to work, to providing tutelage and instruction, to fulfilling a desire for companionship. Florence Cushman Milner, whose father worked in the 1850s as an operative in a coach- and wagon-making factory in Concord, New Hampshire, recalled that she spent "many childhood hours in the shop," where her father taught her "the names of the tools and the use of as many as [her] childhood hands could compass."[17]

Among the laboring class in some factory towns, family togetherness and paternal availability were more usual than in rural areas. Many New England textile mills, for instance, employed the whole family. As late as 1868, the superintendent of schools in Fall River, Massachusetts, reported that "the operatives are for the most part families, and do the work in the mills by the piece, taking in their children to assist." Similarly, in Manchester, New Hampshire, laborers recruited other family members to work in the textile mills and were able to control their placement within the factory's workrooms.[18]

Although fathers continued to work alongside their families in factories until the turn of the twentieth century, as time went on the number of families participating in this arrangement shrank. Even when families did work together, the manager and foreman usually usurped the power of the father. A father might contract for his children and collect their wages, but his authority now counted for less than it had in the past, when family members worked together at home and the father was the business head of the family household. Ultimately, fathers in the industrial work force, who labored ten hours or longer, six days a week, had less time to spend with children and fewer means to participate in elaborate family gatherings than did men like Amos A. Lawrence or even Chester Gurney.[19]

The Missing Father

In cities and towns, as in the countryside, the poorest fathers were most often absent from home. As the factory system took root, and during hard times thereafter, an uncertain economy periodically separated many fathers from their families. Commenting on the situation in the second decade of the nineteenth century, the reformer and philanthropist Matthew Carey observed that "thousands of our laboring people travel hundreds of miles in quest of employment . . . leaving families behind, depending upon them for support. . . . Hundreds of them are swept off annually, many of them leaving numerous and helpless families."[20]

Although most of the men who participated in the nineteenth century's "tramping system" of migratory labor were young and unmarried, a significant proportion were fathers of families in search of steady work. Responding to the republican assumption that the honorable artisan was the family breadwinner, journeymen in a variety of trades traveled along employment networks that sometimes stretched great distances.[21]

It is difficult to know how frequently the unsuccessful search for work led men to abandon their families, but it seems clear that the incidence of paternal abandonment rose in the nineteenth century, as a geographically mobile working class formed and fathers who could not find work where their family lived searched for employment elsewhere. Families of marginally employed fathers were at a sharply greater risk of breaking up, evidenced by juvenile reformatories that were filled disproportionately with the children of unemployed or missing fathers. David J. Rothman has shown that the overwhelming majority of children in antebellum reformatories came from the bottom layers of the economic structure, the offspring of fathers who were common laborers or semiskilled workers. The managers of the New Hampshire House of Reformation, for instance, calculated that in 1860 almost half of the inmates' fathers did not have regular employment. Statistics from the New York House of Refuge indicated that of the 257 children in the institution in 1847, 60 percent were orphaned or had only one parent, with most of them missing fathers. One study of this asylum, using a sample of 500 inmates between 1830 and 1855, found that only 27 percent had lived with both biological parents. [22]

At the bottom of the economic ladder, the line between providing for and abandoning one's family could be exceedingly thin. In the 1840s, John Howlett migrated through Ohio and Indiana in search of steady and remunerative work. Unable to find employment, he left a wife and two daughters behind in Indiana in the spring of 1850 to seek his fortune in the California gold fields, but without success. Unable to send money home, Howlett concluded that he had little else to offer his wife and children. "Now I do not know what to say to you," he wrote from California in 1851. "I can not give you any advice. I wish I could. You must do the best you can. God forgive me for making this foolish trip to better my condition."

Howlett remained in California more than eight years, unwilling or unable to return home. Eventually he managed to rejoin his family, but he spent little time at home once back in Indiana, where he worked as a teamster.[23]

Family abandonment is not to be confused with work-imposed absence. Nonetheless, abandonment was sometimes the final and most desperate departure for men who had established a pattern of leaving home in search of work and economic security. The story of Israel Pastor, a Jewish immigrant to Cleveland, illustrates this pattern. Pastor, who had grown to manhood in the East End slum district of London, departed from home for the first time soon after his marriage, in the 1880s. He left behind a pregnant bride and his preadolescent stepdaughter, Rose, in order to find work and to establish himself in South America. Failing at that, Pastor returned home to a family that had grown to include a six-month-old son, but he soon left to try his luck again, this time in America. After settling in Cleveland, Pastor sent for his family, who joined him in the autumn of 1890. There he worked as a junk peddler until the Depression of 1893 ruined his business. His family's finances crushed, Pastor sank into despair and alcoholism. After a series of unannounced and unexplained absences from home, Pastor finally abandoned his family.[24]

Pastor's life story helps to explain why nineteenth-century working-class fathers were more likely than mothers to end their lives as boarders, in service, or in the poorhouse, rather than living with their children. While aged parents residing with their children was the norm in the nineteenth century, widowers were much less likely than widows or married elderly couples to reside with their children.[25] Part of this discrepancy is explained by the fact that men in old age were likelier than women to have the economic means to live independently. The overrepresentation of elderly men in poorhouses, however, reflected other social trends, not least the masculine tendency to break ties with family and move away from home. These rovers likely were joined by men discredited as failures in their children's eyes. A mother, after all, had been supported by her husband. Grown children, therefore, saw fit to continue to care for her in old age. They did not necessarily extend the same sentiment to a father who had been unable to meet the expectations of masculine responsibility and independence bound up in his role as family provider.

Across the social structure, then, the provider role established expectations about paternal availability and determined how much time a man had to spend with his family. As far back as one can trace in the nineteenth century, economic responsibility and earning money to support the family topped the list of masculine priorities. Whatever child-rearing responsibilities a father assumed had to conform to the availability and rhythms of work, whether on the farm or in the city.

The Fireside Father

Agrarian work rhythms differed from the regimentation imposed by the factory bell or the counting-house clock. When farm children were not in school, fathers were freer to include them in their work routines. Especially during less busy seasons, these men were more available to children than were their counterparts in factories and offices. Whether they were in fact also more involved parents is harder to assess. What is certain is that in rural and city homes alike, fathers were part-time parents.

Consider the diary of George A. Slayton, a forty-one-year-old farmer in Salem, Nebraska, who kept a rather complete record of his activities in 1888. Slayton was the father of five children, a daughter, who at the time was eight, and four sons between the ages of six and fourteen. Slayton's diary, which records both work and family activities, offers little evidence of substantial participation in child rearing. He was, at best, a spare-time parent. Most diary entries focus on work he had accomplished or that needed to be done. Slayton was more likely to mention his hired hands, Eddie and Hamlin, by name than any of his children, if only because his oldest sons were just reaching the age (generally about fourteen) when they would be expected to put in a full day's work on the farm. Most of Slayton's time with his children seems to have been spent during nights or on Sundays, especially during the slack winter season, and involved his role as a companion. "I read in P.M. & bound some of the children's magazines. In evening showed the children their magic lantern pictures," he recorded on January 13. On Sunday, August 12, he noted: "A pleasant day, but I did not feel very well, so I remained pretty close to the house, read a little & visited with the children."[26]

Slayton's diary is representative. A striking feature of personal reminiscences recalling nineteenth-century agrarian childhoods is how often paternal closeness is associated with slack work seasons. E. Lakin Brown, for instance, remembered a Vermont childhood in which "winters were made seasons of business and pleasure" by his father.[27] Autobiographical evidence also confirms that the fundamental cadence of paternal availability was relatively unchanged by industrialization: nineteenth-century fathers were available to children primarily at night and on Sundays.

Frequently, fathers were recalled presiding at the supper table, where they might interrogate children about their day's activities. "My father was always plumping surprising questions at all of us—questions about our work, and our play, and especially about what happened at school after we began to go," recalled the muckraking journalist Ray Stannard Baker, who grew up in northern Wisconsin in the 1870s. "He often asked these questions at the table, sometimes greatly to our confusion."[28]

Fireside rituals after the evening meal were a time of family togetherness and paternal availability in many middle-class homes. Charles Weller, who grew up on farms in Michigan and Wisconsin in the 1840s and 1850s, recalled: "Our winter evenings were largely spent by the fireside, mother sitting with her sewing and mending, and the boys seated on the brick hearth fashioning with their jackknives cunning little cedar boxes, listening as father read to us." Florence Cushman Milner, the coach maker's daughter from Concord, New Hampshire, also had especially vivid memories of her father's nightly fireside presence. She recalled that in winter, after the dishes had been cleared, the family gathered in the dining room, where her father stared silently at the fire in the stove. "If the opened door revealed a fine bed of coals, he reported the fact laconically. He was a man of few words. The remark was enough to send my sisters to the cellar for apples which my father pared, quartered and divided equally."[29]

While these memories document active engagement by fathers in domestic life, they fundamentally recall rituals of authority. It is the father who dispenses food from the cellar, the father who reads aloud while others listen, the father who is the child's interlocutor at the dinner table. To a large extent, nightly family rituals organized themselves around the father's availability. By voice and gesture, fathers used this time to confirm their family leadership, letting other family members know who was in charge. In earlier times, religious ritual had served this function. Fathers who led their families in home worship or catechized their children symbolically displayed their moral authority as heads of household. Some fathers in the nineteenth century continued to exercise such religious authority, but in an increasingly secular society fathers more often used time at the fireside and dinner table as occasions for ritualized displays of family leadership.

Significantly, these leadership rituals were enacted in homes that were becoming a less masculine space, the site of more feminine and child-centered activities. In the first half of the nineteenth century, the social meaning of home as an independent economic unit headed by the father gave way to a concept of home as a place where the mother's household management could enable the father and his family to get ahead. This definition, emphasizing women's domestic labor in the service of men and children, was embodied in the earliest suburban homes designed by Catharine Beecher and Andrew Jackson Downing in the 1840s. As women assumed control over domestic space, the house became, in the historian and social commentator Dolores Hayden's apt phrase, a "stage set for the effective gender division of labor." At the same time, the home was valued as a meeting ground of the sexes. Many middle-class men took a significant interest in the details of furnishing and running their household. Within the house, certain times and places were reserved as backdrops for displays of masculine authority, if only to bolster masculine self-respect by acknowledging the father's domestic presence.[30]

The Sunday Father

Just as evening gatherings were organized under a father's supervision, so was a father's presence crucial to the way a family spent its Sundays. Indeed, it is impossible to overstate the importance of Sunday to fatherhood in the nineteenth century. Cultural historian Ann Douglas has observed that in Victorian America, "every day was Mother's day." Sunday, however, was an exception. From children's perspective, it was the day when they had the most sustained involvement with fathers, who were at other times preoccupied with work. From a father's point of view, Sunday was a time to reorder priorities away from work and focus on religious and familial engagements. As a storekeeper from Princeton, Massachusetts, reflected in 1836: "On a Sabbath day at home, relieved from the cares and anxieties of the week, I can set down in the full enjoyment of the domestic fire side."[31]

For middle-class men, Sunday's domestic leisure almost always involved devoting time to children. As a Michigan jurist, separated from a family that included five children between the ages of two and ten, put the matter in a letter to his wife on a Sunday in 1862: "I would give a good deal to have the children here today. Sunday—of all the days in the week—seems unnatural unless I have them about me."[32]

Time and again men's personal documents afford evidence that children were a large, if not the dominant, feature of men's Sunday domesticity. On Sundays, more than any other day of the week, children suffused middle-class masculine consciousness. To cite just one more example: Alexander Winchell, a geology professor at the University of Michigan, for many years devoted a part of each Sunday to mourning the deaths of three young children. "I have spent a dark and rainy Sunday upon a couch of sentiment," he recorded one day in 1863. "This forenoon before the rain commenced I visited the resting places of my dear little lost ones and communed with their spirits for an hour with the suggestive associations telling their spirit tales in my hearing."[33] Winchell led a busy and productive professional life; but his Sunday diary entries, unlike most during the week, are preoccupied with thoughts of his children, both the living and the dead. Indeed, the nineteenth century's cult of childhood seemed to demand children's Sabbath presence.

Just as children were much on a father's mind, so too did children associate Sundays with their father's availability. Whether or not a father accompanied his family to church (and a growing number of fathers did not), it is the rare childhood reminiscence of Sabbath activities that does not include an account of time spent with him. Whether the account emphasizes a father's authority or his companionship depends largely on the nature of his religiosity. Consider the rather rosy reminiscence of Nancy Atwood Sprague, who was born in 1837 and grew up on a Vermont farm. Sprague devotes an entire chapter of her childhood reminiscences to her family's activities on Sunday, an account in which her father, Ebenezer Atwood, is the central figure. From her perspective seven decades later, she recalls the entire day having revolved around his presence and activities. Before breakfast, Atwood's children gathered to watch him shave in a corner of the kitchen.

After breakfast, he taught his children Bible lessons and led family devotions. Chores and church attendance followed. After meeting, Atwood led singing in the Sabbath school, returned home with his family to dinner, and spent much of the rest of the day in the company of his children. "After dinner there were a few leisure hours, generally very happy intimate ones," his daughter recalled. "Father nearly always, and Mother, when she could leave the babies or take them, would wander over the farm, a pleasure the working days had no time for." Sprague recalled her father exchanging "confidences" on these walks, offering her marital advice on one occasion.[34]

Not all recollections have such a honeyed tone. Invariably, though, whether recalled fondly or with a grimace, a father's Sunday presence left lasting impressions. A girl who grew to womanhood in New England during the 1830s recalled a Universalist father who enforced a strict Sabbath observance. "Children were not made companions of and their needs of occupation and interest seemed not to be ever thought of," she recollected. "If we got a pair of scissors we were told to put them away for it was Sunday. We were not even allowed to sit and look out of the windows . . . but were told to take a book and look at that. Yet mine was a loving kind father, only we could not discern the affection hidden by such a veil of strictures. So we feared where we should have been led to love him."[35]

Sunday's redirection of children's attention toward their father was as pronounced in secularized households as in the religiously observant homes that the foregoing narratives recall. The diaries of Alice Stone Blackwell of Dorchester, Massachusetts, and Walter Curtis, of Detroit, illustrate this point. Alice's journal for 1872, the year she turned fifteen, and Walter's for 1887, when he turned thirteen, offer rather complete records of their daily activities. A very rough index of parental engagement in a child's life and imagination is the number of times that parent is mentioned in a child's diary. Both Blackwell and Curtis mentioned their mother more often than their father, roughly by a ratio of 60 percent to 40 percent. In part, at least, this is because the routines of middle-class urban life involved them more with their mother on a day-to-day basis. A similar analysis that excludes weekdays and focuses only on Sundays, however, reverses the proportions: in both journals the ratio of references shifts decisively in favor of father, whose sustained, day-long presence at home registered with these children.[36]

Whether or not fathers attended church with their families, they were generally available to children afterwards. In addition to being a time when all family members were together to visit or receive relatives and friends, Sunday afternoons were an occasion for father-child activities in many middle-class homes. As we have seen, Ebenezer Atwood and his children walked the fields of his Vermont farm. Ray Baker's father read aloud to his six sons on Sunday afternoons and took them on "tramps" in the Wisconsin woods. Alice Blackwell and her father frequently took carriage rides together, to visit his friends and associates or to hear a lyceum lecture. Walter Curtis also anticipated his father's company on Sunday. Disappointed when his father was required, for a time, to work on Sunday afternoons, Curtis carefully logged the absences in the diary of his youth.[37]

The Differentiation of Family Time

To a surprising extent, the experiences of rural and urban fathers converged in the nineteenth century. The enduring significance for fatherhood of Sunday and nightly family rituals, in homes as disparate as Nancy Atwood Sprague's in Vermont after 1837 and Walter Curtis's in Detroit in 1887, highlights fundamental stability in the outward rhythms of family life, even in the face of massive economic change. More than it rearranged the way men divided their time between work and home, market activity altered the inner experience of family time.

The deeper men were drawn into the commercial economy, the more striking the difference between work time and family time became. In a rapidly commercializing society, many men in the business and professional middle class came to see competition in a world of anonymous, self-seeking "strangers" in sharp contrast to the cultivation of bonds of solidarity among "friends"—wife and children—at home. This opposition amplified the emotional importance of family and family time to middle-class men, but it also limited their sense of domestic responsibility. For if paying the bills was a man's duty, family time was his reward, sometimes even his salvation. Men swept into the vortex of the masculine marketplace came to think of family life as an alternate realm of sympathy and affection, to whose benefits their economic sacrifices entitled them. For at least some middle-class men, moreover, nineteenth-century ideals of masculine achievement were at odds with their desire to participate more fully in the emotional warmth they saw embodied in the lives of their wives and children.

Albert G. Browne of Salem, Massachusetts, testified to this dilemma. Married in 1833 and the father of six children born between 1835 and 1853, Browne was a partner in a prosperous ship chandlery firm, which required him to travel extensively. On a trip in 1838, he told his wife, Sarah: "I regret my protracted absence on many accounts, but it would be the height of folly to let a little anticipated hardship turn me from my purpose. I could not respect myself. *You* could not respect me, were I to do so. Altho at times I feel homesick & babyish, less so, however, then [*sic*] at first."[38]

Browne counterposed his "babyish" longing for home to a manly endurance of hardship. His self-respect and his image in the eyes of his wife were clearly bound up in the role of family provider. At the same time, he was obviously torn between a home-based world of friends and kin, with his wife and children at its emotional center, and the business world in which he was immersed. The economic arena was stimulating, full of challenges and rewards, but could not, he claimed, satisfy his deepest needs for emotional attachment. "More then [*sic*] a month has passed since I left you, my children, my friends," he wrote his wife from Kentucky in 1842:

> Absent from you I know better how to appreciate my blessings. It would seem strange indeed if I did not, for never had one so undeserving as I am, such a wife, such children & such friends. The people I meet with every day are kind, considerate, attentive, polite, but they are not my dear friends, they cannot fill the void place in my heart. I want sympathy, affection. At home I have it. I should be a wretched being without it. I would not have you suppose that I am unhappy. Far from it. I am too much employed, my mind is too much engaged to permit despondence & unhappiness to enter.[39]

Browne was not alone in the tangle of his emotions. He was among the growing number of fathers in the first half of the nineteenth century whose participation in the market economy opened a chasm between home and work. Navigating the distance was an emotionally complex experience. Certainly, market relations magnified the felt need to get ahead or risk disreputable (and unmanly) failure in the scramble for success. Viewed through the prism of Victorian domesticity, however, the world of commerce was as alienating as it was engaging. Even the most work-obsessed men, or perhaps those men most especially, anticipated a spiritually salutary transition to family time when they crossed the threshold of home.

William Appleton, a well-to-do Boston merchant, was distressed by his inability to leave the office behind at night or on Sunday. "My mind is much, quite too much, engrossed in business," he confided to his diary in 1836. "I fear it will be my ruin. I try to devote some time every day to the all important subject, my future existence, but when I get into the vortex of business I find my mind so much engrossed that I can hardly free it when I return to my family or even on the Sabbath."[40] Such attitudes accorded with nineteenth-century stereotypes that proclaimed the moralizing influence women and children had on men. Fathers looked to their families for access to a moral life they felt they could not lead on their own.

Men like Browne and Appleton were among the first parents to experience the opposition between family and work. They were spared, however, the conflict of roles that has aggravated the massive movement of mothers into today's paid labor force. While many nineteenth-century fathers felt torn between work and family, fewer felt the same tension between child-rearing responsibilities and work. More often than they spoke of being unavailable to guide their children, absent fathers spoke of missing their children's company. "Few people have pleasanter children than I and none, certainly, love them better," the Boston educator George B. Emerson told a daughter in 1847. "Yet how little time during the year have I to enjoy their society. All last winter and spring I was looking forward to some arrangement which would give me more of your society than I had previously had."[41]

Emerson could impose this construction on family time because few parents in the nineteenth century doubted that children could be raised properly by mothers at home, notwithstanding limited paternal involvement. As early as the second decade of the nineteenth century, correspondence between parents began to testify powerfully to belief in the superiority of maternal child rearing. Women sometimes protested the burden that this understanding imposed, especially when husbands used such reasoning to justify long absences from home. The logic of expanded maternal responsibility, however, identified paternal nurturance with the work men did away from home. "I have heard it abroad that a Mother does more towards forming the character of children, than the father," a Congressman from Massachusetts told his wife in 1811. "In this respect I feel happy, because, I know, not only your anxious desire for the happiness of your children, but your ability to instruct them in the way which they ought to go. Oh, how I long to see them. . . . But I console myself, in some measure, with the thought, that altho' absent, I shall become more acquainted with the world and be better able to lay the foundation for their future happiness and prosperity, than if always at home."[42]

As has been detailed in Chapter 2, beginning in the 1830s, a religiously oriented school of family advisers castigated such thinking, chiding fathers who used work commitments and the importance of motherhood as excuses for "paternal neglect." Writers such as Theodore Dwight Jr., William Alcott, and John Abbott had the matter half-right. Although men used breadwinning and the power of maternal influence to justify absence from home, few people other than the advisers themselves seem to have thought of this absence as a form of "neglect." Within the family, masculine concentration on breadwinning elicited much less skepticism than the rhetoric about paternal neglect suggests. There is little evidence to indicate, for instance, that a father's routine absences from home in pursuit of a living provoked much concern that children were being raised without adequate paternal supervision. In part this is because the absence that family advisers began to decry in the 1830s and 1840s, when professional and commercial life in the cities was beginning to remove men like themselves from home, had been a fact of family life in many other rural and urban households for quite some time. Then, too, many parents shared the view that becoming "more acquainted with the world" prepared men to convey lessons on how to get ahead in society. A father's absence on business, in this respect, contributed both to his family's present sustenance and to his children's future prospects.

For a variety of reasons, then—belief in maternal competence, traditions of work-related absence, a lack of emphasis on family "togetherness," and the identification of absence with paternal nurture—routine leave taking was seldom contested. The breadwinner ideal had coalesced quite early in the century across many ranks of the social structure. By 1810 artisan journals were proclaiming loudly that the honorable artisan was expected to be the family breadwinner.[43] Accordingly, family dissension became visible primarily when the father's separation was exceedingly long, often a matter of years.

The maritime culture of the New England whaling industry is a case in point. In the industry's heyday, from the 1820s to the 1870s, whaling voyages could last upwards of three years. Ships' officers (who were older and more likely to be married than common seamen) justified such prolonged absences from home both to themselves and to their families ashore as acts

of affection and devotion. They viewed being at sea not as a sign of estrange-
ment but as in keeping with their domestic responsibilities. Wives consigned
to virtual single parenthood sometimes protested this narrow view of masculine responsibility. Young wives most often emphasized the emotional
costs of separation. Repeated voyages also inspired protests about the lack
of family leadership resulting from a father's absence. Some women pressured
seafaring husbands to give up whaling altogether. However, the overall impact of such complaints is difficult to assess. The historian Lisa Norling found
that the willingness of wives and mothers to tolerate long paternal absences
ultimately sustained the whaling industry.[44]

In other places, prolonged absence seems to have summoned the same
grudging acceptance. James Birney, a Michigan father seeking his family's
fortune in the California gold fields, was pointedly reminded by his wife,
Bridget, in 1859 that his children required "both a father and a mother's care."
Bridget Birney, with the aid of a brother-in-law, assumed management of
the family farm in her husband's absence. While she lamented and sometimes
resented his being away, she also saw the authority she had assumed as tem-
porary. Upon his return from California, James Birney resumed his family
leadership role with apparent ease.[45]

Like the farmer who left home for a season to find employment or the
businessman who traveled frequently to tend his accounts, Birney was
thought to be caring for his family's economic needs rather than avoiding
his child-rearing responsibilities. It was taken for granted that mothers bore
the major responsibility for children, especially young children. When fathers
were away working, nineteenth-century men and women alike assumed that
these men were fulfilling their primary family responsibility. "I wish you
could be with me," a mother in New Jersey wrote in 1858 to a husband whose
work for a book publisher frequently took him from home, "but still I am
rather proud to see you persevere with business. It is better than to yield to
the feeling of least hunger that would send one rushing home."[46]

The Nursing Father

A major exception to this general rule, and one that casts a particularly revealing light on the father's role, is the part men played when their children
were ill. Although women bore primary responsibility for nursing sick family members at home in the nineteenth century, the gender line did not bar

fathers from their sick children's bedsides. Indeed, cases of serious illness demanded a father's presence and care. Work commitments notwithstanding, fathers were expected to rise to the occasion during a family health crisis and rally to their children's sides. The attention that men devoted to children who were gravely ill reflects an intermittent but persistent and deeply felt aspect of fatherly care beyond breadwinning.

Expressions of concern for children's health and advice about maintaining it are among the most common features of the correspondence of nineteenth-century fathers. The following excerpt from a letter written in 1841 by a merchant in Syracuse, New York, to his wife, who was visiting family in Spencer, Massachusetts, is representative: "You write that it is somewhat sickly particularly among children in Spencer. I hope you will be careful of the health of yourself and child and remember that good health is not a sure safeguard against sickness except it be treated with care. I should be sorry to learn that any unnecessary exposure or neglect had placed either of you under the care of a physician, though it often happens that sickness takes the place of health without being able to trace it to any cause. Should such be the fact with either of you, I trust that I shall be duly notified."[47]

Routine illness did not ordinarily trigger paternal involvement in childcare. But as the foregoing excerpt suggests, in an age when the etiology of most diseases was shrouded in mystery and child mortality rates remained painfully high, illness provoked a great deal of parental anxiety, especially if symptoms persisted for more than a few days. Despite some advances in medical science toward the end of the century, doctors remained unable to cure the era's killer diseases: influenza, tuberculosis, diphtheria, and yellow fever. Even at the beginning of the twentieth century, death rates remained extraordinarily high. By one demographic estimate, one out of every ten white infants and one out of every five black infants died by the age of one. Death struck children most often in the first few years of life, but mortality rates in later childhood and adolescence also remained high by late-twentieth-century standards. Overall, therefore, few parents were unacquainted by personal or proximate experience with the death of a child, and all feared the possibility.[48]

Historians have debated, somewhat inconclusively, what effect this high child mortality had on the emotional investment parents were willing to make in their children. Some argue that parents withheld affection as an emotional hedge against such an overwhelming loss. Others maintain, more persuasively, that the loss of a child had no such psychologically distancing effect.[49] In the nineteenth century, a child's illness clearly heightened paternal solicitude. Diary evidence reveals that nineteenth-century fathers cared greatly about their children's health and closely monitored the symptoms of sons or daughters who were ill. To take but one example, here is what a father in Boston recorded in 1852 about a two-year-old son's illness: "My dear little Amory has been ill since last Monday. His first symptoms were a stiff neck, and fever on Monday afternoon; but he was soon over it, and was bright again on Tuesday until afternoon. It was not until Thursday that we called Dr. Homans (Dr. Warren being absent) and he pronounced it bronchial fever. It has gone on, and he is considerable [*sic*] reduced in strength, not having eaten any thing but a little piece of biscuit for a week."[50]

Fathers not only worried about and closely watched the condition of sick children, they actively cared for them. Personal documents abound with cases of fathers participating at a sick child's bedside. Fathers stayed up with children at night, monitored their condition, helped to bathe them, administered medicines and poultices, and consulted with physicians about their symptoms and treatment. The frequency of such paternal participation is difficult to measure, but a good rule of thumb is to ascertain the involvement of a physician. Ordinarily, once an illness warranted a call to the doctor (sometimes a last resort), fathers became involved in the child's care.

Alexander Winchell, a geology professor at the University of Michigan, usually left the responsibility of treating sick children to his wife. But when his small daughter Stella became gravely ill in 1859, he became personally involved. Winchell's record of his daughter's illness and the treatment she received is emblematic of prevailing expectations and attitudes surrounding paternal care. "I went to bed, but was frequently awakened during the night by the sickness of Stella," he noted. "At half past three I got up to examine her at her mother's request. It was always very hard for me to be aroused in the night to attend to any case of illness in the family. I got into bed with Stella, saying I was no nurse & did not expect to be. Her mother then lay down . . . & rested."[51] Stella's illness eventually proved fatal. As the seriousness of her condition became more apparent, Winchell became a full partner in her care, staying up with her at night, taking her pulse, giving her medicine, applying mustard plasters, bathing her, and consulting with her physician.

Winchell did not consider himself a "nurse," the family role was too gender coded for that, but he acted as one on this and other occasions. His active participation and the similar involvement of many other fathers who shared his desire to attend to sick children represented an episodic but substantial commitment of time and care. Illness was a family crisis, and fathers were expected to reorganize their priorities to deal with it. Whenever possible, fathers abandoned work commitments and returned home when they learned that children were seriously ill, all the more so if the condition was assumed to be mortal.[52]

In children's memoirs and diaries, some of the tenderest references to fathers highlight their participation as nurses. Recalling his family's migration from Michigan to Kansas in 1886, when he was in his late teens, Clayton B. Wells noted that the family was stricken by typhoid fever. Struggling with the illness for several weeks, he wrote: "I was very close to death. Just at that time, fortunately, we had an old doctor who was capable. The principal reason for my recovery, however, was the faithful nursing given me by my father and stepmother. I owed my life to them." Similarly, Abel Regal, a youth who grew up in Ohio and Michigan, recorded in his diary in 1854: "I still continue to grow worse and Father is compelled to be up with me all night. No one else can handle me so gently or soothe my pains so well as he."[53]

Correspondingly, some of the tenderest passages in men's diaries and letters are reserved for the contemplation of children who were seriously ill or who had succumbed to death. The sentimentalization of a child's death is among the hallmarks of nineteenth-century culture. The death of Eva in *Uncle Tom's Cabin* and that of Little Nell in Dickens's *The Old Curiosity Shop* are outstanding expressions of this tendency, which Ann Douglas has identified as an element of the "feminization" of nineteenth-century culture.[54] It is important to recognize, however, that men as well as women were touched by Victorian sentiment and that it spoke to men most directly in their capacity as husbands and fathers. Where fatherhood is concerned, men clearly used the illnesses and deaths of children as occasions for the contemplation of their own softer emotions. Upon the death of his daughter Stella, in 1859, for instance, Alexander Winchell composed a 40,000-word reminiscence of her short life, which he titled "Tears over the Tomb: Recollections of My Little Angel Child." In this outpouring of grief, remarkable more for its length than for its intense emotions, which other fathers shared, Winchell declared that the death of his daughter affected him more profoundly than it did any other family member, including his wife. "Oh it wrings my heart to think how much love and tenderness I have lost," he asserted. Other fathers left similar, albeit shorter, records of their desolation when a child died.[55]

While the illness or, especially, the death of a child had particular salience in men's emotional lives by opening a window on tender feelings, they were not the only medical emergencies that jogged fathers from their accustomed work routines and economic preoccupations. A wife's illness, too, urged men toward greater domestic engagement. But a spouse's illness was less often an occasion for fathers to participate directly in childcare. "You are greatly needed at home now I am sick," a Massachusetts mother of two boys, aged nine and six, wrote to her seafaring husband in 1823. "I hope before the end of this week I shall hear of your arrival."[56] The expectation was clear: in spite of sex-role stereotypes, men would lend a hand about the house when needed. Availability of a daughter old enough to help her mother greatly mitigated the need for a father's assistance, however. When mothers were ill or otherwise unable to handle domestic chores and childcare duties, added responsibility devolved primarily on older daughters, who acted as their mothers' surrogates and assistants, rather than on fathers.

Modernizing Fatherhood

Like the Sunday father or the fireside father, the nursing father was a part-time participant in domestic life. Throughout the century, most middle-class men worked long hours, which took them away from their homes and families most of the day. Such work-imposed absence was seen not as a rejection of fatherhood, but as a necessary (even salutary) element of a father's care. A socially imposed division of labor thereby excused fathers from the home as certainly as it tied mothers to it. Nonetheless, many nineteenth-century fathers were able to combine work with substantial involvement in family life. The nature of this involvement was a new dimension to men's domestic lives that added just as much to fatherhood as the time away from home subtracted from it.

Men drawn into the commercial economy idealized family life as a realm of sympathy and affection, the center of an inviting world of friends that contrasted sharply with the marketplace's impersonal world of strangers. Cultivating relationships with wife and children promised both an emotional respite from the market's aggressive competitiveness and a spiritual healing.

In a secularizing society, and at a time when men in particular were reluctant to participate in organized religion, family ties resonated with moral meaning—exaggerated, perhaps, but real. Ironically, then, the same material conditions that drew men out of their families redirected their deepest emotions back home, placing a new premium on family togetherness.

This effect was most pronounced among middle-class men.[57] It occurred where the separation of work and family intersected with romantic images of wife and children, idealizations at the heart of bourgeois attitudes toward domestic life. Indeed, new understandings of the value of family time were part of the manufacture of a new kind of male identity, part of the creation of what it meant to be a new kind of man. This modernization of masculinity was tied, in turn, to the emergence of a new class identity. The image of "home as refuge" was, after all, principally a middle-class ideal, a conceit of middle-class men.

Heightened expectations of family togetherness coalesced in this construction of domestic life, rearranging the family calendar to highlight the times when fathers were home. Thus holidays such as Thanksgiving and Christmas acquired new domestic content and grew enormously in importance during the nineteenth century. The celebration of Christmas, in particular, was a middle-class invention whose new rituals and imagery drew on changing conceptions of the father's role. Beginning in the antebellum era, but especially in the decades after the Civil War, a day that had once occasioned sometimes boisterous public revelry became an elaborate and expensive celebration of child-centered domesticity and consumption.

Significantly, the modern Christmas celebration was preeminently an urban phenomenon, with a surrogate father at its core. According to a recent historian, the holiday came to embody familial and public rituals fashioned by middle-class city dwellers in order to feel at home in a society of strangers.[58] At the symbolic heart of this new domestic holiday stood Santa Claus—a consummate father figure, the protector and rescuer of children, laden with toys and treats. A protean figure (successful factory owner, philanthropist, and secular saint), Santa Claus absorbed the dual aspects of modern fatherhood. Demanding goodness but seldom chastising children, he was the embodiment of nurturant male love, an ideal Victorian parent. At the same time, he reflected the work-centered life of American fathers, a man whose business—the preparation and annual delivery of toys to children in other families—seemed much more important than his own home life.

The tension between nurturance and absence enveloped a wide range of family-oriented activities, which, like the holidays, increased pressure on men to spend leisure time with their families. In the latter half of the nineteenth century, parlor games, croquet, church socials, and family picnics all became increasingly popular pastimes.[59] Middle-class men neither wholly embraced nor entirely rejected this expansion of family time. Increased participation in family activities was matched by massive participation in fraternal associations and lodges, which took men away from home one night each week, immersing them in a world of masculine ritual. The solace that men found in organizations such as the Red Men, the Odd Fellows, the Freemasons, the Knights of Pythias, and hundreds of smaller orders was at least partly an expression of male frustration with the increased social pressure to embrace family togetherness.[60]

In the last century as today, some fathers spent more time with their children while others spent less. Some fathers were taskmasters and disciplinarians, while others were more inclined toward play and companionship. For every father who was emotionally present and available when home, another remained distracted by work and psychologically distant. Apart from biographies, there is little one can say about these variations. In its broad outlines, however, fatherhood is constituted in socially determined ways. In nineteenth-century America, norms surrounding paternal availability helped to shape a sometimes contradictory but distinctly modern style of fatherhood. Fathers were primarily breadwinners, excused from the fireside by economic necessity, but they also were expected to participate actively in family life when they were not at work and to act decisively during times of family crisis. Middle-class men craved the companionship of their wives and children. In the final analysis, if the structure of work and household responsibility circumscribed fathers' participation in the essentials of child rearing, it also heightened the emotional importance of time that family men spent at home.

Chapter 4

Becoming a Parent

The Transition to Fatherhood

You know it is the sentiment of Dr. A. Clark that a man
is really but half a man till he gets a wife.

R. R. Richards, 1849

For men and women alike, marrying and eventually having children are
pivotal life experiences, culturally defined points of entrance into new social
roles and responsibilities. Psychologists working within a family-systems
framework suggest that patterns of family life are established within the marital relationship.[1] We can therefore learn a great deal about parenting roles
by first exploring the husband-wife bond, where those roles are initially constituted and continually grounded. When the object of investigation is fatherhood in the nineteenth century, such a strategy is all the more important; for, as we have seen, paternal responsibility became increasingly
mapped onto the husband's social role.

I suggested in Chapter 2 that this conflation of identities represented a
strategy to fortify fatherhood at a time when feminized parenting ideals had
weakened the cultural authority of masculine child rearing. In addition, the
demography of family formation tended to unite the identities of spouse and
father. In early America and throughout the nineteenth century, marriage
and parenthood were closely linked. The average age at which men and
women married in 1890 was essentially the same as in 1800. Young men typically left their parents' homes, married, and set up their families while in

their mid- to late twenties. Almost all nineteenth-century men and women eventually married (more than 90%, with the proportion rising somewhat toward century's end). Consequently, the vast majority of men expected to wed and, having done so, anticipated becoming fathers in short order. For, at a time when abstinence and withdrawal were the chief means of birth control, first children often entered the world without delay.[2]

What did the birth of a child mean? To be sure, fathers in the last century, like fathers today, took pleasure in begetting children and seeing them develop into variations of their own image. They wanted their children to grow up and live as adults in accord with family traditions: to become, in psychologist Daniel J. Levinson's apt description, "their personal legacy."[3] But becoming a father entailed historically specific social meanings in an age that celebrated motherhood so intensely. Becoming a mother in Victorian America was the quintessence of femininity, the preeminent symbol of womanhood. Woman-centered birthing practices supported this cultural understanding. Until childbirth was removed to hospitals in the early part of the twentieth century, women relied on a network of midwives, female relatives, and friends to manage labor and delivery at home. Over the course of the nineteenth century, expectant mothers increasingly requested the attendance of a male physician in the birthing room as well, in the (often misguided) belief that he would assure their health and safety.[4]

There was, however, another male figure present in the birthing chamber all along—namely, the father. The traditionally female nature of the home environment where children were born has largely obscured the father's inclusion from historical view. Nonetheless, many nineteenth-century men participated actively in the rituals of childbirth, not so much to celebrate the biological event of becoming fathers as to lend assistance and moral support to their wives. Rather than being the harbingers of fatherhood, pregnancy and childbirth could be, and often were, medical crises in which men were called upon to act as attentive husbands. Family formation in the nineteenth century thereby helped to establish expectations that family men would rise to the occasion when called upon at these critical times. Because the role that men played at childbirth was defined largely by their understanding of what it meant to be a good husband, discussion of the transition to fatherhood begins with a look at marriage.

Marriage and Manhood

In July 1815, twenty-two-year-old Charles Russell, a storekeeper in Princeton, Massachusetts, took pen in hand to respond to a friend's congratulatory
letter upon his recent marriage. "I return to you my unfeigned thanks for your
wishes respecting my future happiness through life and sincerely hope the
same blessings will attend you after you have entered the marriage state," he
told his friend Joshua Dillingham, of Camden, Maine. Russell went on to explain that there was "no real happiness" in being single. "A man may enjoy the
greatest affluence in life and be crowned with honours superior to any earthly
being yet if he is a single man there will be something wanting," he opined. A
wife, Russell told his friend, was a "bosom friend," someone who soothed a
man's anxieties and partook of both his enjoyments and his misfortunes.[5]

Russell's friend Dillingham shared his belief that marriage was necessary
for complete masculine happiness or at least was capable of summoning sentiments that his recently married friend was sure to find congenial. Continuing their correspondence, he told Russell that wealth and honor were hollow achievements without a wife at one's side. "A bosom friend to whom we
can open our hearts without reserve is necessary to complete happiness," he
echoed, all the more so because a woman's refined nature and "delicate
mind" inspired affection that few masculine hearts could withstand.[6]

The exchange embodies a world of gender stereotypes and role expectations, neatly summarizing widespread views about the moral superiority of
women and the salutary effect of female influence on the male character. Russell and Dillingham were true believers in the companionate marriage ideal.
For them, a wife was the central figure in a domestically constituted circle
of "friends" guaranteed to enlarge a man's happiness. While their language
and sentiments are high-flown and, to the modern ear, suspiciously effusive,
we have no reason to doubt the sincerity of their beliefs about either the advantages of wedlock or the perils of bachelorhood. Like many other middle-
class men of the nineteenth century, Russell and Dillingham took to heart
the message espoused by numerous family advisers—that men both needed
and benefited from a settled domestic existence.

Something else about the friends' correspondence is particularly intriguing. At age twenty-two, Russell had married somewhat earlier than most

of his contemporaries, but in one important respect he conformed to the demographic norms of his era: parenthood promptly followed marriage. When he wrote to Dillingham, Russell's wife was four months pregnant; their first child, a son, was born five months later, within a year of the couple's wedding. Nowhere, though, does Russell mention the prospect of becoming a father.

Given the relatively quick transition from marriage to parenthood that characterized family formation in the nineteenth century, one might expect that as young men and women thought about marriage they also discussed children. But they did not. As historian Ellen K. Rothman has shown quite definitively, the images of married life in nineteenth-century courtship letters focused largely on husband-wife companionship, not parental roles. The issue of children was almost never mentioned.[7]

In this one respect, at least, what young women and men talked about when they talked about marriage corresponded to what young men discussed among themselves. This preoccupation with conjugal companionship is featured as well in the thoughts that men confided to their personal diaries. One searches long and largely in vain for reflections about becoming a father in the diaries of young men in the nineteenth century, although diarists devote ample and sometimes agonized attention to the topic of getting married and becoming a husband. How can we explain this disparity?

To some extent, Victorian sexual reticence inhibited discussion of pregnancy and parenthood, a social norm nicely illustrated by one diarist who managed to broach the subject but encrypted references to his wife's "delicate condition" in a numeric code. Numerous practical considerations served to fill the void created by what modesty left unsaid. As marriage approached, middle-class men became preoccupied with the task of finding a place to live and conducting the business needed to secure a home. Once a house was found, a man's main task was to earn the money needed to support married life. This duty to provide goes a long way toward explaining the close identification of marriage itself with middle-class manhood. The obligation a man assumed the moment that he married, to support a wife and establish a new and independent home—"commencing housekeeping," as nineteenth-century Americans spoke about it—signaled a youth's progress to manhood. Children would soon require support as well, but most men simply took it for granted that, once married, they would become fathers.[8]

Marriage signaled something else besides assumption of the status of household head. It recognized men publicly as sexual creatures. Although some nineteenth-century men were sexually active before marriage, such behavior was not culturally sanctioned, and in fact was condemned. At a time when premarital sex was not yet the norm, marriage officially inducted middle-class men into the sexual tribe. Fatherhood, of course, confirmed this status, but there is little evidence that married men who desired, but did not have, children considered childlessness a reflection on their masculinity. Fathers were touted as superior masculine types by popular medical writers, but Victorian scientists had no conception of male infertility. Accordingly, if a married couple was unable to have children in the nineteenth century, the blame and guilt were carried exclusively by the "barren" wife.[9]

The association of marriage with household leadership, sexual initiation, and manhood was decidedly a middle-class conceit. Being "manly" in urban working-class culture had less to do with marriage and the "family man" ideal, and was more closely tied to masculine peer groups and the saloon. In a recent study of working-class culture in antebellum New York City, for instance, Richard Stott points out that the autobiographies of married working men expressed a sense of longing for youthful days spent in such all-male groups as volunteer fire companies. Marriage for these men seems not to have matched the emotional intensity and excitement of the single life.[10] Such nostalgia for youthful male camaraderie was expressed less often by middle-class men. Many middle-class males formed intense same-sex friendships in youth, but they assumed that their close ties would be broken by manhood. E. Anthony Rotundo calls attention to the fact that many young men thought of their intimate friendships as the functional equivalent of marriage and expected wedlock to sever those male bonds. Rotundo's perceptive examination of letters and diaries uncovered not a single instance in which male friends maintained their former intimacy after marriage, and his study found some whose relationships did not survive at all.[11]

None of this is to suggest that prospective middle-class husbands entered marriage without a backward glance or any apprehension. As they approached the altar, young men expressed serious concerns about the pressure to provide. Given nineteenth-century sexual stereotypes, they also had understandable misgivings about the emotional difference between men and women and sometimes doubted their ability to forge a mutually satisfying marital bond. A growing body of scholarship has shown rather clearly, however, that middle-class men generally overcame such apprehensions and looked forward to marriage, expecting it to enrich, rather than restrict, their daily lives.[12] Once a marriage date was announced, for instance, a man was generally more eager than his betrothed to have the wedding take place. For a variety of reasons, women were more likely than men to view the transition to marriage with foreboding or trepidation. Women were motivated to prolong the period of engagement, in part because marriage brought an end to a time in their lives of relative independence and freedom, while entering marriage placed fewer restrictions on men. Women also seem to have had greater misgivings that marriage would efface the intimacy of courtship and its aura of romantic love.[13]

Men like Charles Russell and Joshua Dillingham clearly did not share these concerns. Rather than emphasize the freedom of the single life, they tended to view bachelorhood in negative terms, as an emotionally impoverished, if not morally perilous, state. Their apprehension reflected persistent cultural criticism of bachelors in colonial and nineteenth-century America. Although a prominent strain in this culture imagined marriage as a painful arena of masculine subordination (much literary humor, for instance, focused on the resistance of male characters to female domesticity), a countervailing tendency condemned bachelors as hard-hearted "pleasure seekers" and men afraid to assume the manly responsibilities of married life.[14]

Such negative stereotypes had a lengthy pedigree. Community leaders in early America, concerned that a population of unattached men living without paternal supervision lacked the family ties necessary to maintain social order, imposed fines and taxes on bachelors and enacted local laws requiring single men and women to live within established households.[15] Nineteenth-century moralists continued to stigmatize spinsters and bachelors. Lamenting a perceived repression of marriage, especially in fashionable society, social commentators suggested that the luxury, indolence, and extravagance of young women deterred men from assuming the financial risks of matrimony. Men were correspondingly chided for being unwilling to set aside personal pleasures in order to marry, pursuing instead a path of licentiousness and vice. Writing in 1837, the English traveler Harriet Martineau reported growing concern with "the increase of bachelors" in the nation's cities. American men were delaying marriage, she commented, "because they have learned to think other things of more importance than the best comforts of domestic life."[16]

In subsequent decades, singleness became increasingly respectable for men. In cities, a highly visible minority resisted matrimony, turning instead to the many clubs, lodges, and taverns that provided an alternative source of comfort and camaraderie. Henry Adams, the writer and social critic, was among those who chose to forsake fatherhood in the period after the Civil War. While Adams was a self-described "believer in the necessity of propagating our kind," he was happy to leave the task to "all [his] able-bodied friends and relations devoting themselves to this end." As for Adams himself, he stated: "Nothing can reconcile me to the position of head of a family. . . . I have myself never cared enough about children to be unhappy either at having or not having them."[17]

Such voluntary childlessness swelled the chorus of popular criticism against bachelorhood. "Many virtuous young men are withheld" from marriage by the "incompetence and the extravagant habits and tastes of those they would otherwise seek for wives," Catharine Beecher chided in 1872. Another large class of men, she added, "shun the toil, self-denial, and trials of married life, and prefer their ease and the many other enjoyments wealth will secure."[18] It is no small irony that Beecher herself, the chief apostle of domesticity, never married. More to the point, the heightened criticism of bachelorhood masked the fact that the proportion of ever-married men remained above 90 percent in the decades after the Civil War, rising slightly, in fact, among successive birth cohorts born after 1865. The reality of marriage's continued viability mattered less than the growing anxiety about consumerism and the apprehension that new urban amenities and leisure activities seemed to have made bachelorhood a more desirable estate, rather than a life stage to be gotten through as quickly as possible.

By the 1870s, the bachelor and the family man came to be seen as opposing social types, the one diverting himself with urban amusements while the other held fast to the home circle. A cartoon in an 1871 edition of *Harper's Weekly* underlined the point. In it, two men converse in front of a department store toy counter. One, a bachelor, comments that the other, a married man shopping for a toy, is no longer seen at the club. "No," the married man replies, "the fact is I've got a little Club at Home which takes up all my spare time nowadays." Lest the moral be lost, the illustration is captioned: "Home Circle versus Clubs."[19]

HOME CIRCLE *versus* CLUBS

SMITH. "Why, JONES, we don't see you at the Club any more."

JONES. "No. The fact is I've got a little Club at Home which takes up all my spare time nowadays."

Fig 3. From *Harper's Weekly*, December 30, 1871.

As a permanent estate, bachelorhood had limited appeal, the allures of club life notwithstanding. For every Henry Adams, many more men set aside their ambivalence about marriage to embrace the obligations of settled heterosexuality at home. A week after his wedding, in 1834, William Lloyd Garrison told his brother-in-law, George Benson, how pleased he was to have "sunk the character of a bachelor in that of a husband."[20] So closely identified were marriage and bourgeois conceptions of manhood that even a formerly married man could experience a resurgence of masculine feeling upon reentering the bonds of matrimony. A minister in Detroit named R. R. Richards had precisely that reaction upon remarrying. Although it is impossible to establish the fate of Richards's first wife on the basis of scattered correspondence, we know that he had been previously married and was probably a widower when he wed in November 1849. Within weeks of his marriage, he wrote to friends that "I feel a little more like a man." He continued: "You know it is the sentiment of Dr. A. Clark that a man is really but half a man till he gets a wife. . . . I have endeavored to render myself as agreeable as possible to Mrs. R. this fore noon while she has been employed in mending my coat. So you perceive she has begun to make herself useful."[21]

The sense of marital manliness to which Richards alluded rested on an understanding of the companionate marriage ideal as an arrangement that served men's emotional needs as well as their creature comforts.[22] We know that, for men in the nineteenth century, family became, in theory at least, a haven from the cold formality of the world, an arena in which love, especially between husband and wife, was to be realized.[23] From this perspective, sentimental domesticity was part and parcel of the secularization of men's motives for choosing family life. Where marrying and raising children had once been considered religious duties, family life was seen increasingly as an opportunity to seek personal happiness. This view of marriage's utility to men was neatly summed up in the letter a twenty-five-year-old teacher, a graduate of Wesleyan University, received from a female cousin two weeks after his wedding, in 1849: "You are now a husband," she wrote, "and allow me to congratulate you upon having a kind spirit to mitigate your sorrows, to share your joys and to make your home your greatest enjoyment."[24]

Notwithstanding the nineteenth-century identification of the home with women, Victorian domestic ideals enjoined men and women alike to cultivate strong family feelings.[25] Marital companionship, moreover, was entirely compatible with masculine dominance of the household. Rather than thinking of marital affection as a basis of feminine power, many men and some women considered it a tool that men could use to cement their family leadership. "Now then hear one word of advice if it be a clue to promote your happyness," a mother in Hamilton, New York, told her eldest son. "Have you a wife do you wish to have your opinion her law (which is I think natural for men to want) then be careful not to rule by lordly . . . power nor be allways doing some disagreeable thing just to show that you dared do it or to please a fool." Rather, she urged, "be faithful kind and affectionate and allways try to cherish that affection that forges united hearts and a married life may be the happyest part of life."[26]

By viewing romantic love and spousal friendship as modern means of exercising domestic authority, many middle-class men had little difficulty incorporating companionate marriage ideals into their definitions of manhood. The experience of Henry Parker Smith of Schoolcraft, Michigan, in the years before his marriage, in 1854, is a case study of the way that marriage and masculinity were intimately linked in the minds of many middle-class men.

Henry Parker Smith's Story

From age twenty-one to age forty-two, Smith kept diaries that provide a detailed account of the transitions both to marriage and to fatherhood at mid-century. His diaries, spanning the period 1848–68, are unusually revealing. Unlike many male diarists, Smith not only recorded events of the day but also used his diary-keeping to explore how he felt in a variety of situations and at various times of transition in his life. If his self-examination distinguishes him somewhat from his contemporaries, the details of his biography ground him firmly in the life experiences of many other middle-class men. Smith's ambitions, desires, and struggles to get ahead were representative of his time and place.

Born on May 15, 1826, Smith began his diary shortly before his twenty-second birthday, a time when he was living at home and working alongside his father on the family farm in Schoolcraft. As the eldest child and only son in his family, Smith could reasonably have expected to inherit his father's farm, although the possibility is not mentioned in his diary. In 1848, when his diary began, his father was only fifty-two, in good health, and apparently in no hurry to convey his property. Besides, for Smith, as for many other young men of his generation, alternative opportunities in the West and the expanding cities were a powerful incentive to forge his own path in life.

In his diary, Smith soon began to refer to his hometown as a "graveyard." He was restlessly casting about for the ways and means to leave Schoolcraft and establish himself on his own. A young acquaintance named Isaiah Pursel, who would eventually become Smith's brother-in-law, had gone to California to seek his fortune. Smith wondered about Pursel's fate and whether his own fortune, too, might lie in the West. For a time, he contemplated moving to Minnesota.

The evidence of his diaries leaves little doubt that finding his fortune was a great object in Smith's life when he was in his early twenties, but it was not the only one. With mounting urgency, Smith's diaries chart his desire to find a wife. "Mother and I had one of those delicious luxuries in a family, a very affecting discussion on my intentions to marry," he recorded on May 12, 1849, shortly before his twenty-third birthday. Until the day he married, in 1854, at age twenty-eight, the topic of marriage never strayed far from his thoughts.

Smith believed that a window of matrimonial opportunity would close if he had not found a wife by the time he turned thirty. That prospect troubled him, for his diary testifies to the belief that remaining single would deal a crushing blow both to his social standing and to his self-respect. As a moderately devout Baptist, Smith also believed that bachelorhood posed a moral risk: "I am a natural hypocrite with all sorts of passions & selfish desires to keep down," he confessed on a Saturday in June 1850. "I am afraid I shall become so callous to gentle & sensitive feelings as to walk through life from thirty to the grave a cold, heartless, selfish, unhappy devil: uncared for & not respected even by myself."[27]

While Smith acknowledged that he might "never get to heaven except through the influence of my partner through life," he despaired of finding such a mate in Schoolcraft.[28] In November 1850, at age twenty-four, he left his father's farm to take a position as a clerk in the Woolworth's store in Seneca Falls, New York. The job did not work out, but he remained in Seneca Falls, where he found another clerical position and boarded with his employer's family. Smith spent a somewhat lonely sixteen months in Seneca Falls. He complained of feeling like a "greenhorn" and was troubled by an on-again, off-again romance with a woman from Schoolcraft named Sofia Root. "Will my present fancy ever amount to anything & if it does can I maintain her through life?" he pondered in November 1851. By the following April, the relationship seemed headed toward marriage, prompting him to reflect: "I am full of doubts now about my making my *wife* happy. I am [coarse?] and she is delicate. I am out of business, but before fall I will have something on the carpet by which I can support us two and pay the remainder of the debts."[29] Just a month later, on his twenty-sixth birthday, Smith concluded that nothing would come of the relationship, a recognition that rattled his self-confidence.

"I am now twenty six years old and have not settled on a home for life yet. My prospects of altering my mode of life are diminishing every day," he reflected disconsolately in May 1852. "I am *in debt, independent, inflexible*, my determinations *inferior to others* that prosper more in love & *out* of pocket, *out* of confidence *out* of a home with numerous other outs. Just thank God I am not out of health."[30]

Sick at heart, Smith returned to Schoolcraft several months later. Home again, he began to work for Isaiah Pursel, who had married Smith's sister and established himself as a storekeeper. Smith's life soon became a whirlwind of economic activity. While clerking in Pursel's store, Smith simultaneously began to improve land adjacent to his father's farm, and, through business contacts he had made in Seneca Falls, supplemented his income as a sales agent.

Although Smith was working ferociously to establish himself, his expanding sense of manhood is associated most explicitly in his diary with his romantic fortunes, not his economic struggles. By the spring of 1853 Smith had met Harriet Amelia Johnson, a twenty-one-year-old schoolteacher in Maumee City, Ohio, whose family had migrated to the Midwest from Massachusetts. As their courtship blossomed, Smith's spirits—and, more to the point, his sense of masculinity—expanded. Just weeks before he first proposed marriage, Smith wrote of feeling "more like a man than I have ever done before." Smith asked Harriet to marry him in June 1853, but received no definite answer. In July he repeated his proposal. Harriet's acceptance prompted him to reflect: "I feel this is the most eventful period of the early life."[31]

Smith's engagement lasted nearly a year. As he lingered on the doorstep of married life, however, his ambivalence grew and concerns about masculinity marched across the pages of his diary. Smith believed that marriage would contribute to his happiness, but he also feared that his youthful vitality was attenuating as he contemplated family life. "They say I grow old too fast, which is true, for youth seems to me the only happy time in life," he reflected in November 1853. "The more *manly* I grow the more deadened become the pulsations of my *heart* and when I become a *man* I'm just fit for earth and to be crushed blotted from existence when the soul is left without a tenement."[32]

To allay his fears of death in life, Smith drew on cultural understandings that associated virility and "true manhood" with family responsibility. As we have already learned, nineteenth-century medical advice constantly reassured men that marital responsibility redounded to their favor. Perhaps as a result of the phrenological lectures that he attended, Smith imbibed the belief that domestic life tempered the impetuosity of youth with the steady purpose of mature, or virile, masculinity. "I am 28 yrs old and single. How time flies," he marveled in May 1854. "I am as young today in feeling as I was 7 years ago though not so volatile, more of a *man*. I am a man and can bear responsibilities I never dared to before."[33]

Most telling of all, until the day he actually assumed the responsibilities of married life, Smith considered himself to be still a boy. At age twenty-eight, on the eve of his wedding day, he reflected: "How strangely matter of fact I am in taking [this] step and how wild it makes me when the thought comes rushing through my mind that this is my last boyish day."[34] Marriage, then, secured Smith's sense of manhood.

Some recent scholarship has tended to stress the disjunction between domesticity and masculinity in nineteenth-century America.[35] But the testimony of men such as Henry Parker Smith, Reverend Richards, Charles Russell, and Joshua Dillingham indicates that a middle-class ideal of marital manliness existed alongside feminine domesticity. These were men who found confirmation, rather than contradiction, of their gender identities in the private sphere. Any number of reasons can be adduced to explain the eagerness with which many middle-class men embraced marriage. Marrying generally meant an end to a time of life that historian Joseph Kett described as "semi-dependent," a period marked by frequent departures and returns from the home of one's birth.[36] A desire for stability combined with Jeffersonian ideals of independent freeholding doubtless led many young men to look forward to leading a more settled, autonomous, and emotionally rewarding life in a home of their own. Finally, nineteenth-century men did not usually define their masculinity as antithetical to private emotions or to the companionate ideal of marriage. As Karen Lystra's analysis of private correspondence has demonstrated, affectionate marital relations and sympathetic emotions were "an integral component of the male role."[37] How, then, did the strong identification of manhood and being a husband affect men's attitudes toward pregnancy and childbirth and their behavior during the transition to fatherhood?

Pregnancy

We have come to think of the nineteenth-century birthing chamber as a woman's place and, likewise, of pregnancy as an event that marshalled the support of female friends and kin. Without controverting these stereotypes, all available evidence suggests that nineteenth-century wives also valued their husbands' moral support during pregnancy and desired their presence during childbirth. Take, for example, the case of John and Louisa Park of Acton, Massachusetts. Louisa Park was five months pregnant when her husband, a naval physician, left on a sea voyage to the West Indies in the winter of 1800. January found John Park two weeks out to sea, on a voyage scheduled to last until July. The baby was due to arrive in April. "Anticipation looks no further forward than Spring—and from that I turn with horror," Mrs. Park confided to her husband soon after his departure. "I have always from the first had a presentiment that I would never live to see May, and it grows stronger every day. . . . Could you be with me all the time, I should be less anxious, though perhaps not more safe, but I think I should. . . . You must not think I blame you for leaving me—I am sure I do not. I have only to regret the necessity and bear it. I wish I could with more fortitude."[38]

A second example, this one from 1851, features the same sentiments. Louisa J. Curtis of Yarmouth, Maine, was pregnant with a third child when she informed her seafaring husband in August that she had recently purchased a carpet for her bedchamber. She explained: "I thort that it would be better for me to do such wirk while I can. I exspect to have to occupy the chamber myself part of the time this winter, perhaps the last time. That is not for me to know but hope that you will be with me that triing day."[39]

Such letters, mixing anxiety with the desire for a husband's comforting hand, suggest that pregnancy heightened the emotional impact of a spouse's absence. Seldom, however, did wives insist that their condition was reason for a husband to delay or alter economic plans. A husband's work, after all, was his top priority, and in most cases there were female relatives and friends to rely on for care during the months preceding childbirth. As the nineteenth century advanced, a growing segment of the middle class also added a physician to their list of those consulted during pregnancy, if his attention were thought necessary to assure a woman's safety.[40]

The social rules guiding a husband's activities during pregnancy affirmed the priority of economic commitments, but that did not mean that men were indifferent to their wives' condition. There is little diary evidence to suggest that men carefully monitored the early stages of their wives' pregnancies. When the fact of pregnancy was noted, however, it was almost invariably accompanied by expressions of deep concern for a wife's health and safety. In many (perhaps most) households, pregnancy heightened a husband's solicitude. Most men welcomed the prospect of becoming fathers for the first time. Scattered evidence suggests that the birth of a son was particularly desired, both as a reflected image of the father and to carry on the family name.[41] Nonetheless, men and women alike viewed pregnancy as a potentially dangerous condition.

While a decline in fertility during the nineteenth century reduced the exposure of women to the risks of childbirth, maternal mortality rates remained high. Demographers estimate that, shortly after the turn of the twentieth century, one of every thirty women might still have been expected to die in childbirth over the course of her fertile years. To Victorian Americans, the odds seemed even greater, if only because the horror of maternal mortality exaggerated their fear. Having witnessed a mother's death or heard it described even once, men and women remembered it for a lifetime. As a consequence, the perception of childbirth's dangers haunted the minds of pregnant women and their families throughout the nineteenth century.[42]

For many men, the possible loss of a spouse cast a heavy shadow over the prospect of paternity. Consider, for instance, the reactions of Henry Blackwell and Henry Parker Smith to news of their wives' first pregnancies. Blackwell, a businessman and advocate of woman's suffrage, was married to the prominent suffragist Lucy Stone. His work for an agricultural book-publishing company during the early years of their marriage demanded frequent travel and time away from their home in Orange, New Jersey. February 1857 found Blackwell on business in the Midwest, at a time when he strongly suspected that his wife was newly pregnant. He wrote to Stone from Chicago, hoping for a letter that would assure him of her health and safety. "After the *strong probability* that exists of your being in *so different a position* from what you were, two short months ago, you may readily imagine that my heart yearns towards you with a painful sentiment of solicitude on your behalf," Blackwell confided. "Lucy dear—if I could take all the pain & suspense, I would not let you have *one pang*. I would gladly take it all for your sake."[43]

Over the next several months, Blackwell told Stone that he considered her pregnancy the "last proof of [her] affection" for him. He would try to deserve that affection, he said, "by doing all I can to act bravely & nobly." Throughout the pregnancy, the peril his wife faced, rather than the prospect of becoming a father, guided Blackwell's emotions. At the same time, he emphasized that the impending birth represented an assumption of mutual parental responsibilities. The expectation of parenthood cast his character in a new moral light, stiffening his resolve to live honorably. The week before their daughter's birth, he wrote to Stone from New York City: "I look out from the dark, mysterious shadow [pregnancy] in which our present life is veiled & see more clearly the defects of my character & purpose. . . . Lucy dear—*however* this great crisis may eventuate, whether it result as I hope & believe, in *our* assumption of new duties & cares, or whether in leaving me *alone* in this strange, uncongenial world—I will try to *meet* my responsibilities *worthily & well*. . . . If God give me the great *privilege* & honor & blessing of your *personal society*, I will try to show my gratitude by living *nobly* in act & thought."[44]

The chilling prospect of maternal death, rather than paternity's warm glow, also colored Henry Parker Smith's reactions to the advent of fatherhood. Far from ratifying his manhood, his wife's first pregnancy prompted a measure of self-recrimination. In August 1854, when Harriet (Hattie) Smith was five months pregnant, Henry Smith confided to his diary: "Rec'd dear Hattie's letter, a long, loving, trusting one. That which we would have shunned and hoped to avoid has already come upon her. Why did I not know the consequences; it was the sin of ignorance for which I may lose my gentle wife. God Almighty forbid, grant that this may not be the cup of bitterness and we will never drink another."[45]

Smith anxiously monitored his wife's condition in the late stages of her pregnancy. As her time approached, his apprehensions mounted. "I am a little uneasy about Hattie," he confided on February 24, 1855, "her time is up in a week or two but I hope she went along through it. *What would I do* should it prove otherwise." Significantly, he assuaged his worst fears by resolving to play an active role when Mrs. Smith was brought to bed. "Hattie feels that her trial is drawn near," he wrote on March 7. "I feel anxious about it sometimes, fear trouble to come but I will trust in the all powerful arm of Providence as we see it exerted in nature, and try to behave myself as a man should and make myself of some use instead of folding my hands and saying Gods will be done." On March 10, four days before a daughter was born, Smith stiffened his resolve: "Hattie feels quite unwell to day & I feel my heart throb every few minutes whenever I think of the trial so near at hand but I will try to abide by the best in the world. 'Sufficient for the day is the evil thereof.'"[46]

The solicitude that Blackwell and Smith so eloquently expressed—particularly, the resolve to commit to fatherhood for the sake of one's wife and the peril that she faced in childbirth—guided the initial response of many nineteenth-century men to the prospect of becoming parents. Scattered evidence suggests that the verbal expressions of care and concern that ring through nineteenth-century men's diaries and letters often were accompanied by concrete actions. Men who were at home as parturition approached often helped prepare for the baby's arrival, making sure, for instance, that the needed supplies were on hand and that the house was in order. Henry Parker Smith purchased diaper flannel and other items for baby care in the months before his daughter arrived.[47]

Similarly, in the weeks and months before the birth of their first child, in 1845, Edmund Churchill, a farmer and storekeeper in Proctorsville, Vermont, launched a furious campaign to make his home more comfortable and convenient. Churchill had been married about a year when his wife, Maria, gave birth to a daughter on September 29. Maria M. Churchill's diary records a frenzy of home improvement undertaken by her husband to prepare for the birth. As parenthood approached, Churchill purchased various household items—an ash pail, a lamp filler, a dishpan, a washbasin, a dustpan, a pail, a dipper, and a server—to make housekeeping easier. He had the tea kettle mended and installed a shelf "behind the sink room door" as a convenient storage place for the lamp filler and matches. "Thus you see we have all things convenient," Maria Churchill commented approvingly, after cataloging her husband's many home improvements. "I think we are getting on finely in the household line."[48]

In the nineteenth century, as today, a certain practicality motivated such masculine nesting. In the past, however, a distinctive set of popular medical beliefs heightened concerns about maternal comfort and safety during pregnancy and after childbirth. The tenets of hereditarian medical thought stressed the power of a mother's imagination to influence the physical and mental condition of her child in utero and during the period of lactation. Since a mother's physical and emotional states were transmissible to offspring, husbands were repeatedly advised to be especially solicitous about pregnant wives and nursing mothers. William Alcott, a physician, educator, and domestic adviser who wrote more than a dozen important books on home life between 1833 and 1857, offered characteristic advice: He urged men to see to it that pregnant wives maintained their health by eating properly and exercising. Husbands, he continued, also needed to lavish affection on wives and new mothers, since a woman's "cheerful spirits" were essential to the development of both the fetus and the nursing child.[49]

Such medical thinking had crosscutting effects on men's experience when their wives were pregnant. John Gillis has recently suggested that middle-class men in nineteenth-century England became less involved in pregnancy, less likely to monitor their wives' condition, and, because it had become a medical matter, much less concerned with antenatal care than were their eighteenth-century forebears. In earlier times, Gillis maintains, fathers made arrangements for the delivery and were generally more attentive and involved in birth preparations. Although they were barred by custom from attending the birth, fathers were the center of public attention after the child was born. They were the first men to enter the lying-in chamber, where they took possession of the child as their own. Fathers also accompanied the infant to church for baptism, while their wives remained secluded at home.

According to Gillis, the father's more prominent role in the past owed

largely to negative images of the pregnant woman as a polluting or dangerous presence whose condition removed her from the wider community. In
the nineteenth century, this image was reversed. Due in part to new medical
understandings that emphasized the importance of the female role in reproduction, the pregnant woman came to be seen as the epitome of femininity. Her condition now associated her with a higher rather than lower
state. As women became the center of attention, Gillis concludes, nineteenth-
century fathers were displaced and marginalized as the "other" in the reproductive process.[50]

The American experience suggests that, even at the margins, men played
a significant role. Fears surrounding maternal health and safety were potent
goads to active involvement in the passage toward parenthood, and, as Gillis
acknowledges, middle-class men felt a powerful need to support their wives
at their moment of greatest danger. Such concern reinforced masculine domesticity, and, to an indeterminable but real extent, the commitment to fatherhood as well, if only for the sake of the mother.

Childbirth

The period of heightened spousal solicitude inaugurated by a woman's
pregnancy culminated during childbirth. Scholarly understandings of childbearing in the nineteenth century emphasize the female-centered practices
of childbirth and the male physician's gradual entry into the lying-in chamber at parturient women's behest. Even before physicians were invited to the
bedside, however, husbands were already there. Many men in both rural and
urban households were present when their children were born and participated actively in the births.[51] These men entered the birth chamber less in
their capacity as fathers (to witness the birth or receive the child as their
own) than as husbands (to lend a hand because their wives valued their presence and wanted them to assist). Husbands lent moral support and helped
in the delivery by performing sundry tasks. They built and tended fires,
heated and carried water, supported the laboring woman as she walked
about, and attempted to soothe her pain.

Typically, it was the husband's task to summon the network of female
friends and relatives who were to attend the birth as well as to call on the
physician. Here, for instance, is the way Lavius Hyde, a minister living in

Ellington, Connecticut, described the circumstances surrounding the birth of a son in 1831:

> About 4 o'clock the mother observed that she felt some like inviting some of her friends, and having a little party. I accordingly, called on a neighbour about 15 rods from us, and asked if she would sit with Mrs. Hyde. I then walked to the Doctors about 100 rods. He had company and was just placing the chairs around the Tea Table. I told him I thought he had better take his cup of Tea and asked his wife to accompany him, soon after. On my return, I found the first invited lady, Mrs. Smith, with Mrs. Hyde, and she hurried me to another neighbor about 20 rods distance, and while I was absent, the Lord committed to our care the little plump looking young gentleman. He came in very good style, and when I entered the room was making acquaintance with his neighbour Mrs. Smith, and seemed to feel quite at home. The doctor soon arrived and all the party proceeded very pleasantly. The mother and little son are very well today but I am expecting she will feel more unwell for some days to come.[52]

Hyde composed that description in a letter to his wife's parents. Almost invariably, it was a husband's task to announce the birth of a child to distant relatives and friends, while his wife convalesced. Very few birth announcements were written by mothers themselves.[53]

Hyde was an especially voluble correspondent. The announcements that most men wrote are noteworthy for their brevity and emotional restraint. Typically, for both the writer and the recipient, the wife's condition was of equal concern with the child's arrival. Here, for instance, is how a baker in Salem, Massachusetts, announced the birth of a daughter in 1818 to his brother, a storekeeper in Princeton: "We have had an addition to our family since you last heard from me of a fine daughter which we have thought of naming Sally. [My wife] has been quite unwell for near two months with a broken brest but it is now getting some better. I cannot write you so much near as I wish. It is now growing late in the evening and I am obliged to be up at half past twelve every morning to work on my bread but shall take an opportunity to write you again."[54]

Another announcement, written in 1870, by a farmer and sometime sawmill operator in Glen Arbor, Michigan, to his father-in-law in Chicago, follows a similar pattern: "We are all quite smart. I was presented with a young son, Oct. 6th, 12 o'clock in the Day. He weighed $7\frac{1}{2}$ lbs. A bouncer. Both

Ettie and the baby is quite smart. His name is John Edward Fisher. John is for you, and Edward is for Father. . . . In regard to sending those potatoes. I will first send you some sitron, about 2 bbls. and then if you can, dispose of them and send me 15 of those Gunny bags, 2 Bu Bags. I will immediately send you the potatoes. I am preparing them now. No more at present. We all send Love."⁵⁵ This note could stand for many others. Seldom did men have the leisure for elaborate discussion of a child's birth. Depending on who was being informed, the news was generally conveyed alongside other (frequently economic) concerns.⁵⁶

Although Reverend Hyde was so busy gathering attendants that he missed his child's birth, other husbands did not. Like Hyde, however, who willingly deferred to the authority of his neighbor Mrs. Smith once she arrived on the scene and took charge of the delivery, they did play auxiliary roles. A man's level of involvement in childbirth seems to have been more closely related to the availability and quality of a female support network and professional medical assistance than to any other single factor.

Henry Parker Smith's participation in the births of his first three children again offers a rare, intimate glimpse into what was expected of men when their wives gave birth. Both the presence of competent birth attendants and Smith's own expanding comfort level as he attended repeated deliveries shaped the nature and extent of his involvement with childbirth as his family grew. The scene in the Smiths' Schoolcraft, Michigan, home on March 14, 1855, mustered a standard cast of characters. Gathered to attend Harriet Smith after she went into labor were three female relatives, including her mother-in-law, as well as a physician and her husband, Henry. Here is Henry Smith's account of the delivery, written five days after the birth of their first child, a daughter:

> All has [turned out?] much better than I had anticipated, as well as I could have hoped. Wednesday evening Father called for me to go to the house to assist them and it was with doubt & misgiving that I went but I did go and stood by my own dear wife through her great trial. She gave birth to a girl weighing 9½ pounds, about half past eight in the evening after which we (Aunts Jane & Mary, the Doctor & I) took our supper with a relish, while mother was dressing the child. I ate like a bear for it seemed that a load of many tons was removed from my heart.⁵⁷

Smith played a more prominent, and far less tentative, role in the births of his next two children, who were born on a homestead in Missouri. Without the dense network of social ties available to the family back in Michigan, Smith had no choice but to act a leading part when his second child, a son, was born, in 1859. On the afternoon of June 5, Smith discovered that his wife was in the early stages of labor. As Harriet Smith's labor intensified in the evening, he sent for two women neighbors to sit with her. Somewhat later he also summoned the doctor. Smith picks up the story: "About 11 or 12 o'clock the child was born and as neither of the women present could act I tied the string & cut the cord and waited until the afterbirth came. It is a fine healthy boy. Did not close my eyes in sleep during the night. Doctor Dade came about two hours [after] the child was born."[58] When his third child was born, in 1861, Smith again acted as midwife in the absence of other competent birth attendants.

Men did not often act as midwives, of course, but they played significant and occasionally central roles as long as childbirth occurred at home. Barton Taylor, a Methodist minister living in Plymouth, Michigan, for instance, seems to have delivered a son in 1873. "Went to bed about ten o'clock suspicious of a change in the programme," Taylor's wife, Elizabeth, recorded in her diary on July 24. "At two A.M. [Barton] got up built a fire & c. At about four [he] went for Mrs. Morrison, and before she got dressed & over we had a young laddie here."[59]

Barton Taylor filled the breach until the midwife arrived—an unusual circumstance perhaps, but in keeping with expectations that a husband would do whatever was necessary in a crisis. More to the point, Taylor's participation (building a fire, summoning the midwife, being present during the delivery) reflected a level of involvement commonly expected of nineteenth-century men. Although men's diary descriptions of their children's births are not often detailed enough to determine their role with precision, one commonly finds the time and date of a child's birth recorded, along with sufficient description of the confinement to indicate clearly that a husband had been present at the birth. "A little daughter was born to me at 2:15 A.M.," Alexander Winchell noted in his diary on September 17, 1867. "Labor began at 8:30 last evening—severe labor at 1:45 this morning—birth at 2:15—placenta expelled at 2:30. A fat, healthy, child, weighing 11 pounds."[60]

Winchell, Taylor, Smith, and many other nineteenth-century men were present when their children were born because their wives wanted them by their sides, and because it accorded with their duties as companionate husbands. What beliefs about becoming fathers guided these men as they gathered networks of birth attendants, built fires, assisted in the delivery, and afterwards informed relatives and friends of the outcome?

Masculine Attitudes toward the Birth of Children

We have already noticed that men did not reflect as often about becoming fathers as they did about getting married. One must turn many pages of nineteenth-century letters and diaries for the rare glimpse of a man's thoughts on the arrival of his child. The reactions one does discover, however, are often quite revealing. Not surprisingly, perhaps, the birth of a child, especially that of a first child, could occasion an outpouring of tender emotions. When Charles Russell of Princeton, Massachusetts, had his first child, in 1816, he told his brother Ephraim in Malden: "I am now a Father. God of nature what a gift. A fine son, the picture of health, the bud of human nature with what pleasure do [I] press to my lips the offspring of one whom I love." Russell went on to describe the pleasure he took "in clasping the dear little cretor [*sic*] in my arms and singing to him lol o by o baby by."[61]

Such fatherly feeling was frequently mixed with, and sometimes overshadowed by, husbandly solicitude. By now it is a historical commonplace to remark that fathers were odd men out in the nineteenth century's romantic reevaluation of family life. The celebration of mothers and children in Victorian America went hand in hand, the argument goes, but the father's role was too freighted with patriarchal baggage to undergo the same sentimental treatment.[62] As we have already discovered, however, spousal devotion was thought of in much the same terms as maternal love and childhood innocence. Men were expected to experience the warmth of family emotions in their capacity as husbands, a sentimental requirement that encompassed the birth of a child.

Within the context of the companionate marriage ideal, a child's entry into the world frequently brought out expressions of sympathy in men for the ordeal through which a woman had passed and the burden of care that had devolved on her. "What trials these young mothers have; especially those who have never thought or [been] educated [to] have the care of a home, without means to keep servants," Henry Parker Smith reflected a month after his daughter Isa was born, in 1855.[63] Similarly, Abijah Bigelow, an attorney from Worcester, Massachusetts, sympathized with his wife upon the birth of a daughter, their fifth child, while he was serving as a representative in Congress: "I have long felt a very deep interest for the trial I was sensible you had to endure," he told her. "Indeed you do not know how much I have felt for you. But I sincerely hope that your health and strength will soon be restored, that your little daughter will prove a blessing and a comfort to us."[64] Bigelow's new daughter was his wife's to care for but a source of blessing and comfort to them both.

As children arrived, most men took pride in becoming fathers. They looked forward to the companionship of their newly enlarged families and embraced paternal responsibility by shouldering the increased burden to provide. "I shall be glad when I can have a little more time to devote to my family," Henry Parker Smith went on to reflect after the birth of his first daughter, "and when the baby gets old enough to help itself some and not have the colic and when Hattie gets strong and return of buoyant spirits." Eyeing the future, Smith also anticipated providing his growing family with the comforts of a new home. Isa's birth cast his mind forward to the time when "we are forehanded enough to live in a little cottage of our own, 'a little farm well tilled,' and able to hire a girl &c &c. Such are my cogitations nowadays."[65]

Postnatal Care

As men adjusted to their new identities as fathers, family support began to come first on their list of priorities, and they conceptualized the time they spent at home, especially with their children, as a periodic commitment. Even so, childbirth, like the sickness of a child, was a domestic moment tinged with crisis. It therefore afforded men the opportunity for heroic family intervention, prompting some to participate in a limited but significant period of postnatal care before returning to the task of making a living.

The burden of caring for newborns and infants fell upon mothers, of course. Frequently women, especially first-time mothers, arranged for someone to assist them for a time as they gathered strength after giving birth. Female kin—mothers, mothers-in-law, or sisters—lent support in many households; when hired help was affordable, a domestic servant or nurse might be hired. Although a husband's care was desired and valued, men were rather quickly reabsorbed into their work lives after childbirth. What assistance they did lend their wives supplemented, rather than replaced, the support of female relatives and friends, but their participation was clearly welcomed.

When she was about to give birth in 1845, Maria Churchill, the Vermont woman whose husband, Edmund, had undertaken so many home improvements, asked her sister to come live with her for a while. After a daughter was born, Maria's sister acted as nurse and helped out with housework.[66] Nonetheless, five days after being brought to bed, Maria noted: "E[dmund] took care of baby & me last night & got along *admirably* & were it not for keeping him awake so much I should prefer him for a nurse every night for I feel so much more at home & can rest better when he is *near, say, in the same bed*, but I must not be a baby on the subject."[67] Maria could not depend on having her husband at her side, however. Less than a fortnight after his daughter's birth, Churchill left home for a week on one of his frequent business trips.

The period of time a husband devoted to heightened domesticity and care after the birth of a child could be quite short. Henry Parker Smith's experience mirrored Edmund Churchill's. Like Maria Churchill, Harriet Smith relied primarily on a female relative (in this case her mother-in-law) for postnatal care after her first child was born. Henry did, however, help out with infant care, nursing, and household chores.

Smith spent the day after his daughter was born "with [his] wife & child watching Hattie's symptoms." The next day, a Saturday, he was back to work at his store. But for the next several weeks Smith tried to be an active parent. "It is rather new business to raise children," he wrote ten days after his daughter was born. "At night mother left us to ourselves and I took off my clothes for the first time since Isa's birth & went to bed with her upon my arm. During the whole night I slept about two hours and my little Isa was as good as she could be. It would have been a ludicrous scene to see us change her diapers three times in the night. We are *very* awkward to be sure."[68]

The births of subsequent children again involved Smith at home, nursing mother and child and assisting with such house chores as washing bed clothes. But the demands of farm work and other business soon pulled him away from home. Two days after the birth of his second child, in 1859, for instance, he left home on a four-day business trip. The pattern of heightened domestic involvement followed by absence repeated itself after the birth of a third child, two years later.[69]

In well-to-do households, a husband's added responsibility seems to have lasted only as long as it took to employ a domestic servant or nurse. Francis Adams White, a Boston tannery owner, was living in suburban Brookline when his second son was born, on September 4, 1858. His wife, Caroline, recorded in her diary: "Mrs. Woodward came to my assistance in the morning of his birth & remained a day or two. Then dear Frank officiated as nurse for a day—till we could procure the services of Mrs. Jones of Cambridge, who is now with me."[70] Thereupon White left home on a week-long business trip. George Slayton, a Michigan native, was farming and teaching school in Salem, Nebraska, in the 1870s and 1880s when his fourth child, a daughter, was born. Like the White family, the Slaytons relied on hired help. Of his daughter's birth, Slayton recalled: "Helen was born on Sept. 3 so we had to have a hired girl most of the winter and next summer as I had very little spare time for house choring."[71]

The foregoing accounts are representative of others; they suggest the existence of a fairly clear set of expectations about a man's obligations after the birth of a child. House chores, nursing, and infant care were female responsibilities, but in the absence of relatives, friends, or hired help to perform these tasks, responsibility was passed on to husbands. Because this was female work, however, men seem to have had a great deal of latitude in setting the limits of their involvement. Sometimes this left wives and mothers in the lurch.

Barton Taylor, the Methodist minister from Plymouth, Michigan, whose son was born in 1873, participated in baby care after the boy's birth. But when his son was several months old, Taylor unilaterally relinquished responsibility. As his wife noted: "Lizzie [a hired girl] has come and, doing well what she does, is better than no help, but does not do enough to relieve me so very much, for [Barton] has given up baby-tending, & having the ironing to do, makes so much more to be done."[72]

Men like Taylor rather matter of factly went back to the task of making a living soon after the birth of their children because that was how they perceived their major responsibility in life. This did not prevent men, however, from viewing parental responsibility as a mutual burden and the role of parent as a social identity that men and women shared. During his daughter Alice's first year of life, Henry Blackwell continued to travel on business a great deal, sometimes leaving home for months at a time. Not long before Alice was born, he had given up a bookkeeping position in New York, which would have kept him closer to home. His wife, Lucy Stone, who thought it her responsibility to stay home with the child, supported Blackwell's decision, which she described as both necessary for the family and required for her husband's self-respect.[73]

As sharply as Stone's and Blackwell's roles diverged, however, Alice's birth invested the couple with a shared parental identity. Their mutual identification with parenthood was somewhat abstract, perhaps, but it was a real meeting ground for their individual roles as mother and father. Mothers and fathers might undertake different tasks, but the efforts of both parents, Blackwell professed, were required to impart the qualities of mind and heart (responsibility, self-control, and perseverance, to name a few) summed up in the nineteenth-century notion of character. When Alice was six months old, Blackwell wrote to his wife from Janesville, Wisconsin: "May we both be spared to give her all the help that parents can give their children. I am sure that the responsibilities of our position will make us very anxious to live nobly & to infuse into her little soul none but brave & true thoughts."[74]

Blackwell's sentiments upon entering fatherhood echoed the high-mindedness with which a host of Victorian moralists and family advisers approached the task of raising children. Other men as well responded to the importance insistently ascribed to parenting. The next chapter will show how such lofty sentiments played out in the actual relationships that fathers established with their young children. Before turning to that topic, however, it will be useful to consider briefly how infants were named.

What's in a Name?

Historians have occasionally looked to naming practices as evidence of shifting power relationships and values within families. Before the American Revolution, about three-fifths of all first-born sons had been named for their fathers, whereas by 1790, that amount had fallen to only one-quarter.[75]

The meaning of such a trend is almost impossible to determine with any degree of confidence. At least one historian has speculated, however, that the break with tradition was associated with changing parental aspirations. Rather than expecting a son to carry on his father's name and craft, turn-of-the-century parents may have given their children more latitude to pursue other opportunities and develop their individual potential.[76]

Choosing a child's name may be related only loosely, if at all, to aspirations for his or her future. Scattered literary evidence hints, however, that nineteenth-century naming practices were indeed associated with declining patriarchal control. Fathers seem to have had greater authority over naming children early in the century than they did later. While the (admittedly unscientific) sample examined here provided several examples of fathers clearly having a unilateral prerogative to name a son before 1820, no instances of such authority were evident in later decades. Throughout the century, family consultation was the rule when choosing a child's name. In some cases a father chose the name for a son, after a mother had named a daughter. More frequently, though, names were agreed upon jointly, after consultation with other family members. The name of a spouse's brother or sister were particularly popular choices.[77]

The following examples illustrate how paternal authority over naming seems to have diminished over time. When a first child, a son, was born to the aforementioned couple, Louisa and John Park of Acton, Massachusetts, in 1800, the father, a physician, was away from home on a naval voyage. In his absence, a family friend had baptized the infant with the name "Tuwarrow," which Louisa found both strange and unacceptable. She wrote to John: "The boy cries too loud—do send me a name for him—I don't like the savage name Tuwarrow, which Captain Hoit gave him."[78]

Again, when a second son was born to Joshua Gray, a ship's master from North Yarmouth, Massachusetts, in 1817, his decision that the boy would bear his name was unassailable by his wife. "Our children are well," she wrote him soon after the boy's birth. "The babe grows finely. I expect you are determined on the name as you wished me to take good care of Joshua Adams."[79]

Later in the century, paternal fiat in the choice of a name was more likely to be contested. John Evarts Tracy, the only son of an attorney in Green Bay, Wisconsin, reported the dispute after his birth, in 1880: "There was a family argument over my name. My father insisted on naming me after his father, Ebenezer Carter. My mother fought this plan with determination and finally succeeded in having me named John Evarts."[80]

Whether or not parents agreed initially, mutual decision making was most often the order of the day. The procedure followed in the Littlefield household in Farwell, Michigan, when a son was born in 1892, seems to have been standard practice in most homes for much of the century. Littlefield, a lumberman, recalled: "As is quite often the case, there was some little discussion before deciding on a name for the baby. His mother and I talked it over and we thought it would be nice to name him for her brother."[81]

Periodic Domesticity

By either choosing a name or assisting in childbirth, many nineteenth-century men played surprisingly active parts when their children came into the world. Their behavior pushes to the margins images of aloof Victorian patriarchs so preoccupied with breadwinning that they placed little or no significance on other family obligations during the earliest phase of a child's life. Female-dominated childbirth practices cast men into a supporting role when children were born, but the crisis of childbirth also encouraged men to associate domestic responsibility with manly action. By inviting husbands into their birthing rooms, wives intentionally blurred gender boundaries to gain moral support at a perilous time. They created expectations that men could and should play an active, even heroic, role at home when they were not at work.

Once a woman was safely brought to bed, fathers resumed their customary work roles rather quickly; it was not unusual for a man to leave home on business within days of a child's birth, as the burden of infant care rapidly devolved on the mother and those summoned to assist her as she convalesced. Given the importance placed on masculine provision, this is hardly surprising. It was crucial to the history of fatherhood, however, that childbirth was often viewed as a medical crisis. By summoning men to action, childbirth practices helped to establish the fact that domesticity would play a periodic but significant role in men's lives.

Far from viewing childbirth as an event transpiring in a separate "woman's sphere," many middle-class men felt called upon *as men* to take an active part, because lending assistance and moral support was crucial to being a good husband. Ironically, then, even as his children entered the world, a man's paternal identity and understanding of his responsibilities as a father were shaped decisively by the relationship he had with his wife. Such husbandly participation still left open the question of how fathers would engage themselves in the everyday lives of their young children. Exploring how men answered that question is the subject of the next chapter.

Chapter 5

A Frolic with Father

Small Children, Play, and Paternal Identity

My youngest child is an infant about 15 months old, with about the intelligence common to children of that age. It has for some months been evident, that he was more than usually self willed, but the several attempts to subdue him, had been thus far relinquished, from the fear that he did not fully understand what was said to him. . . . Still I had seen enough to convince me of the necessity of subduing his temper, and resolved to seize upon the first favorable opportunity which presented, for settling the question of authority between us.

Francis Wayland, "A Case of Conviction,"
American Baptist Magazine, October 1831

He said to me concerning the baby, "And has your husband a theory? Because if he has this child is ruined."

Eunice Tripler, recalling a remark of General Winfield Scott
upon the birth of her first child, ca. 1841

On the subject of raising children, Francis Wayland, president of Brown University and a nationally noted Baptist minister, was fast becoming by the 1830s, if he was not already, a paternal anachronism. When his fifteen-month-old son one day refused the offer of a piece of bread, the "favorable opportunity" that Wayland had been waiting for to subdue the toddler's will had at long last arrived. Over the next thirty-six hours, Wayland withheld food from the small child, starving him into submission. Wayland has left us a detailed account of this incident. Writing in the *American Baptist Magazine*, he represented himself as a model father whose reluctant duty, however harsh it seemed, was to subjugate the will of a stubborn child. "There can be no greater cruelty than to suffer a child to grow up with unsubdued temper," Wayland wrote. Such indulgence would serve only to spoil the child and would ill prepare him to live in a world where he would be called upon to submit to the authority of "more powerful beings than he."[1]

Wayland may have considered himself a model father, but his methods struck some of his readers, as they would most parents today, as a form of child abuse. Indeed, his article, which he chose to publish anonymously (uncertain perhaps of its reception), was greeted with as much scorn as assent. Responding to "A Case of Conviction," one reader labeled its author "little better than a brute [who] should not be allowed to preside over the destinies of infants. His own acknowledged brutality towards his own offspring should gain for him the anathema of the public and the indignation of every parent."[2]

Francis Wayland's harsh conception of paternal duty swam against the nineteenth century's tide of domestic reform, which exalted the kindness, love, and tender care of the mother as the instruments best suited to shape the character of children, especially while they were young. By the 1830s, what would become the long heyday of the mother had arrived. Unlike the domineering patriarch of "A Case of Conviction," most fathers played an auxiliary role in the moral development and training of their young children.[3]

As the father's responsibility for moral instruction receded in the nineteenth century, new modes of paternal behavior came to the fore, not least the image of father as a companion and play partner to young children. The future of fathering lay not with Wayland's rigorous involvement in the upbringing of his infant son, but with the ideas embodied in General Winfield Scott's remark to Eunice Tripler, the wife of his company surgeon: A father with a "theory" of infant management, Scott maintained, was more a menace to the training of young children than a model parent; such matters were best left to mothers. As the less responsible, because supposedly less capable, parent, nineteenth-century fathers were left to cultivate the playful aspect of parent-child relations. Indeed, new understandings about the emotional value of family life for middle-class men urged them to do so. To use a nineteenth-century term, fathers were encouraged to *frolic* with their children.

Images of fathers at play are a prominent feature of family documents from the earliest decades of the nineteenth century. Strikingly modern scenes of fathers rolling on the carpet with children, carrying them on their shoulders, entertaining them with toys and playthings—in short, routinely initiating or responding to demands for play—belie the one-dimensional stereotypes of work-obsessed and emotionally aloof Victorian patriarchs. Middle-class men did not simply beat a hasty retreat into breadwinning after the mother's role expanded in the early nineteenth century. Their response to social change was both more human and more complex.

Nineteenth-century men were caught in a dilemma. Husbands who competed vigorously at work to earn a living for their families also were expected to adhere to the emergent conventions of companionate households, which meant cultivating intense familial bonds. Accordingly, the history of fathering in the nineteenth century is best understood as a dialogue between opposing tendencies: withdrawal into breadwinning on the one hand, and greater involvement with children on the other. Although men had less time for fatherhood than in the past, they were still encouraged by moral opinion makers to cultivate more substantial emotional ties with children than had earlier generations of fathers.[4]

Fathering young children in nineteenth-century America straddled another cultural contradiction as well. Parents in that period held profoundly conflicting attitudes toward children.[5] At times, children were celebrated with Wordsworthian fervor as angelic innocents. Close association with children, considered in their sentimental aspect, was thought to benefit parents. The moralizing influence of childhood innocence could be especially salutary for fathers, since men by definition needed such ethical uplift more than did women. The companionship of one's children, moreover, was understood to replenish spirits harried by competition in the economic marketplace. Such sentiment notwithstanding, nineteenth-century parents also thought of children as impulsive and self-centered, small beings unable to distinguish between reality and imagination or good and evil. These less sanguine appraisals of children's nature suggested that the first order of business for mothers and fathers alike was not to cultivate a child's friendship but rather to assure prompt conformity to parental wishes.

Controlling the Young

In an era when children and how they were to be raised were subjects of mounting concern, fathers could not easily evade issues of discipline and control. Increasing demands on children for conformity and obedience in the nineteenth century were matters not readily left to mothers alone, however weighty the maternal role had become.[6] Notwithstanding new reliance on mothers and their nurturant methods, the objects of parenting had not shifted dramatically. The central child-rearing precept of most nineteenth-century parents, as it had been for earlier generations of parents, was obedience.

For all the contemporary discussion of affection as the best mode of winning children to correct behavior, affection itself was never the top priority. Rather, it was the means for forming the child's conscience, understood as an internalization of the parents' discipline. Children in the model nineteenth-century family still offered implicit and prompt submission to their parents' wishes, but now out of love instead of fear of punishment. The ideal mother in child-rearing literature was strict but loving; the ideal father supported maternal authority, intervening whenever a stronger or more consistent discipline was necessary.

As historian Mary Ryan has observed, nineteenth-century parents endeavored to implant in the child's personality the bourgeois virtues: honesty, industry, frugality, temperance, and above all, self-control.[7] These prudential values, designed to reproduce a model child "infused not with the spirit of a daring, aggressive entrepreneur but with, rather, that of a cautious, prudent, small-business man" shifted somewhat later in the century, when strenuosity and the exercise of will power in youth became more highly regarded.[8] Over the course of the century, such values and aims left considerable scope for fatherly participation in a child's upbringing.

At a minimum, the fact that many nineteenth-century mothers were paying more attention to child rearing and supervising their children more closely stimulated paternal concern with issues of child development. Husbands' letters to their wives are full of interest in the behavior and training of young children, and it was the rare child who received no warnings from an absent father to obey his or her mother. This guidance, however, tended to exalt maternal exertions on behalf of children and reinforce the mother's primary role in the child's life, rather than laying claim to the role of preceptor in chief.

The substance of such advice can be illustrated with excerpts from letters written by Abijah Bigelow and William L. Hudson, both fathers of young children during the first half of the century. In 1811, Bigelow, a lawyer and politician who then had a son and two daughters, all younger than six, wrote to his wife in Massachusetts:

> I wish you, as I know you will, to pay that attention to [the children] which will be useful, by impressing upon their minds, so far as it is practicable, at their age, the importance of obedience and good behavior. With familiarity, which I think very necessary, they should still have that respect which will induce them to mind instantly. You see I can preach well, but I confess to practise is very difficult, and I have often thought that I had not so good a faculty of managing children as I ought to have. Tell the little rogues that their papa thinks of them every day, that they must be good children and mind their mama.[9]

Bigelow, as this excerpt attests, was concerned about the new "familiar" mode of maternal child rearing, fearing that it would undermine filial respect. More to the point, maternal child-rearing methods led him to question his own "faculty of managing children." That nagging doubt did not prevent him from offering his wife, Hannah, a great deal of unsolicited child-rearing advice, but it did reinforce his decision to play a secondary parenting role and to refer to his wife as "head" of the household. Eventually, Mrs. Bigelow came to resent her husband's steady flow of suggestions about how to raise the children, interpreting his running commentary as tacit criticism of her competence. She complained, moreover, that Bigelow's epistolary advice was not matched with a corresponding degree of parental attention when he was home and available to his children.[10]

Not all men shared Bigelow's misgivings about maternal child-rearing methods. William L. Hudson, a naval officer, positively glorified his wife's parenting ability, lauding her devotion to her children. In a letter written in 1850, he observed that nothing gratified parents' hearts more than "seeing their children obedient, kind and loving to them and living in harmony and love with each other." The basis of such order and affection was the nearly sacred power of a mother's love to elicit corresponding emotions in her children. "If there be anything I anxiously covet of our dear children," he wrote, "it is that next to love & devotion to their maker, they may appreciate your great care and love for them and make you the best return in their power by doing everything on their part that will please and gratify you."[11] Such sentiments, one suspects, helped Hudson justify to himself the distance that military service imposed on his own parenting.

Although Bigelow and Hudson differed in their assessments of mother-hood and the companionship on which the new parenting was based, both men understood their task as fathers in much the same way—namely, as a duty to reinforce maternal authority in the family. Especially where young children were concerned, many men conceptualized the father's role as being a friend of motherhood, someone who, by reminding children of their mother's sacrifices, could enhance the disciplinary influence of her love. In their capacity as fathers, they sought to establish mothers as the focus of fil-ial affection. As a Connecticut woman widowed in 1865 said of her late hus-band's parenting: "He taught them [their eight children] kindness and rev-erence to me."[12]

By highlighting the importance of the more available parent, this con-ception of the father as a cheerleader for motherhood helped to mitigate emergent conflicts between men's work and home responsibilities. Adopt-ing an auxiliary role, however, did not allay all psychological discomfort and in fact raised anxieties all its own. Feelings of impiety troubled some men as they joined in the praise of moral mothers. Equally perplexing was the ques-tion of whether men who fit the pattern of nurturant child rearing were truly men. Could they still compete aggressively at work? And what of the new parenting methods themselves? Were gentle techniques adequate to ensure obedience, especially of unruly sons? What should fathers do specifically to guarantee that children conformed to their mothers' will?

As we have seen, Abijah Bigelow doubted his "faculty of managing chil-dren" and left matters mostly to his wife. Many other fathers followed suit. Albert G. Browne of Salem, Massachusetts, had similar misgivings, which his religious doubt compounded. Browne married in 1833, at age twenty-seven, and spent the years before the Civil War building his ship chandler's firm into a prosperous and far-flung enterprise that required frequent and extensive travel from home. On a business trip in 1842, he reflected on his role as parent of a young son, telling his wife that he sometimes felt "unfitted to convey lessons of wisdom or instruction to his tender susceptible nature." Browne went on to assure himself that his son would receive such lessons from his mother's lips. He feared, however, that the small boy's impetuos-ity would defeat her best efforts to impress him with the need to "govern & subdue his constitutional instability." Above all, Browne wrote, he wanted to have his son's "young mind thoroughly imbued with religion," a wish that troubled his own conscience. "It has ever been a source of unhappiness to me that I am wholly unqualified to afford him this instruction," Browne confessed. "Tho not religious myself, I see its necessity, its imperative necessity."[13]

At a time when parents considered religion an essential tool of child nurture, differences of faith influenced how active a role fathers chose to play in establishing the principles of family governance. Evangelical fathers like Francis Wayland were more likely to involve themselves directly than were religious skeptics like Browne or the majority of men with more moderate religious views. Like Francis Wayland, the nationally renowned Presbyterian minister Lyman Beecher embodied the principle of discipline in his family from the time his children were very young. "Our mother was gentle, tender, and sympathizing, but all the discipline of government was with father," recalled Catharine Beecher, his eldest daughter, born in 1800:

> With most of his children, when quite young, he had one, two, or three seasons in which he taught them that obedience must be exact, prompt, and cheerful, and by a discipline so severe that it was thoroughly remembered and feared. Ever after, a decided word of command was all-sufficient. The obedience demanded was to be speedy, and without fretting or frowns. "Mind your mother; quick! no crying! look pleasant!" These were words of command obeyed with almost military speed and precision.[14]

To judge by the autobiographical evidence of other nineteenth-century childhoods, Catharine Beecher's testimony accurately represents the more activist engagement of evangelically oriented fathers in the management of young children. Her reminiscence hints at a limited use of corporal punishment by her father to establish the principle of prompt, unquestioning obedience to parental authority. Overall, though, the sources afford scant evidence that corporal punishment was a pervasive fact of family life. My reading of the autobiographies and personal papers of ninety-four individuals who grew up in the nineteenth century uncovered only four accounts of corporal punishment. In two cases the disciplinarian was the child's father; in the other two, the mother. Generally speaking, neither parents nor children wrote much about punishment in their reminiscences, and discipline is seldom discussed in children's diaries.[15]

What the evidence does suggest is that fathers remained concerned about the training of young children, especially the matter of instilling principles of obedience, even after maternal authority expanded. They were quite will-ing, however, to play a supportive role. Although maternal child rearing could provoke paternal anxiety, prompting some men to question their ap-titude as parents, such feelings should not be exaggerated. Fathers such as Abijah Bigelow and Albert Browne tended to brush aside their discomfort and go about their work with the assurance that mothers knew best how to manage the children.

Indeed, fathers whose work commitments distanced them from home used maternal child rearing to define their lessening personal responsibility for children's behavior. This relinquishing of authority, however, was a mat-ter of degree. Attitudes toward discipline varied and were shaped impor-tantly by religious belief. While evangelically oriented fathers sometimes played leading and punitive roles as family disciplinarians, many more men abjured the exercise of dominance and control over young children for the cultivation of tenderer ties. This trend in fathering, which first emerged in urban middle-class households, found its foremost expression in the ex-pansion of the father's role as his children's play partner.

Father's Play

For middle-class mothers and fathers in the nineteenth century, home was a shared space with multiple, sometimes contradictory, meanings. A site of feminine work and masculine relaxation, the home was also a nursery for children's development. The ideal home was a place purged of worldly char-acter. Here mothers were expected to supervise their children intensively. This protected enclave where children grew up was also a cradle of child-hood innocence, a place where adults enjoyed the pleasure and benefit that close association with children could provide.[16] This latter formulation had particular salience for men. Fathers, who were less burdened with children's daily care, were encouraged to view home as a "utopian retreat," a source of spiritual refreshment and after-hours escape from the daily rigors of bread-winning.[17] By midcentury, the return from work was a newly important as-pect of family life. Idealized images of the event depicted men leaving be-hind the noise, strife, and selfishness of the world for the serenity of home. There, as one writer imagined the scene, a loving wife and the "sweet voices" of children greeted him.[18]

To experience the tonic effect of children, men needed to enter into the spirit of childhood. Nineteenth-century gender stereotypes suggested that fathers had less natural sympathy for small children than did mothers. They could, however, find access to the child's world through play. Historians of play and playthings point to the middle of the eighteenth century as a time when adult fears and suspicions of children's play began to relax. Earlier, play had been accepted to a limited extent as an antidote to idleness and disorder. In an intellectual atmosphere dominated by religion, however, colonial parents had feared play as potentially selfish, irresponsible, and irrational. Samuel Moody summarized this ambivalence in a sermon in 1721, when he allowed that children should "play sometimes a little, and there is no hurt in it, but they are often thinking of Christ, while they are at their play."[19]

From about the middle of the eighteenth century, parents began to see in children's play greater potential for good. As historian Bernard Mergen observes, children born after the middle of the century "found themselves in a society much more tolerant of play."[20] Material culture reflected these beliefs. Entrepreneurs invented new games and toys, which appeared on the shelves of milliners' shops and general stores. Books for children, such as John Newberry's best-selling *A Little Pretty Pocket-Book Intended for the Instruction and Amusement of Little Master Tommy and Pretty Miss Polly*, published in London in 1744 and reprinted many times in England and America over the next fifty years, described games and offered accompanying moral lessons.

Positive valuations of children's play greatly expanded in the 1830s. The writers of moralistic juvenile fiction such as Jacob Abbott, author of the popular *Rollo* and *Lucy* series for young children, depicted childhood as a period of play and pleasure that prepared girls and boys for the responsibilities of adulthood. Such preparation, however, could not be accomplished by children themselves. Rather, it required the intervention of a sympathetic adult to establish order and teach lessons of character, a moral endlessly repeated in Abbott's books.

By the standards of modern children's literature, the world of Rollo and Lucy is exceedingly mundane. Entire plots turn on cleaning a toy closet, sorting nails, or, somewhat more eventfully, building a duck pond. Parents in Abbott's stories are first and foremost authority figures who insist on prompt and unquestioning obedience as a precondition for their affection.

And yet they are not martinets. Within the uneventful and emotionally con-
strained world of Abbott's books, children could expect parents to respond
positively to demands for play, a lesson not lost on his young readers. Abbott's mothers and fathers are portrayed in remarkably similar terms. They
employ the same gentle modes of discipline, teach similar lessons of character and self-control, and are equally sympathetic to children. Abbott's fathers, who are away from home most of the day, are eager to teach their
children lessons when they return in the evening, occasionally through the
medium of play. In a rather typical vignette from one of the *Lucy* books, a
father sitting by his fireside is asked by his young children to "have a play."
He agrees, but rather than play the "noisy" game his daughter suggests, the
father insists that they play "college" and proceeds to offer his children a
lecture.[21]

Abbott's fathers (and mothers) had a limited sense of fun, but the author
was not alone in linking fathers and children through the play spirit. From
the century's earliest decades, fathers were singled out for special treatment
by the purveyors of children's books and toys, who commercialized and
circulated images of father's play. In an advertising pamphlet distributed by
a juvenile book store that opened in New York City in 1825, for example,
fathers were urged to "Come buy a little pleasing toy, / It's done up very
neat, / 'Twil please a little girl or boy; / I'll sell it very cheap." An accompanying poem titled "My Father" glorified the father's role as play partner with
his children:

> Who in my childhood's earliest day,
> Before my tongue one word could say,
> Would let me with his watch chain play?
> My Father.

> Who call'd me first his little boy,
> His source of hope and future joy,
> And bade me not those hopes destroy?
> My Father.

> When seated on my Mother's knee,
> Who us'd to play at peep with me,
> Hiding where baby could not see?
> My Father.

And oh! when I could read my book,
Who gave me such a tender look,
And such a heartfelt pleasure took?
My Father.

Who took me in the fields to walk,
And listened to my infant talk,
Making me chains of thistle's stalk?
My Father.

And when my kite I wish'd to try,
Who held the string to make it fly,
While pleasure sparkled in my eye?
My Father.

The poem concludes with the young speaker's promise to reciprocate his father's playful affection by being a prop and comfort to him in old age.[22]

Parent advisers also urged fathers to make play with children part of a new and more affectionate style of parenting. Horace Bushnell's famous book of parenting advice, *Christian Nurture* (1847), recommended that a father "show a generous sympathy with the plays of his children" and act as their occasional play partners, entering "into the frolic of their mood with them."[23] By the 1850s, family advisers, reacting in part to the austerity of their own childhoods, were urging fathers who had been born in the first decades of the century to adopt a "childlike spirit" and cultivate more affectionate relations with their children than their own fathers had sustained toward them. Too much emphasis on instruction and reproof by the earlier generation of fathers had sacrificed filial affection on the altar of reverence and respect, said moralists such as Artemas Muzzey.[24]

Beneath the salesmanship and prescription lay the reality of father's play. The testimony of diaries and letters confirms that fathers in middle- and upper-middle-class households acted as play partners with infants and young children from at least the turn of the nineteenth century.[25] The emotional importance of play's role, however, seems to have expanded after about 1820, when it was linked to the recreational and escapist possibilities of domestic life—that is, to images of home as a refuge for men from the aggressive competitiveness of the economic marketplace. Evidence for this proposition is contained in the letters that fathers wrote to their wives and children.

For a variety of reasons, personal correspondence (especially, perhaps, the letters that families have chosen to preserve for inquiring eyes in historical archives) tends to express more positive than negative emotions. Fathers away on business are not likely to write home to tell wives and children how glad they are to be away or to express relief from the vexations and responsibilities of family life. Consequently, we must interpret cautiously the sentiments about home's appeal in the letters that absent fathers wrote to their families. The attraction of home, however, can be expressed any number of ways, and the particular form it takes reveals a great deal about the aspects of family life that a correspondent values. Absent husbands, of course, seldom failed to mention their missing a wife's warmth and affection. Equally often, fathers of young children also expressed intense desire to participate in their play or otherwise enjoy their companionship. Indeed, Victorian Americans had a specific word to describe this activity: Fathers were said to *frolic* with their children, a word that seems to have assumed this particular meaning toward the middle of the eighteenth century.[26]

For long periods between 1825 and 1834, John Davis was away from his home in Worcester, Massachusetts, while he served as a representative in Congress. A lawyer as well as a politician, Davis married in 1822, at age 35. His first child, a son named John, was born within a year, and by 1826 Davis was the father of two small boys. In this period, Davis rarely wrote home without inquiring about his "frolicsome boys" or otherwise casting home's attraction in terms of his desire to participate in their play. When his wife stated in 1825 that the "gaiety and fashion" of life in Washington would make home seem poor by comparison, Davis endeavored to mollify her concern by enumerating the gratifications of home. There he could eat, drink, and sleep when he pleased. Above all, he said, home was a place "where you can sit and look into the fire and feel under no obligation to speak to any one—can lie down and roll on the carpet and frolic with the boys." Such domestic ease surpassed "your five o'clock dinners, your whiskey and your Champaine."[27]

Whatever special pleading went into this statement, Davis's decision to anchor home's charm in the image of rolling on the carpet with his young sons reflected the growing appeal of a playful style of fatherhood in elite and middle-class households. For Davis, the possibilities for informality and spontaneity in his relationship with his young sons contrasted sharply with the social straitjacket of political life. Complaining of the numerous invitations that Washington etiquette required him to accept, lest he be thought "odd," Davis told his wife in 1826, "I would change them all for a play [with] John and George."[28]

As his family expanded, Davis remained the play partner of his youngest children. By 1832, a third son, Phillip, had been born. "As for Philly," his wife told him, "you are in his little thoughts more frequently than with either of the others. He often talks of you and tells how you play with him."[29] The comment is revealing. For Davis, the heyday of paternal playfulness seems to have lasted until his children were six or seven years of age. As they grew older, concern for their education and securing their future began to crowd out images of play in his letters.

Davis's pointed contrast of the warmth and spontaneity of a home with children to the demands of breadwinning and the cold formality of the workplace is part of a recurrent theme in men's reflections on the value of domestic life from as early as the 1830s and onward. When Boston educator George Emerson decided to move his wife and young children from the city to suburban Brookline in 1836, his father, a physician from Kennebunk, Maine, told him that his new home would help "soothe & quiet" his mind after the demands of a busy day. In the country, his father said, he could "run away from the dust & bustle of the City" to enjoy "the soothing smiles of [your wife] Mary & the dear lambs of your flock."[30] This understanding of suburban family life as a pastoral antidote to the agitation of the city was a distinctly masculine invention: Men created it, and men were its chief beneficiaries.[31] Adherence to the pastoral view of settled domesticity was a class marker as well, a conceit of middle- and upper-middle-class men that emphasized the sentimental, rather than economic, value of children.

Oddly enough, this conceptualization of domestic life retained a peculiarly economic logic. For now home life and, especially, the relationship with small children became a commodity for masculine consumption. In many homes, the cult of childhood enthroned the youngest child of the house as an object of intense affection. Frequently, the baby of the house was referred to as a "pet" or "plaything" and was indulged accordingly in even the strictest families.[32] While young children were objects of affection for all the family, they seem to have been viewed in this light especially by their fathers, who had little responsibility for their physical care. When the father returned from work in the evening, young children could be trotted out almost like toys for his amusement. A Providence, Rhode Island, woman wrote to her sister in 1840: "The children are all well and three of them go to school every day. . . . John stays in the parlour with me when I am at home and Frank is brought down in the evening to have a frolic with his Father."[33]

Such involvement with child's play was consistent with definitions of middle-class manhood throughout the nineteenth century. Even as standards of masculinity changed later in the century to stress single-minded devotion to business and pursuit of the strenuous life, engagement with child's play retained its grip on the masculine imagination. Thus Theodore Roosevelt, the Progressive era's paragon of virility and upright manhood, could take unabashed pleasure in the company of children. "Children," he enthused, "are better than books."[34]

In the early and late nineteenth century, such attitudes toward children were stamped indelibly by class experience. A playful style of fatherhood developed first in the most literate households, among those parents most likely to be exposed to new ideas about the sentimental value of children. Economically advantaged families also had more time and means for elaborate paternal play than their working-class counterparts. A house with a parlor was not a prerequisite for a frolic with father, but such a home certainly facilitated the type of paternal intimacies shared during a family's leisure hours in the evening.

Within the upper and middle classes, fathers who acted as play partners with young children were quite common. Even in religiously orthodox households, where one might expect to find playful attitudes circumscribed by more rigorous understandings of family government and discipline, images surface of paternal play. Ebenezer Atwood, a well-to-do farmer and local politician from Vermont who served as superintendent of his church Sunday school, was recalled by a daughter who grew up during the 1840s in the following terms: "My father was distinctly puritanical in his character and habits but was not austere. He had stern ideals of conduct and integrity and was strict in the discipline of his family, yet genial and friendly with his children, often sharing our sports. It was not unusual for both my father and mother to join us as we cracked our jokes and our butternuts before the big open fire, or played our game of 'Blind Man's Bluff' in the old kitchen."[35]

Two previously encountered examples of the behavior of fathers further reinforce this point. One would hardly expect Francis Wayland, the abusive disciplinarian who starved his fifteen-month-old son, to enact the role of frolicsome papa. And yet Wayland was able to unbend in play with his children, indulging them at home and in public. In their reminiscences, Wayland's sons recalled that when their father met them on the college green returning from his study, he would "carry them home on his shoulders much to the amusement of those who witnessed this exhibition of parental affection." They recalled as well the surprise of visitors calling upon the college president at his residence, only to find him "stretched at full length upon the floor engaged in a frolic with his boys and abundantly enjoying their wild delight when they were allowed to believe that they had conquered their father."[36] Similarly, Lyman Beecher, as domineering a parent as one could hope to find, was recalled primarily as a play partner of his young children. "His chief daily recreations were frolics with his children," said Catharine Beecher. "I remember him more as a playmate than in any other character during my childhood. He was fond of playing pranks upon us, and trying the queerest experiments with us, for his amusement as well as ours."[37]

Beecher's children were exceptionally literate and so have left us with unusually detailed descriptions of their interactions with their father. The record unintentionally illuminates the complexity of father's play and the extent to which it embodied new tensions between affection and control. As Catharine Beecher recalled, her father's "experiments" included once swinging her out of a garret window by the hands "to see if it would frighten [her], which it did not in the least." Another time, she reminisced: "As I was running past a wash-tub, he tipped my head into it, to see what I would do."[38] Beecher's play, in fairness, was often far less abusive than this. If play represented a real desire to partake of his children's affection, however, it also reflected his abiding need to exert fatherhood's traditional dominance.

Just as play tugged against religious values that urged men toward emotional reserve and distance, so did it counter economic and work priorities. If ever there was a candidate for the stereotypical starched Victorian father, it was James Valentine Campbell. Born in Buffalo, New York, on February 25, 1823, Campbell came to Detroit with his parents in 1826. After graduating from an Episcopal college in 1841, he was admitted to the bar in 1844 and practiced law in Detroit until being elected to the Michigan Supreme Court in 1857. He remained on the bench, serving as Chief Justice until the time of his death, in 1890. Campbell had an extremely active professional life: He taught law at the University of Michigan during most of his judicial career and served for a time on the Detroit School Board. He was frequently away from home, and there can be little doubt that work was the primary focus of his life. Yet his letters to his children belie stereotypical images of nineteenth-century fathers' remoteness from their families.

These letters trace a revealing emotional trajectory. When his children were young, Campbell mixed regular doses of advice about obedience and schooling with lighthearted banter, demonstrating a great sympathy for childhood. Childhood, in Campbell's mind, was largely a separate but parentally supervised world of play, not unlike the small and uneventful world depicted by Jacob Abbott. A letter from 1857 to his son Harry, age three, captures Campbell's characteristic tone:

> My darling little Harry . . . Nelly [age five] is lying down on papa's bed fast asleep on two big pillows. She sends her love to Harry and wants you to give Jimmy and mama each a good kiss for her. She is a very good little girl and wants very much to see her little brothers. You must play just as much as mama will let you while you are at aunt Sophie's and be a good little boy. You know papa thinks a great deal of his dear little Harry. Have you had any rides yet with the pony? You must recollect all about it so that when you come home you will have ever so many nice stories to tell Nelly.[39]

We smile; by modern standards, Campbell entertained a rather saccharine view of childhood. Yet he corresponded regularly with his children, was intensely interested in their activities, and derived great personal satisfaction from providing his small children with toys and opportunities for play. When he was away from home, which was often, his letters became full of the imagery of his children at play. "I have been thinking a good deal today of you and the children," he wrote his wife in 1856, as a thirty-three-year-old father separated from home and his three young children. "I wish you were here or I at home. At times I feel strongly tempted to turn round and go home instead of spending the time up here. . . . I should like to see Nelly and Harry tumbling about on the grass or picking up pebbles on the beach. I suppose baby would hardly engage in such occupations yet."[40]

Campbell imagined watching his children at play, but he was much more than an interested bystander, a voyeur of childhood contented to observe from a distance. He spent a great deal of time with his young children, accompanying them to the park, taking them on errands, and enjoying their company around the house. In the process, he acquired practical parenting skills. Campbell was perfectly capable, for instance, of managing a fretful toddler. In the summer of 1866, when his wife was away from home on a visit, he noted that their two-year-old son, Eddy, had taken a long nap with him one afternoon. When Eddy woke up, he missed his mother and was about to look for her, until his father intervened to allay the little boy's fears of abandonment. "I got him engaged before he had time to fret and he remained quiet," Campbell informed his wife.[41]

Campbell corresponded with his children all his life, but the letters he wrote to them later—full of newsy accounts of neighborhood events, family matters, social life, and political developments—are noteworthy for their emotional restraint. The affection he so easily, if somewhat sentimentally, expressed for his "darling little" children was a lost chord in the letters he wrote after they had grown up. As was the case with John Davis, Campbell's interest in and capacity for play concentrated rather narrowly on young children.

There are several reasons for this circumscribed focus, not least the romantic fascination with youthful innocence. As children grew up, moreover, their lives changed in ways that subverted the spirit of fatherly play. In rural homes, by age seven or so boys had begun to help their fathers with farm chores. This, in turn, emphasized the father's role as adult companion and model of those sober traits needed for work. Girls correspondingly were integrated more fully into the social world of their mothers as they grew older. In the cities, later generations of boys drifted into an independent world of outdoor activities as they grew older, a peer-oriented subculture that was relatively free of adult supervision. Similarly, a semi-autonomous girls' culture distanced daughters from fatherly play.[42]

Frequently, men in old age recaptured the sense of paternal playfulness. Cultural understandings that young children should act as sources of comfort to the elderly resurrected the playmate role, and images of grandfathers responding to young children's demands for play and initiating play themselves are not hard to find. To take but one example, James Draper, a farmer and teacher from Spencer, Massachusetts, was especially fond of his smallest grandchildren. On a visit home in 1841, his daughter described the following scene to her husband in Syracuse: "Bubby is on the floor *surrounded* with *play rings*, as father calls them. He plays with him just as I told you he would. *Bumps his head* against the door. Strikes it with a paper and sings *particular* tunes to him that he always sings to babies."[43]

Playful Togetherness

Source after source attests to the benefits that fathers anticipated receiving from close association with young children. As a thirty-year-old man in Illinois, separated on business from his wife and two-year-old son in Massachusetts, remarked in 1841: "How I wish I could see him if it were but for a minute. . . . It would do me good to hear his ringing laugh & have a good frolic with him."[44] Or as a printer from Portland, Maine, phrased it more floridly, in a letter addressed in 1858 to his youngest daughter: "I love to see those tender hands extended, those toddling limbs, that tiny body, those orient eyes, those talking lips, for they tell me of thy Maker and of mine. So fearfully and so wonderfully made are all thy parts; thou tellest me of *wisdom*, of goodness, and of love, and so I ponder on."[45] Similar statements exalting how men stood to gain by intimate association with children can be adduced with relative ease, but how children were thought to benefit from their father's attention is somewhat harder to discern in family documents.[46]

While play could be instructional as well as entertaining, there is scant evidence that parents had education uppermost in mind when they spoke of fathers frolicking with their children. Quite the contrary, rather than making father's play acceptable by giving it a didactic gloss, parents seem to have valued it primarily for the pleasure that such companionship gave both father and child. The new purpose of father's play in the nineteenth century was to contribute to family cohesion.

Fathers earlier had been capable of sustaining warm and affectionate relations with small children and expressing their fondness in the form of play. Such behavior probably dates to the relaxation of attitudes about play in the middle of the eighteenth century, if not before. But not until the nineteenth century was play seen as a way to bring families together. The tremendous increase later in the century in the number of toys, games, and other family pastimes—from building blocks and board games to stereoscopes and magic lanterns—sustained this new home entertainment.[47]

Even before manufacturers realized the potential profits to be made from marketing family togetherness, however, fathers among the professional middle class, especially men who worked partially at home, pioneered a form of play that highlighted adult-child companionship. Just as Lyman

Beecher was recalled by his daughter Catharine principally as a playmate, so was Nathaniel Hawthorne a close companion of his children. A recent study of Hawthorne's notebooks concludes that he was an engaged and affectionate father little interested in exercising dominance and control. Although he devoted his mornings and sometimes his afternoons to his writing, Hawthorne's notebooks and letters record almost daily walks with his daughter, Una, and son, Julian. He especially enjoyed watching them play and playing with them. As Julian recalled, he and Una could not "remember when their father was not their playmate, or when they ever desired or imagined any other playmate than he."[48]

Fathers like Beecher and Hawthorne conditioned young children to expect enjoyment from adult companionship and to act and think playfully themselves. Such lessons were problematic. If they bolstered family togetherness, they also awakened fears about indulging children and aroused the corresponding longing for strict patriarchal control. Take, for instance, the comments of Sarah M. Foster, the seventeen-year-old daughter of an academy principal in Erie, Pennsylvania, who went to visit an uncle in New Hampshire in 1850. In a letter to her parents, Foster described her uncle's relationship with his children in the following terms: "I never saw any children receive more attention than uncle devotes to his. He thinks their every wish must be attended to before everything else, but I do not think they are any happier for being indulged so much."[49]

As the century progressed, such apprehensions relaxed and a doting father came to be seen as someone whose society could contribute significantly to a young child's happiness. The indulgence that Sarah M. Foster viewed with suspicion, Edna Ormsby positively celebrated. Ormsby was married to a school principal in suburban Chicago. She gave birth to her first child, a daughter named Esther, in 1891, followed by a son, Stewart, three years later. A journal Ormsby kept to chronicle her daughter's growth and development offers a clear portrait of her husband, Fulton, as an indulgent and tender father. More to the point, Edna Ormsby *expected* her husband to dote on his young children.

Fulton Ormsby led his family in daily home prayer and Bible reading. Beyond that, he had little practical responsibility for the care of his young children. When it came time to put the children to bed at night, to organize their birthday parties, to decide about their schooling, or to take them to the dentist, Edna Ormsby took the lead. Although she wanted little assistance in handling the day-to-day demands of raising Esther and Stewart, Mrs. Ormsby expected one significant involvement from her husband: to be his children's emotional and social companion. This was his paramount role, and to Mrs. Ormsby's mind, it was all but impossible that by fulfilling it her husband would spoil his children.

In her diary, Mrs. Ormsby makes a point of noticing the various ways in which her husband indulged their daughter. When Esther was two, Mrs. Ormsby noted with approval, her father permitted her to finish meals on his lap, where he fed her bits of dessert. When Mr. Ormsby learned from his wife that Esther seemed lonesome, Mrs. Ormsby was pleased to report that he went out the very next day to buy his daughter a kitten. All of this paternal attention accorded with Mrs. Ormsby's belief that "Home is the most blessed thing in the world and I want my children to have only precious memories of theirs."[50]

Fatherly devotion was an essential element of this sentimental plan. In July 1893, when Esther was nineteen months old, Mrs. Ormsby proudly recorded: "[Esther] and her papa are the *best* of friends and if ever a child was blest in a father Esther is in hers. It does not seem that she can ever be anything but grateful to him for all his devotion. He is never to [*sic*] tired to take numberless steps for her nor too occupied to stop to amuse her. He is always so gentle with her and so pleased when she is happy and well."[51]

Fulton Ormsby's affectionate regard for his daughter was hardly something new in the history of fatherhood, but the positive value ascribed to his tenderness was a nineteenth-century innovation. Behavior that had once raised fears about indulging children and undermining family discipline came to be valued as a way to promote family togetherness and thereby assure children's happiness.

Play and Children's Attitude toward Their Fathers

Father's play quite clearly fulfilled a masculine craving for familial warmth and affection, but what meaning did it hold for children themselves? In particular, how did it affect children's attitudes toward their fathers? Autobiographical evidence suggests that play softened children's perceptions of their fathers, moderating the extent to which attitudes toward mothers and fathers diverged, but it did not often close the emotional gap.

The amalgam of love, companionship, training, and governance that parenting involves is bound to arouse mixed emotions in children. How these parental attributes and responsibilities are culturally assigned goes a long way toward determining how children respond to their mothers and fathers. In the nineteenth century, children considered their mothers to be more confiding and affectionate parents than their fathers, who were often perceived as correspondingly stern and withdrawn. Descriptions of fathers more honored than loved abound in the source material. In the pages of personal narratives, we encounter fathers who were recalled as "disciplinarians," or as parents who "possessed few attractions for a child." Again, we find a father who was remembered as "a bitter opposer to innocent amusements," or as someone who believed that "work and implicit obedience were the things most needful in a son," or simply as someone "in his deepest emotions unexpressive." Collectively, such memories clearly demonstrate that a child's deepest affections were reserved for mothers, who were described characteristically as the more confidential parent, someone to whom children could unburden their hopes and fears, a parent who was "of a gentler turn," more "benevolent and kind."[52]

While this maternal preference was quite real, it was also, partly at least, an artifact of memory. Because paternal play focused so exclusively on young children, autobiographical accounts that could shed light on the child's point of view are rare. Indeed, for the very smallest children, they are lost to history. Psychologists have found that long-term memory does not develop until about age four, and then only imperfectly, so it is not surprising that few personal reminiscences include detailed accounts of experiencing paternal play as very young children. However, autobiographies do confirm the importance of nighttime fireside rituals that engaged fathers in older children's lives as well as the importance of a father's companionship on Sundays.

Autobiographical evidence reveals that paternal playfulness was less developed in agrarian households than in urban middle-class homes. Farm children often associated home with the work they did there. As a child who grew up on a farm in western Michigan in the 1860s and 1870s recalled: "School life afforded larger opportunities than the home for the play spirit to express itself. That one fact made my early school days tolerable and even happy."[53] On one level, the association of home and work simply reflected the realities of farm life. So long as the family remained a corporate work unit, the father acted primarily as its economic leader. More pointedly, paternal behavior may have differed in rural households because one of the chief ideological supports of father's play—the idea of home as urban retreat—was absent.

Where father's play was lacking, attitudes toward mothers and fathers contrasted sharply. Horatio Earle, born in 1855 and raised on a farm in Mt. Holly, Vermont, recalled his mother through the warm glow of memory as "the bravest and best woman [he had] ever known," someone who "watched over and cared for" them all, and a parent "ambitious for her children's welfare." Memory's embers were banked, however, when Earle spoke of his father, a man he described as a "stern, Vermont farmer." He recalled: "I never touched his hand after I became old enough to remember. He didn't know how to play, or to join others in playing, and actually could not play with us children." In attempting to explain his father's lack of sympathy, Earle located it primarily in his obsession with work: "Riding the grindstone seems to be a delight for farmer fathers, when one of their boys is turning the stone. How my arms used to ache! I dared not say a word. . . . And when a rainy day would come and I would think there was nothing we could do on the farm, and that fish would bite mighty good—I would ask father, 'Can I go fishing?' He would reply, 'No, I guess we will clean out the hog pen.' Then my heart would almost break."[54]

Not all rural fathers were so bereft of the play spirit, but images of paternal companionship and play emerge most vividly in the diaries and letters of urban, middle-class children, especially those born after midcentury. Two excerpts stand for many others. Walter Curtis, born in 1874, grew up in Detroit, where his father was an affluent white-collar worker. In a diary he kept at age thirteen, he noted: "Ma was gone all day, and when I got home at noon Pa hid behind the pantry door just for fun, and I looked all over for him." Similarly, Henry Blackwell devised games to play with his daughter, Alice, who was born in 1857. In one such game, which the family called "drunk," Blackwell chased his daughter and her friends around a table "tumbling back upon us in a tipsy manner, [with] . . . gesticulations on his part, and howls on ours." One time the game got so out of hand that Blackwell crashed through a set of glass doors. On another occasion, when the family was staging a mock trial with Blackwell as the judge, he donned a green lampshade "which was put on to give him a Judicial aspect." In many respects, Blackwell emerges in his daughter's journals as a more affectionate figure than her mother, who kept her on a tighter rein and was more likely than her father to govern her behavior.[55]

The parenting styles of Henry Blackwell and the father of Horatio Earle stood near the outer limits of paternal playfulness in the nineteenth century. Neither man was a "representative" father. Viewed side by side, however, they represent a tendency in fatherhood history closely associated with the creation of urban middle-class family culture—namely, the demand for, and men's increased capacity to sustain, playful interactions with their children.

Play and the Modernization of Family Life

It is possible to exaggerate the importance of father's play in setting a tone and direction for paternal relations with young children in the nineteenth century. To some extent, play's salience depends on which view of the nineteenth-century child one chooses to highlight—the romanticized innocent whose companionship afforded men an antidote to the competitive demands of the workplace, or the callow youth in need of training and guidance. Of course, neither image solely determined paternal behavior. Fathers veered between companionship and affection, on the one hand, and dominance and control, on the other, as circumstances warranted. The two faces of Francis Wayland's fatherhood, as, alternately, disciplinarian and playmate, testify nicely to that fact. Nonetheless, in the period 1820–50, when images of childish innocence were joined to the escapist possibilities of family life for men, father's play took on heightened meaning. Fathers, especially men in the urban middle class, came to seek spiritual refreshment by spending time close to their small children.

The timing is significant. A growing consensus dates the amplification of motherhood and the emergence of the so-called moral mother during the period 1785–1830. From this perspective, the growing importance of the father's playmate role responded to the rise of maternal dominance within middle-class homes. Indeed, father's play is most accurately seen as the vehicle through which men relinquished their interest in exerting patriarchal authority over young children, as they became increasingly content to reinforce maternal authority over child rearing.

Nineteenth-century father's play underscored the extent to which feminine control was paramount in the lives of young children. New and expansive concepts of the mother's importance permitted fathers in the professional and commercial classes to resolve mounting tension between the competing demands of family life and work commitments that separated them from home. Men such as Abijah Bigelow and Albert Browne used maternalism to redefine their relationship to young children, and play was integral to that redefinition. The growing importance of play contributed to a reduced definition of personal responsibility for the socialization and training of young sons and daughters.

As this process of redefinition unfolded, fatherly play became part of the manufacture of a new kind of middle-class male identity, one less tied to exerting domestic authority than it had been when family leadership was seen as a religious and moral obligation. The frolicsome father became acceptable perhaps because patriarchal power had become less personal and more institutional, more tied to secular public spaces and economic matters outside the home. Thus, the playful dad was part of the modernization of masculinity: A father's personal power became benign, perhaps latent, as his institutional power grew more obvious but more distant from the home.

For most of the century, images of *frolic*, with the word's connotation of an enjoyable but somewhat inconsequential pastime, determined the meaning of father's play. Fathers, especially men in the urban middle class, sought spiritual refreshment by spending time close to their small children. On the positive side, play provided men with access to tender feeling and the softer side of their masculinity. Less benignly, the frolicsome father helped to buttress patriarchal assumptions about domestic work—the work of wives and mothers. If the home were a refuge, a place of play, then it could not be a place where serious work was done. From this perspective, father's play helped foster what historian Jeanne Boydston has called the "pastoralization of housework," the transformation of domestic work into nonwork.[56]

As the century progressed, paternal playfulness became increasingly intertwined with demands for family togetherness. Fatherly play came to be

seen more explicitly as an expression of companionship that could help assure a small child's happiness. This reorientation of meaning accorded with
and perhaps helped pave the way for the rising valuation of playfulness itself. Belief in the achievement of happiness through play seems to have been
a concept specifically related to changing attitudes toward work and leisure
as a consumer society took shape during the years 1890–1930.[57] It seems
doubtful, however, that paternal playfulness with children was significantly
more common in 1890 than it had been in 1850. While there is no way to
judge the frequency of behavior on the basis of literary evidence, the prevalence of play imagery in personal documents strongly suggests that middle-
class fathers had acted as young children's play partners for quite some time
before the turn of the century. Within the home, play's contribution to happiness was recognized early on and often seen in relation to fathers and children. Parents certainly valued play before the rise of commercial entertainment fragmented the way family members spent their leisure time in
subsequent decades.[58]

In some respects, the prominence accorded to father's play in nineteenth-
century family documents is not at all surprising. Numerous social scientific
studies over the past decade have shown that fathers and mothers alike play
actively with infants and small children. Fathers, in fact, devote a higher proportion of their time with children to play than do mothers. They differ,
however, in their style of play, tending to be more physical and less didactic.[59]
The evidence of this chapter accords with such findings about modern parenting activities, but suggests a need to rethink assumptions that the father's
role as his children's play partner is a recent innovation. In historic perspective, the rise of paternal play attests to the great satisfaction that nineteenth-
century culture encouraged men to take in fatherhood.

The access to tender emotion that play afforded men was entirely compatible with notions of middle-class masculinity in the last century. Ironically, play's prominent place in the relationship between fathers and young
children in Victorian America owed less to ideas about children's needs than
to gendered understandings of home as a place of feminine work and masculine leisure. In those origins lay the limits of play's power to shape children's attitudes toward their fathers. As an expression of companionship,
play softened the edges of fathers' role as breadwinner by engaging men with

their children as work permitted. The rise of father's play demonstrated men's willingness and ability to behave sensitively toward young children, in accord with the precepts of gentle child nurture. But play also confirmed fathers' secondary role as caregivers. If paternal play encouraged children to seek companionship from their fathers, it also directed them toward their mothers for instruction, as well as emotional and physical care.[60]

Chapter 6

Patrimony's Yardstick

What Fathers Provided as Children Grew Older

If it were not for the education of the boys I should not strive much more for money.

John Davis to his wife, 1830

You know that women must learn all the domestic and household duties in order to make themselves useful in life.

Joseph Curtis to his daughter, 1864

Romantic belief in the redeeming innocence of children left middle-class men wide latitude to embrace the tenets of modern parenting when their sons and daughters were young. Even the reliance on maternal authority, so central to the ordering of nineteenth-century family life, permitted, indeed encouraged, men to forge intimate bonds with their youngest children. How were these affectionate ties transformed as those children grew older? What meanings for manhood did raising sons and daughters to maturity have?

The domestic ideal urged mothers and fathers alike to view parenthood as the noblest and purest part of their nature. At one level, accepting fatherhood as his highest responsibility in life reconciled a man to a subsidiary role of backing up and sustaining the influence and authority of his wife. Fathers, however, continued to view themselves as guarantors-in-chief of their children's future prospects. To transmit a full measure of social and economic respectability was the ultimate requirement of a father's care, as well as most men's earnest desire. Measuring up to patrimony's yardstick meant not only providing children with an economic base but also seeing to it that they grew up with the character traits needed to get ahead in life.

These dual tasks took on increased urgency as a number of nineteenth-century economic trends complicated the process of occupational transmission. Long-term developments — including the erosion of the apprenticeship system, decreasing availability of agricultural land, and, in the latter part of the century, the decline of small family businesses — made it more difficult for fathers to transmit job skills and occupational opportunities to their children directly.[1] Ironically, then, by creating new opportunities for success, the nineteenth century's market revolution increased the pressure on fathers to secure a child's life chances while stripping them of the traditional means to do so. As a consequence, a new burden of anxiety settled on fatherhood, bearing down hardest on the relationship between fathers and sons.

Men were equally concerned with the future prospects of growing daughters. They sought especially to ensure a daughter's marriageability, both by policing her sexual conduct and by reinforcing the lessons in feminine behavior conveyed by her mother. Among the urban middle class, growing numbers of fathers saw to it that daughters acquired traits — for instance, musical skills and an acquaintance with literature — that signaled bourgeois refinement. A culture of aspiration, then, shaped fathers' ties with both sons and daughters as they grew older. The inner dynamics of the two relationships were quite different, however. A father's duty to model the sober behavior that would help his sons define themselves as workers and as men opened a gulf of emotional distance between them. The father-daughter relationship, by contrast, permitted greater displays of paternal warmth and tenderness.

Fathers and Sons

If nineteenth-century parents wanted anything, they wanted their children to be obedient and to grow up to lead socially useful lives. These twin goals, established when children were young, did not change much as they grew older. A man from Massachusetts, writing to his grandson in Alton, Illinois, in 1844, nicely summed up what was expected of boys: "Your Father has often written to me how good and useful and manly you [are], and I have been delighted to hear it," he told the child. "You must learn to read

and write well, and know all that is necessary to make a useful and wise man.
. . . You must always do what your dear Father & Mother tell you, and endeavor to assist them all in your power." Boys were to be equipped for a life
of productive labor; girls were to be afforded the training and education appropriate to the role of wife and mother.[2]

For a son to become a socially useful man, his father had to transmit the
practical skills and provide the economic start he would need to make his
way in life. So long as fathers expected sons to follow in their footsteps, either on a farm or in a craft or trade, training a boy for adulthood was a natural extension of a man's everyday activities. His work was a model of manly
behavior. On farms especially, boys measured their growth and development
by the advances they made up a ladder of increasingly complex, strenuous,
and responsible labor. At the top of the ladder stood the boy's father and
other adult males. Typically, a boy's introduction to farm labor began with
simpler jobs, such as hunting eggs, filling the woodbox, and weeding in the
fields and garden. As the boy grew in strength, he tackled heavier work, such
as haying and harvesting. After shuttling back and forth for a time between
his mother's house and garden and his father's fields, a boy finally took his
place in the realm of masculine labor.[3]

Abraham Leenhouts's recollection of growing up in a Dutch immigrant
farming community in western Michigan in the 1870s illustrates how powerfully this progression might allow the teenage son to identify with his father and associate the father, in turn, with his work. Leenhouts, who was
introduced to farm work by weeding the corn, was permitted by his father
to hay with a horse rake for the first time at age twelve. The experience made
him feel that he "really was somebody," and in his expanding capacities that
"somebody" was a clear reflection of his father: "I always anxiously looked
forward to the time when I should be grown up, like Father," Leenhouts
remembered. "I was proud of my father, who, I thought, was the biggest
and strongest man in the world. He could fell the tallest tree in the woods;
he could handle a yoke of oxen or drive a team of horses as he pleased; he could
haul the heavy logs in big piles; he could plow the fields; and most wonder-
ful of all, he could lift me on his shoulders as easily as I could lift a kitten."[4]

Not all accounts are so worshipful, of course, but rarely does the diary
of a teenaged boy raised on a nineteenth-century farm fail to reflect intimate

knowledge of a father's work. Consider, for instance, the diary kept in 1860 by a fifteen-year-old boy named Clement Smith, who grew up on a farm in south-central Michigan. Even when he attended school in the winter and did little farm work himself, Smith was preoccupied with his father's labor:

> Tuesday, Dec. 4—Chopped wood in the forenoon, went to school to Miss Brewer in the afternoon. Pa got the horses shod.

> Monday, Dec. 10—Pa went after a load of corn. Pa took me to school. Snowed about 10 inches last night.

> Monday, Dec. 17—Went to school as usual. Pa drawed logs in the afternoon. Mr. Hosmer helped him.

> Tuesday, Dec. 18—Pa went to Vt'ville. Rainy and cold.[5]

In a year of entries, Smith's mother is mentioned only a half-dozen times, and then only when she had accompanied her husband on an errand or visit. The diaries of contemporary city youth, in striking contrast, contain many more references to a boy's mother and much less knowledge of what fathers did when they went to work.[6]

Despite, or perhaps because of, their practical importance, father-son relations in rural homes did not often include a great deal of emotional exchange, or even warmth. Until a son came of age, married, and established an independent household, he labored primarily for his father rather than for himself. If anything, this obligation tended to attenuate ties of affection, especially when the burden of work came to be seen by the son as an obstacle to self-realization and personal advancement. Even when the yoke of farm work was worn lightly, the evidence of diaries, letters, and reminiscences demonstrates that sons turned more often to mothers than fathers when there were confidences to share. Abraham Leenhouts, for instance, venerated his father, but he felt more affection for his mother, who was "quicker to praise" her eleven children and more demonstrative in her concern for them.

When measured against a yardstick of maternal love and tenderness, even the most honored fathers fall short in reminiscences of nineteenth-century childhoods.[7] Stereotypes of affectionate mothers and controlling fathers that color these accounts are an enduring feature of American family life, antedating the nineteenth century and persisting into the twentieth. No doubt parents were then, and are today, perceived as emotional opposites because they often behave that way. The reasons for this disparity are manifold, but at least one source of difference in the nineteenth century can be traced to traditional understandings of the father's legal and economic status.

From colonial times, the legal system that obligated a father to train and educate the children in his custody also conferred on him complete rights to their labor.[8] Although the father's property rights in his children diminished over the course of the nineteenth century, the labor relationship continued to shape family ties, especially between fathers and sons in the rural North. In thinking about their rights and obligations, fathers habitually invoked the contract prerogatives of masters. Sons correspondingly viewed service for their fathers as a form of indenture, and the relationship itself came to resemble a quasi-contractual bond. Over the course of the nineteenth century, this imagined contract's terms were rewritten to accommodate more egalitarian family ideals, but the metaphor itself proved to be surprisingly resilient.[9]

The Father-Son Contract

Early in the century, the contractual metaphor that guided father-son relations was taken quite literally. Boys growing up in the rural North spoke repeatedly of "owing their time" to their fathers until age twenty-one, a formulation that derived from the traditional terms and timing of indenture.[10] In early New England, children were frequently bound out, especially to relatives, between the ages of roughly seven and fourteen. The assumption was that, up to age fourteen, a boy could compensate for his board and clothing with his labor; thereafter he was considered old enough to perform a full day's work and earn something besides his keep. Accordingly, formal apprenticeships generally began at fourteen and lasted seven years, until a youth reached the age of majority at twenty-one.[11]

This division of the youthful life course roughly by a rule of seven powerfully influenced father-son relations. Boys who might have begun to perform useful work about the house around age seven moved decisively into the sphere of masculine labor at about age fourteen and remained obligated to their fathers until age twenty-one and beyond. Reminiscences of nineteenth-century childhoods frequently document a boy's life having reached a turning point at age fourteen that subjected him more directly to his father's will. Generally, this meant that a boy's schooling was cut back and he was expected to devote full time to farm labor, or he might be apprenticed to a trade. Other transitions were also possible: Charles R. Harding, who was born in 1807 and grew up in Putney, Vermont, recalled, "My life passed quietly, but swiftly away until I was fourteen." In that year his father settled his property, deeding his farm to Charles's brother and providing each of his other children with sixty dollars upon his death. "I was to have my time, take care of myself, and my brother was to take care of the old people," Harding recalled bitterly. "For a boy to be turned loose upon the world without a home, without a dollar, without a parent's care or a friend to protect and guide [him] is in my estimation no great legacy."[12]

Like Harding, many boys felt the weight of their father's authority descend upon them at age fourteen, but few were emancipated so prematurely. Rather, boys were routinely expected to work for their father until reaching their majority. Recalling his youth on a New Hampshire farm in the first decade of the century, John Ball, the tenth and youngest child in his family, noted, "As for the boys, my father claimed their time till they were twenty-one, and they continued to work at home, until of that age." Nathaniel Stacy, a near contemporary of Ball who grew up in a family of seven children on a farm in western Massachusetts, similarly remembered prevailing upon his father to "give me my time" when, at age seventeen, he decided to pursue an education rather than follow the plow like his father.[13]

Notwithstanding the ethos of joint labor that historians associate with the family economy, these reminiscences highlight the power fathers exercised as head of the family enterprise. Farm children participated in that enterprise as members of a team, but it was a team hierarchically ordered and headed by their father. Indeed, so long as the family existed as an economic unit, a boy's youth often amounted to a period of quasi servitude. Consider the experience of Morgan Curtis, who was born in Cortland, New York, in 1810. In order to free himself of his work obligation before turning twenty-one, Curtis had to compensate his father in cash for his time. Curtis was the third child in a family of ten children. His eldest brother had gone off to learn a trade, and the second had died early, so the burden of working for his father descended upon him. Like most rural children, Curtis attended school only in the winter months and worked on his father's farm the rest of the year. At the age of twenty, he decided to start in life for himself, but in order to do so he first had to negotiate an agreement with his father. Curtis agreed to pay his father forty dollars in exchange for his time. Hiring himself out to an uncle for one year at ten dollars per month, Curtis used a portion of his wages to compensate his father for the loss of his services.[14]

Curtis's cash accounting highlights how crucial economics were to the tenor of father-son relations in agrarian households. By the early nineteenth century, however, a father's power to insist on a son's subservience and service was compromised in a substantial number of homes. The following story of a youth's transition from home to work in the 1830s illustrates the point. William Grow was born in 1816 and grew to manhood in Homer, New York, near Cortland. His father, a farmer named Elisha Grow, wanted his son to remain with him on the farm rather than learn a trade. When the boy showed an aptitude and desire to become a carpenter, however, his mother arranged an apprenticeship for him at age fifteen. Grow completed his training four years later, when he purchased his outfit of tools and began to work in and around his hometown for a dollar a day. "Here," he recalled later, as an eighty-five-year-old, "my life may have said to have begun in earnest."[15]

As he neared manhood, Grow became estranged from his father, a breach that was opened, in part, by rising expectations that fathers would support their children's aspirations and by changing power relations in the family. Grow became embittered when his father refused to help him become a carpenter. Elisha Grow, his son later recalled, was someone who "failed to give [his sons] the encouragement which boys should have had in the way of tools and material."[16] Grow's ambition, and the expectations of many sons like him, collided directly with terms of the traditional contract that subordinated filial autonomy to a father's conception of the family's economic need. In this respect, the changing dynamics of father-son relations—especially the expansion of a son's desire to succeed on his own terms—figured prominently in the democratization of family relations. Put another way, economic opportunity tended to loosen paternal control, freeing sons to choose an occupation even in the face of paternal resistance. How much unilateral economic power could a father exercise, after all, when a boy's mother could arrange an apprenticeship for her son? By the time he turned nineteen, Grow could support himself, although he continued to live at home. Other youth, who departed home to work at a trade, lived even further beyond a father's reach than did William Grow.

We may never know how often a son's desire to strike out on his own brought him into direct conflict with his father, but in many households securing paternal approval for a son's choice was a victory to be won. Because sons looked to their fathers to launch them in life, they were apt to view their youth as a long period of subjugation when fathers seemed to be hindrances to success. Autobiographical and other evidence points quite conclusively to the years around age twenty-one as a time of heightened tension in father-son relations. As a son reached his majority, a father's authority began to wane. In terms of the contract metaphor that bound them, the son's accumulated labor had elevated his bargaining position in the relationship. He had fulfilled his half of the bargain, and now it remained for the father to make good on his. This tipping of the scales toward filial autonomy occurred at a time when issues of farm succession and career choice demanded definitive resolution. A son's dissatisfaction with the extent and nature of his patrimony manifested itself in his early twenties as complaints about the quality of his father's care.[17]

In nineteenth-century family documents, which for a variety of reasons frequently contain more positive than negative emotions, the bitterest references to fathers often involve real or perceived failures to provide adequately for a son or daughter when the child came of age.[18] Once they had grown, the children of a farmer named H. S. Fish from Williamson, New York, seldom had a kind word for their father. In their correspondence from the 1860s, Fish emerges as a selfish and difficult man whose children complained repeatedly that he was able but unwilling to do much to advance them in life. When assistance required loosening the family purse strings, his daughter Julia said in an 1862 letter that Fish could never be relied upon to provide it. Julia's brother Dan shared her ill will toward their father:

> Julia, you was speaking something about the old man. . . . I would see them all in h--l before I would give an intch [*sic*] to such a selfish person as him. I should walk on my hands & knees a mile every day before I would ask him for a bite to eat. Now do not let my words turn you against eny [*sic*] one for I am only speaking of what I should do. You may think I am speaking rather rough against the old man but I do not think he has the faculty or will to get along with enyone [*sic*] long at a time, let alone his own family.[19]

Most fathers did what they could to secure their children's economic future without compromising family needs in the present. Strategies for deal-
ing with questions of patrimony, however, changed over time. Nancy Grey
Osterud's careful study of a nineteenth-century dairy farming community
in New York State found that the goal of most families initially was to establish their children on farms in the local community. By the last quarter of
the century, under the pressure of decreasing land availability, most parents
had shifted their objective from helping all their sons establish farms nearby
to ensuring that one of their sons remained on the home farm to care for
them in old age. Adhering to the notion that children should be treated eq-
uitably, noninheriting sons were furnished with an education or with capital to start out on their own.[20]

In the Midwest, ethnic differences helped to shape family strategies. A
classic study of the Midwestern frontier found that German-American fathers and other immigrants with European peasant-farm backgrounds were
eager to see their grown sons established with their families on farms clustered about their own. While immigrant fathers struggled to realize this goal
by purchasing adjacent farms, native-born fathers made no such efforts on
behalf of their sons: "To be a self-made man was his ideal. He had come in
as a 'first settler' and had created a farm with his axe, let the boys do the same.
One of them perhaps was kept at home as a helper to his aging parents; the
rest set out willingly to achieve beyond the mountains or beyond the river
what the father had accomplished in the West of his day."[21]

Prudence determined who remained behind. If only because they came of
age and were living at home when their fathers were growing too old to do
the work needed to maintain the farm themselves, younger sons frequently
were chosen to inherit the family land. Such a son entered into a partnership
with his father, becoming co-owner of the land with full rights of inheritance, in exchange for assuming a variety of family responsibilities. Foremost,
he continued to farm the land in concert with his father and agreed to support
his parents for the remainder of their lifetimes. Here, for instance, is how
a proposal to care for his aging parents was outlined to a son in 1830 by a
correspondent in western New York: "The conditions which he [your fa-
ther] proposes are these. Provided you engage to live with him and see to
the maintenance of him & wife during life, he will on your removal give you
a deed of one half of the farm and you shall have the improvements whole

together with the stocks, farming utensils &c &c while he and your mother are able to labour, you shall return them one half of the produce of the whole." Besides supporting his parents, as this proposed agreement stipulated, it was not unusual for an inheriting son to maintain any unmarried sisters who continued to live at home. If his father died and these sisters married, he provided their dowries.[22]

Because issues of farm succession involved the deeding of property rights, fathers commonly saw to it that the necessary arrangements were made, but decisions were subject to family negotiation. Younger sons who wanted to seek their fortune elsewhere, for instance, could arrange for an older brother to remain on the farm in exchange for relinquishing claims to further support from home. That is what John Ball did before he was able to embark at age seventeen on a path that led from his father's New Hampshire farm to Dartmouth College and a subsequent career as a lawyer.[23]

As a family strategy, the arrangement between fathers and sons was an attempt to provide old-age insurance for one generation and economic security for the next. Scattered evidence suggests that fathers invested relatively more affection in the children they chose to stay behind. Often, youngest sons were described as the "flower of the family." From an early age, they were designated as their father's "hope for the future" or "prop in old age." Writing in 1804, a thirty-nine-year-old Lancaster, Massachusetts, man said of his youngest son: "Francis, a darling boy, will I hope discover always the generosity, fortitude and manliness of mind with the mixture of affection and tenderness he possesses and be a prop to our age and blessing to all around us." Describing the death of a younger brother, in 1829, a man raised on a Vermont farm noted: "The shock to my father was terrible. He had never lost a child before and Joseph was his darling, and in the event of my going away, his hope and reliance in the future." Similarly, a father from Raynham, Massachusetts, wrote of his youngest son, a youth of nineteen who had moved to Philadelphia in 1863: "We hear from Henry every week. He receives for pay now 2.50 cts. per day. I look upon him as the flower of the family and may he be spared to comfort & support us in our declining years for I feel sensibly that I am past the meridian of life."[24]

While conveyance of land was a common way for rural fathers to establish chosen sons and provide for their own retirement, apprenticeships to a craft or clerkships in a store remained, until about the time of the Civil War, favored means to set other sons up in the world.[25] Financial support during his term of service generally constituted the bulk of the son's patrimony, since the apprenticeship itself was considered his ticket to middle-class respectability.

Apprenticeship was a path to the future that made little distinction between blue- and white-collar occupations. Outside the largest cities, a father in one of the professions who secured an apprenticeship for his son in, say, a carpenter's workshop, rather than sending him to college, compromised neither his own respectability nor his son's social standing as late as the 1840s.[26] So long as working with one's hands remained a route to middle-class status, arranging an apprenticeship fulfilled the requirements of a father's care, preparing sons to reproduce a father's station in life. In the middle of the nineteenth century, however, the collar line began to harden. As craft trades declined and became concentrated in larger factories or workshops, blue-collar work lost its respectability, a development with far-reaching consequences for the history of middle-class fatherhood.[27] As the gap between manual and nonmanual occupations widened in the nation's cities, the pressure mounted on urban middle-class men to provide their sons with educational opportunities. Changing paternal attitudes toward schooling, therefore, shine a bright light on the modernization of fatherhood in the nineteenth century and on the divergence of rural and urban modes of fathering.

Fathers and Education

Given how closely a father's care was identified with the efforts he made to establish his sons in the world, one might expect most men to have eagerly embraced schooling as a means of fulfilling their paternal responsibility. In many rural households, however, mothers and sons were quicker than fathers to recognize the economic usefulness of obtaining more than a common-school education. This dynamic accords well with the contractual nature of the father-son bond, which was aimed principally at serving the father's needs until a youth reached his majority. It also fits nicely with what we know about the father's economic leadership of his household. The family's economic security in the present, not a son's future expectations, was the top priority for most rural fathers. Accordingly, they were willing to forgo a son's services to advance his education or career goals only after assuring themselves that this could be done without jeopardizing the welfare of other household members. In short, family safety, not filial aspirations, came first, and fathers were much more likely than mothers to resist prolonged education for their sons.[28]

Paternal resistance to advanced schooling tempered growing acceptance of primary schools as places to train and educate the young. Unlike their colonial counterparts, most nineteenth-century parents expected that children would learn to read and write in the classroom rather than at home. Rising school attendance rates in most areas of the country reflected growing parental support for classroom instruction. Gains were especially sharp in the Midwest, where the patterns of high enrollment already achieved in New England were reproduced. Although nineteenth-century parents were eager to send their young children to school, most were reluctant to have them remain longer than necessary to obtain a basic common-school education.[29]

Fathers' views on the subject of leaving school after a basic education had been acquired were especially pronounced. For where school attendance became a family issue, mothers and children almost invariably were aligned on the side of continued education in academies, grammar schools, or colleges, while fathers opposed such additional schooling. However, it cannot be said that continuing beyond primary school was an issue that divided most, or even many, of the families whose documents provide the source material for this chapter. Irregular and brief attendance was common. Narrators with rural roots generally recalled without comment that their schooling began to be cut back between the ages of ten and twelve, when boys who had attended school sessions in summer and winter began attending only in the winter months because their labor was needed during the summer season. In many households, a child's education was further curtailed or came to an end at age fourteen, as boys and girls began to shoulder increased responsibility at home or in the fields. Nonetheless, an unmistakable pattern emerged in the evidence, demonstrating that fathers were less supportive than mothers of a child's expanded educational aspirations. The documents record not a single instance of a father supporting a son's desire to continue his schooling over his mother's objections, but the reverse situation arose in various households throughout the century.[30]

The principal explanation for this pattern is that many fathers viewed education in academies and grammar schools as unnecessary and at odds with both a son's traditional work obligations and the family's economic welfare. Men who required their sons' labor tended to share the belief of one father who observed that "it was sufficient that boys get a little reading, writing, and arithmetic; they need only enough book learning for 'gettin' on with.'"[31] Moreover, money spent on school tuition was money that could be used to pay taxes, make mortgage payments, and rent or acquire land.

Mothers, whose relationship with sons was focused less exclusively on work, viewed matters somewhat differently. Frequently, children recalled mothers not only as someone who offered home instruction, but as the parent who chiefly stimulated and supported their intellectual development. "My inclination for reading and study was not encouraged as much by my father as my mother," recalled Nathaniel Stacy, whose father struggled to maintain a farm in western Massachusetts at the turn of the nineteenth century. "He thought it necessary to keep his children all at work, with all possible diligence, in order to obtain a subsistence; and, indeed, so it was." Similarly, Maxwell Gaddis, who was born into a large evangelical household in Lancaster, Pennsylvania, in 1811, recalled: "My dear mother took a very special interest in my own mental training, because I had inherited a feeble constitution. . . . She was often devising 'ways and means' to favor her own wishes in securing to me an education while young. She frequently prevailed on father to send me to school in summer, when my little services were most needed at home, on the farm."[32]

There is no way of knowing how often the issue of extended education pitted a father's economic priorities against a mother's greater sympathy for her children's aspirations, but the memoirs of James Oliver Curwood demonstrate that this family dynamic persisted late into the century. Curwood grew up in the 1880s on farms and in the small towns of Michigan and Ohio, where his father was "always under the strain of laying aside enough to pay our taxes and the interest on the mortgage." When Curwood decided at age twelve that he wanted to go away to school, his father demurred. Soon Curwood was plotting with his mother to overturn his father's decision: "Relentlessly she . . . worked to wear down my father's certainty that what I sought was quite impossible. It was not that he didn't understand and sym-

pathize with me, but rather that he saw obstacles which to him seemed in-
superable. . . . If our peach orchard, which the frost attacked so often, would
only bear a good crop he would think about it—but he simply couldn't afford the expense now."

Curwood and his mother eventually won their battle. The winter after his
mother launched her campaign on behalf of James's education, Curwood's
father agreed to place their Ohio farm in the hands of an older son and move
into town. There, he opened a cobbling shop so that James could live with
him and his wife while attending school. The following year James, then
thirteen, was sent to live with a married sister in Michigan in order to attend
school there. However, his mother missed him, so the following year his
parents joined him there and left their older son behind to manage the Ohio
farm.[33]

When fathers refused to bend, sons sometimes rebelled. "My father's bias
against education beyond the three R's figured in my leaving home," recalled
Nels Anderson, whose father, a Swedish immigrant to the Midwest, clung
at century's end to an "Old World model" for his sons' rearing. "He would
have a fertile farm, and near it a like farm for each of his children." Anderson
eventually earned a Ph.D. in sociology at the University of Chicago rather
than live out his father's agrarian dream.[34]

None of this is to suggest that all or even most fathers were considered
obstacles by educationally ambitious sons who grew up in the rural North.
Nor does it mean that fathers were indifferent to their children's intellectual
development. While mothers took the lead in early education—deciding, for
instance, when and where young children would begin to attend school—
there is ample evidence in the sources that fathers as well devoted themselves
to their children's education. Fathers routinely told young children stories
and rhymes, read to them, and rewarded them for learning to read and write.
As children grew older, paternal involvement in their education intensified.
Fathers quizzed children about what they had learned in school, supplemented their education with home lessons, and sometimes took the lead
when arrangements were made for a child to attend school away from home.
That was especially true for sons, whose educations were frequently supervised by their fathers.[35]

What this varied and sometimes contradictory evidence suggests is that
fathers, more than mothers, were guided in matters of schooling by an eco-

nomic calculus. In the final analysis, the usefulness of a boy's labor on the farm and his traditional work obligations to his father dampened paternal enthusiasm for extended schooling.[36] While this pattern is clear, it is easy to exaggerate the level of paternal resistance to schooling. Attendance rates, after all, were rising. Moreover, attitudes were shaped by a father's own education and wealth. Well-to-do farmers, who could afford hired hands, were more willing than fathers with fewer resources to subsidize a son's education in an academy or college. Such an education, however, was understood to constitute a son's patrimony, fulfilling the father's responsibility to provide him with a start in life. Andrew Aldrich Angell, a prosperous farmer in Scituate, Rhode Island, and a member of his state's legislature, provided such a patrimony. When Angell's son James turned fifteen, in 1844, his father offered him a college education. "My father informed me that he was able and willing to send me to college, but in that case would hardly be able, in justice to my five brothers and sisters to aid me further," James recalled. "It was left to me to say whether I should go."[37]

Paternal attitudes toward education in Northern cities differed from those in the countryside. By the 1830s, if not earlier, providing children with the means to an education was, in the minds of many urban middle-class men, among their most important functions as fathers. Indeed, the desire and ability to keep children in school quickly became a sign of middle-class respectability and a marker of class boundaries. Consider how a twenty-two-year-old Brown University student contemplating his life as a man spoke of education in 1833. Elias Nason told his parents: "I long for the time when I can live comfortably—And [keep my] children all at school. . . . Ben's folks are well and he works hard and steady but he don't keep his children at school. They grow up like wild beasts."[38]

Among the emergent bourgeoisie, affording educational opportunity became entwined with the modern breadwinning style of fatherhood and heightened pressure to provide. The testimony of John Davis, a lawyer and congressman from Worcester, Massachusetts, is illustrative. Educating his sons and supervising their schooling was central to Davis's self-definition as a father, an attitude common to urban middle-class men. Davis was forty-three years old and the father of three sons when he told his wife in 1830: "My exertions I feel confident will with prudence keep us above want and we need not care for much beyond this. If it were not for the education of

the boys I should not strive much more for money, but they will be a heavy
item on my hands that will call for constant exertion and I shall cheerfully
devote my labor to them."[39]

Davis's sense of paternal responsibility—his emphasis on working for his
sons rather than on the labor they owed him—reflected both the declining
economic usefulness of children and the rising parental hopes for their future. Throughout the antebellum era, having children became an increasingly costly proposition. Economic historians calculate that by 1860 children
represented a significant drain on a family's economic resources. Even on
farms, more children meant more expense rather than more free labor.[40] In
cities, where children were less valuable as workers, the economic incentives
were even greater to invest more resources in fewer offspring. As distinc-
tions between manual and nonmanual labor took on sharper focus in urban
areas and the social pressure to get ahead in a competitive society intensified, an altered climate of aspiration for children also took shape. Whereas
fathers in rural areas might reasonably view a common-school education as
sufficient for a son to "get on with" in the world, succeeding in the cities,
where middle-class status was linked ever more closely to nonmanual work,
required something more. "I must continue working to educate the boys &
beyond this I have but little ambition," Davis reiterated in 1832. "It is one
of my principal objects to bring them into life in a way that they may make
something of themselves."[41]

Davis was not alone in closely identifying paternal care with the efforts he
made to provide his sons with an education and to launch them in life. If traditional forms of fatherhood highlighted the service a son owed his father
until reaching his majority, a modernizing tendency, emergent in the first
half of the century and more pronounced later, emphasized the steps fathers
took to secure their sons' prospects in a changing and uncertain world. Indeed, heightened anxiety about the ability to place sons in society and raise
them to succeed in a "man's world" was a hallmark of the nineteenth century's new fatherhood.

Various studies have shown that the transmission of occupational status
became vastly more complex in the nineteenth century than it had been earlier. By midcentury, small businessmen became increasingly hard pressed
to put their sons on a sound economic footing by bringing them into a family firm. Mary Ryan's study of Utica, New York, for instance, found that be-

tween the 1840s and 1860s the proportion of family partnerships in that city was reduced to one-fourth its former size. Of all the wills processed in Utica between 1850 and 1865, only five transferred a store or workshop to a second generation. Similarly, Michael Katz's study of mid-nineteenth-century Hamilton found that over the decade 1850–60, a declining proportion of sons followed their father's occupation.[42]

In such unsettled economic circumstances, good fathers were said to put their sons "forward in the way of experience" and to take "great pains" to train and educate them, efforts aimed at the ultimate goal of guiding them into an occupation. At least two rationales were advanced for this fatherly care. The first and older one suggested that the start a father gave his son as he entered manhood would incline the son to reciprocate by supporting his father at life's end, becoming, in the contemporary phrase, his "prop in old age." The new note in nineteenth-century fathering pushed this prudential consideration to the margins, highlighting instead the desire to have a son reproduce or advance beyond a father's station in life.[43]

As laboring to provide children with an education became central to evaluations of middle-class manhood, the self-sacrifice involved created a new vocabulary of filial obligation. Thus Charles Russell, a storekeeper from Princeton, Massachusetts, lectured his seventeen-year-old son at college in 1832: "You know Theodore that your mother is obliged to work every day beyond her strength and should I employ a clerk to do the business in the store instead of doing it myself I doubt whether I should be able to give you the advantages I wish to. We are obliged then to be prudent & work hard for your benefit."[44] Similarly, an upper-middle-class businessman from Salem, Massachusetts, the father of six sons and two daughters, told a sixteen-year-old daughter attending school in Boston in 1857: "Always bear this in mind, my dear daughter. Your parents love their children, and are willing to make sacrifices for their good. . . . They desire for them, next to good principles, & a firm enlightened religious faith, a good education & it is to them a source of the most heartfelt satisfaction and pleasure to know that these greatest & best of all things on earth will be theirs."[45]

It would be easy to misinterpret the new note of self-sacrifice in father-child relations. For one thing, only a tiny handful of fathers labored to put sons through college, although an increasing number sought to provide at least some academy or grammar school education. For another, educational opportunity was provided to fulfill a father's traditional obligation to give children a start in life; sons who received advanced schooling had little expectation of further assistance. Nonetheless, just as injunctions toward self-sacrifice were powerful influences on nineteenth-century mothers, encouraging women to put the needs and interests of others above their own, so too did fatherhood register these child-centered expectations.[46]

Family advisers importuned mothers above all toward altruism, but men and women alike were prompted to demonstrate "parental regard" for offspring. Such solicitude, unlike, say, tenderness, was an aspect of the new parenting easily embraced by men because it was less gender coded. Whereas such stereotypically feminine attributes as gentleness and warmth might compromise the hard side of masculine identity, self-sacrifice was a time-honored component of the Christian fatherhood ideal, and men had little difficulty incorporating it into secularized understandings of a father's care.[47]

Ironically, the emphasis on parental solicitude tended to heighten expectations of filial obligation. A parent's sacrifice exacted a price, to be paid by children in the form of implicit obedience. Whenever possible, fathers continued to insist that their interests be served and that their authority be accorded unquestioning respect in exchange for their efforts to provide.[48] Indeed, mounting pressure to provide tended to sharpen a father's sense of entitlement to filial gratitude. On one level, father-son relations had become more oriented toward the son's prospects than the father's economic needs, and so reinforced affective rather than instrumental bonds. Fathers, however, continued to extend support within the overall context of a contractual exchange, and sons without an economic role to play now brought less to the bargaining table in return for their patrimony. What fathers demanded, absent their sons' labor, was less their affection than their continued obedience and respect.

From this perspective, when a son's obligation to work for his father withered, what remained and became an increased psychological burden was the expectation that he would defer to paternal authority so long as he lived in his father's house. Because city children had less reason to leave home for schooling or to find work, sons in urban households tended to stay under the paternal roof longer than did their rural counterparts, and as long as they resided there issues of deference and respect were central to the relationship with their fathers.

This psychological dynamic is shown nicely by an incident in the life of James Barnard Blake, a young man born in 1827 to a prosperous Boston family. Educated in public schools and a private academy in Boston, Blake finished his schooling at age eighteen. He then went to work in an uncle's engineering firm in Boston, where he remained for the next six years while he continued to live at home with his family. Blake's diary for 1851, the year he turned twenty-four and left home to take a job as superintendent of the Worcester Gas Light Company, documents an emotionally fraught relationship with his father. In a year of entries, nothing unsettled him more than the thought that his father suspected him of disrespect. His diary entry for New Year's Day reflects his father's towering importance:

> During the past year which I have now left behind, I have enjoyed very much. Nothing has occured [*sic*] to mar the beautiful symphony of feeling, or to ruffle the finer affections of the family circle; everything has moved quietly on under the direction of my highly respected and much beloved Father; and I thank my God that he has been spared me now in the morning of my manhood as a pattern, and adviser and a guide. God grant that he may live long in this world happily, and that I may be spared and situated in such manner that I can be a comfort to him in his declining years and in part reciprocate the blessings and cancel the debt which he has so kindly imposed upon me.[49]

The passage is noteworthy in several respects. Here is evidence that fathers continued to loom large on the mental landscapes of sons entering manhood in upper-middle-class urban households. Blake speaks of his father as a role model, adviser, and guide, in language that echoed contemporary family advice. The most telling metaphor comes at the end of the diary entry, however, when he notes the "debt" that his father has "so kindly imposed upon me." Blake is using the language of contract, which had guided father-son relations from the beginning of the century. By their mid-twenties, sons in rural areas had gone a long way toward cancelling that debt with the accumulated labor that they had undertaken on behalf of their fathers. Consequently, when they entered manhood they tended to think more in terms of what their fathers now owed them.

In urban middle-class families, however, the terms of the traditional contractual bond between father and son had been altered. Sons now came to manhood more beholden to their fathers, whose self-sacrifice imposed a heavy psychological burden. As a consequence, emotional relations between fathers and sons in city homes did not warm appreciably, but rather reproduced the somewhat strained and distant relationships we have already noticed in rural households. James Barnard Blake said that his father was both "highly respected" and "much beloved," but respect more than love structured their relationship. Deep ambivalence churned below the ostensibly unruffled surface of family emotions orchestrated by the senior James Blake.

In June, a discordant note entered Blake's "symphony of feeling." The circumstances are unclear, but Blake's father seems to have interpreted his son's choice of a straw hat, a style he disfavored, as a sign of disrespect. This charge anguished James: "I am fully convinced that he little knows the motives which govern my actions," he confided to the pages of his diary. "To say that I have not proper respect for my Father is a grave charge to me. I had rather be branded as a villain, than to be told that I have no respect for my Father. I cannot think he meant what he said, but that it was uttered in a moment of weakness."[50] The following day James returned to this theme, noting: "I felt quite sad all day owing to the gross charges which my Father laid upon me last night, so unexpected and so very hard." He reiterated that he felt misjudged and misunderstood. "Most happy am I to have him advise me, and chide me, but it hurts me sorely to have such a volley of imaginary sins put upon my shoulders at once," he said. "Ah little does he know his son's character, little does he know the respect he bears for him."[51]

Blake's tense relationship with his father, balanced precariously between veneration and resentment, was hardly unique. Punctilious regard for a father's wishes was the first rule of conduct for sons well into their twenties. When fathers detected insubordination (real or imagined), censure quickly followed. Indeed, chastising older sons seems to have come easier for many men than expressing tenderness. For only with a tight grip on their emotions could fathers prepare their sons to take their place in a "man's world" as fully masculine adults, equipped with self-control and respect for authority, perseverance, hard work, and the other practical virtues required to get ahead.[52]

In 1834, Charles Russell, the Princeton storekeeper who had reminded his son Theodore of his parents' sacrifice to put him through college, asked him to investigate and report on the price of hats in Boston, information he needed for business. Days passed with no response, and on the assumption that his request had been ignored Russell sharply criticized Theodore for his (supposed) negligence, only to receive the information he required in a subsequent mail. Late one Saturday night, Russell sat down to write his son an apology of sorts, explaining that if he had received Theodore's letter more promptly it "would have prevented the unpleasant censure" he was obliged to impose. His own harshness prompted Russell to reflect on a father's role. "You know not, you never can know until you are a Father and are placed in a similar situation, the fear the anxiety the solicitude that is felt on your account," he said. The words then began to tumble from his pen in an unpunctuated stream of emotion: "You are separated from our watch and care amid a thousand allurements & temptations & then again the anxiety that is felt for your health & future prospects all combine to swell the bosom with a thousand tender emotions mingled with fear & hope & could you but stand behind the curtain & see the tender emotion felt on the mention of your name or receipt of your letter, the tears that drop from the cheeks of a tender mother, the gathering round and anxious watchfulness of a beloved brother & fond sister, but enough my own weakness interrupts the pursuit."[53]

Russell's letter articulates more eloquently than most the deep anxieties that nineteenth-century parents came to share. Similar apprehensions about children's moral well-being (particularly when they lived in cities), about their physical health, and about their future prospects ring through the letters of mothers and fathers alike. While fathers lectured their children about all these matters, emotional reticence guided their relationships with sons. Accordingly, there is no evidence that Russell actually shared his feelings with his son Theodore. The letter in which he unbosomed these sentiments ends abruptly, is not signed, was never addressed, and probably was never sent. It was one thing for a father to have tender feelings and anxieties about his children's prospects, quite another to share the depth of his emotions with his son.

While men could be highly expressive in their relations with wives, daughters, and young children, emotional relations with older sons remained relatively cool and distant, oriented toward overseeing their transition from the family circle to the world of work. Urban middle-class fathers in white-collar occupations were less able than their agrarian and artisanal counterparts to transmit job skills directly, but their primary role remained the same: socializing their sons to work by overseeing their education, guiding career decisions, and instilling business values. A man's success or failure as a father, and therefore his sense of masculine self-respect, hung on the outcome. Accordingly, the correspondence of middle-class fathers with sons who were at the beginning of their careers contains a steady flow of practical guidance on such matters as the importance of conscientious work habits, finding jobs, and negotiating wages. Fathers repeatedly urged sons to combine hard work with moral fiber, but their correspondence reflects little emotional exchange. As the son of a paymaster's clerk in the federal armory at Springfield, Massachusetts, summed it up: "Father trained me to do my work punctually and well."[54]

Fathers and Daughters: The Quasi Wife

Expectations governing fathers' relationships with daughters were less antagonistic to affection. While tight-knit mother-daughter bonds tended to hold fathers at bay, the distancing impact is easily exaggerated and frequently misunderstood. Just as the nineteenth century's "female world of love and ritual" accommodated the interdependence of husbands and wives, so too were the lives of fathers and daughters mutually entwined.[55]

As girls became teenagers, their role in housekeeping and the care of younger siblings expanded. In effect, daughters, especially eldest ones, became deputy mothers, or what the contemporary family adviser Lydia Sigourney dubbed "mother's viceroy." Commenting on this acquisition of maternal duty, Carroll Smith-Rosenberg has observed aptly that the roles of mother and daughter shaded into one another.[56] Even as a girl's life came more and more to resemble her mother's, however, she retained significant ties to her father. Indeed, she developed new ones. For the transformation of the daughter's role had an ironic consequence: Rather than cut her off from her father, a daughter's new responsibilities as she grew older frequently placed her in a quasi-wifely relation to him.

Much evidence indicates that, even before they became teenagers, daughters were substantially involved in their father's life. Just as boys between the ages of roughly seven and fourteen from rural homes inhabited a common world of family labor, so did girls in late childhood and early youth shuttle back and forth between their mother's and father's spheres of work. Especially on the frontier, where labor was scarce, girls frequently participated in such "masculine" activities as planting or harvesting. Anna Howard Shaw, who moved to the woods of western Michigan at age twelve in 1859, even helped to build her family's log house. The "dearest treasure of [her] childish days," she recalled, was a saw and hatchet her father gave her. "I was to use [these] tools as well as my brothers did, as I proved when I helped to build our frontier home." Similarly, David Ward, who grew up on a farm in Essex County, New York, in the 1820s and 1830s, recalled that until he was large enough to help, his two older sisters "assisted [his] father much in his farming, in spreading, raking and loading hay and grain, making and weeding the garden, digging potatoes, pulling flax, driving team, etc." He continued: "As soon as my strength would in any measure permit, I was put into the harness of work, and largely took the place of my sisters in doing men's work."[57]

Recent scholarship suggests that when girls crossed gender boundaries to work alongside their fathers, the consequences for their development were profound. On the frontier further west, girls who herded, harvested, and hunted with their fathers and brothers had an especially troubling passage to womanhood, when they were expected to give up these masculine activities for what they took to be more mundane and limiting household work.[58]

Scattered evidence from the Midwest confirms that girls found an unaccustomed freedom in performing masculine labor, which could lead, in turn, to a romanticized identification with a father and his work. Consider the testimony of Bertha Van Hoosen, who grew up on a farm in Rochester, Michigan, where she was born in 1863, the youngest of two daughters. While her older sister helped her mother, Bertha accompanied her father everywhere, helping him husk corn, plant potatoes, pull stumps, and shear sheep: "I spent little time in the house and had no conscientious feeling about helping Mother with housework," she recalled. "I was the dog-like companion of my father and, in consequence, acquired an empirical foundation in agronomy and animal husbandry. When father announced, 'Well, lambings over and the creek is pretty high so I guess we better shear next week,' I trembled with delight."[59] Similarly, Florence Hartsuff, whose father was an army surgeon, was his constant companion at various postings throughout the Midwest and West after the Civil War. "All memory except life with my father is blurred. My mother was a vague person who presided in a kitchen over Diggins freezing cream and a shadowy cook," she recalled. "Most of all I loved snuggling close to my father's heart, secure in his protecting arms, sheltered under his army cape against snow and wind."[60]

The point of these admittedly rhapsodic recollections is not that companionship and mutual labor necessarily translated into veneration (although they clearly sometimes had that effect). Rather, we see that work brought fathers and daughters together in unexpected ways. Sometimes, of course, that labor bred only resentment and could intensify a girl's identification with her mother. Lucy Stone, who grew up to become a prominent abolitionist and suffragist, smarted under the yoke of laboring for her father as a girl. The eighth of nine children in her family, Stone was born in 1818 and raised on a 145-acre farm near West Brookfield, Massachusetts. Along with her three sisters, she helped her mother with the housework and sewed shoes to be sold in the local store. She also shared with her brothers such outside chores as driving the cows to pasture and filling the woodbox, but she was regarded by her father as the boys' inferior. Not surprisingly, she found little pleasure in her domestic labor and less affection for her father, whom she came to blame for her mother's difficult life.[61]

In some respects, Lucy Stone's fraught relationship with her father was an exception among exceptional women. Specialists in nineteenth-century women's history have observed that ambitious, independent women, those who pushed gender boundaries beyond the confines of domesticity to establish public careers, frequently had supportive fathers as guides and inspirations. The fathers of such women did not serve as role models exactly—certainly not in the way that they modeled manly behavior for their sons—but they were uniquely positioned to enlarge a daughter's sense of possibility. As an authority figure inhabiting the public sphere, a father could offer assurance and approval that sanctioned an ambitious daughter's forays beyond her mother's world. Such a father was able to stiffen a girl's backbone, providing the reassurance that she needed to overcome personal inhibitions and the sense of social impropriety.

Clara Barton's career is a case in point. At the beginning of the Civil War, Barton's desire to be of service to the Union cause as a volunteer nurse stirred up conflicted feelings. Fearing that soldiers would treat her like a camp follower, she was paralyzed with doubts about the propriety of an unmarried woman serving on the front lines. According to a recent biographer, Stephen B. Oates, Barton's father liberated her to follow her calling. "With her father's approval," Oates writes, "she could challenge any attitude, go anywhere men were fighting."[62]

Most fathers, of course, had no such liberating effect on their daughters' lives. As girls grew older, they had many opportunities to be involved with their fathers, but this interaction tended to reinforce, rather than challenge, conventional gender norms. Most men considered it part of their fatherly duty to uphold womanly virtues, seeing to it that their daughters grew up to become good wives and mothers. Because a daughter's responsibility to her father often resembled that of a surrogate wife, her training for these roles was a natural extension of their relationship. The quasi-spousal bond uniting father and daughter came to the fore especially when a girl's mother was sick or away visiting friends and relatives, not infrequent occurrences in nineteenth-century America.

By age seventeen, Sarah Partridge had assumed many housekeeping responsibilities on her father's farm in Bay City, Michigan. Like other girls her age, she cooked, baked, washed, and ironed. On the evidence of her diary, she can fairly be described not only as deputy head of the household, fully responsible for its operations when her mother was absent or incapacitated, but as a substitute wife. Part of her entry for March 17, 1881 reads: "The first Saturday that Ma was sick, I washed 12 pieces for Pa and made bread besides lots of other work. I baked the bread and ironed Pa's clothes Sunday. I 'pulled the ox out of the pit.' James [her brother] said something about that."[63]

Such accounts pepper the diaries of teenage girls. By age seventeen, Jessie Phelps recognized that it was her responsibility as eldest daughter to take her mother's place when called upon. On March 2, 1888, she noted: "When I got home last night I found Papa sick, Mama away and I to do it all. I doctored Papa to the best of my ability and also tried hard to keep the children quiet." Elizabeth Gurney had similar obligations to her father. For example, on May 31, 1857: "This morning Father must be up at 5 o'clock, so I must get up & cook his breakfast. Ma & Clara [her sister] both took medicine last night, and not feeling well, did not get up till of the 7."[64]

The emotions associated with these spouselike role expectations were as varied and complex as those incorporated in the marital bond. A daughter's obligations to her father could be experienced as oppressive, or they might cement bonds of affection. Elizabeth Gurney did not much like caring for her father, who abandoned his family in 1858 and whom she came to regard, with good reason, as a religious hypocrite. Ellen Regal, the eldest daughter in a family of four children, on the other hand, adored her father, an itinerant evangelist. The diary she kept for the year 1857 suggests that their relationship shared some aspects of a companionate marriage. On March 23, 1857, she wrote: "Children a little better. Worked in the kitchen. Folded & ironed clothes to keep awake while sitting up with Father."[65]

As the foregoing examples attest, the bond between mother and daughter doubled back to reinforce a girl's obligations to her father as well. This emotional system, in which filial relations shaded into spousal ones, found its ultimate expression in the case of a mother's death, when the eldest daughter in the household was expected, temporarily at least, to fill the maternal role. Generally, this was a transitional responsibility, lasting until a father remarried or made other arrangements for the care of dependent children. The task of mothering the family, however, could fall on the shoulders of a girl as young as thirteen, and might last for a period of years.[66]

Time and again, girls whose mothers died expressed the belief that it was up to them to "carry on" by assuming parental authority over children and, not incidentally, increased care for their fathers. Emily Ward, whose mother died during the family's migration from Vermont to Kentucky in the winter of 1817, recalled: "I used to lie awake at night thinking of my mother, wondering if she knew how hard I tried to be a mother to the children, to make Father happy, and to do my duty." As the eldest daughter, Emily was indeed shifted into a maternal role. "I felt that my responsibility to the younger children was great, and I tried to do everything for them that my mother had usually done."[67]

Eventually Emily Ward's father placed her two younger sisters with a family in Ohio, taking Emily and her brother to live with him in Michigan. "I wanted them to go with us," Emily reflected, "but Father said I was too young to manage young girls. I didn't think I was too young, and I thought it would be better for them to be with us. But I was only thirteen, I couldn't make much impression on Father." Emily, of course, had no choice but to acquiesce. Maternal death enhanced a girl's parental authority over siblings without breaking down the hierarchy between father and daughter. Following a mother's death, her tasks devolved on daughters but not her power in the marital relationship. Daughters, in any case, frequently experienced the added responsibility they assumed when a mother died more as an obligation to their siblings and to their mother's memory than as a duty to their fathers. It was not unusual, for instance, for younger siblings to be committed to the care of an eldest daughter as a mother's dying request.[68]

Fatherly Advice

Daughters whose family responsibilities thrust them into ongoing involvement with their fathers became the recipients of frequent paternal advice. Mothers clearly served as their daughters' chief counselors, and nearly all men believed that mothers were their daughters' best and most appropriate role models. Because they were less responsible for girls' development, fathers were less involved in bringing up daughters than they were in raising sons. As Joseph Curtis, a Maine father of five boys and two girls, told his wife in 1864: "Remember that Willie [their nine-year-old son] must go to school and at the one where he will learn the fastest and be the least exposed to bad habits. The girls can better take care of themselves with your advice."[69]

Nonetheless, fathers counseled their daughters on a wide variety of domestic and personal topics, both while they were growing up and after they had married and moved away from home. Such advice might extend even to the intimate details of infant and toddler care. Asa Emerson Foster, a school principal from Erie, Pennsylvania, told a married daughter in 1862 how to proceed now that her two-year-old child had been weaned: "I am glad to hear you have got along so well in weaning Julia. Now is the time to lay the foundation for moral character. Never before could she realize her dependence on others for comforts. Food from nursing she considered her natural right. But it must be line upon line, precept on precept. Here a little & there a little & administered with affection."[70]

Such advice was not unusual from fathers. Other fathers as well counseled daughters on such "feminine" topics as pregnancy and childbirth, household furnishings, and other matters that one might expect to have been the exclusive preserve of mothers.[71] Just as fathers admonished sons to uphold manly ideals, they lectured daughters on correct feminine behavior. Massachusetts father Abijah Adams struck a characteristic note when he told his fourteen-year-old daughter Maryanne in 1808 that it was "of the first importance to cultivate all those virtues which tend to embellish the mind & fit it while young for the qualifications of a good child, a good Wife, a good Mother, a good friend & a good Christian." Adams went on to advise his daughter that modesty was "peculiarly requisite in a young lady. . . . It is one of the brightest ornaments in the female character; and the want of it has been the ruin of many."[72]

Other fathers offered similar advice, instructing their daughters to be "always social and lively, but never rude" and to "remember that a smiling cheerful countenance in a female is very pleasing and interesting and gives pleasure to all around." Later in the century, an employee of the Freedmen's Bureau told a fourteen-year-old daughter, "Be as womanly as possible. Respect yourself. Never do anything you would not wish to be known." Similarly, Stephen Foster, husband of the noted abolitionist Abigail Kelley Foster, told his sixteen-year-old daughter Alla on New Year's Day 1864: "You are just stepping from the platform of youth to womanhood & the passing months will each leave a mark & permanent impress upon your future character & destinies." Foster advised his daughter to cultivate especially her powers of conversation. "This is the faculty which charms; & you must remember that to charm is to captivate & that to captivate is to command. This, then, is the chief source of power, especially to your sex." If she followed his advice, Foster assured his daughter, "I trust you will not fall far below your mother in what I regard as her great accomplishments & what is I am sure the chief source of her great influence."[73]

Whether their advice was to cultivate modesty, pleasing manners, or powers of conversation, fathers habitually urged daughters to conform to conventional gender norms. "You know that women must learn all the domestic and household duties in order to make themselves useful in life," Joseph Curtis told his daughter Josephine in 1864. "Book education is pleasant and useful to improve the mind but domestic knowledge is equally necessary."[74]

What fathers hoped to achieve by all this advice is plain enough: they wanted their daughters equipped for marriage. The choice of a spouse, however, could be as perilous to father-daughter ties as was the choice of an occupation to the father-son relationship. Issues of courtship heightened latent tensions with daughters because, as young women approached the altar, fathers policed the double standard of sexual morality ever more vigilantly. Just as boys entering manhood tended to feel the added weight of their father's economic authority, young women were pressured to conform to a father's sense of appropriate courtship behavior. Whether the issue was dancing, dating, or simply writing to gentlemen friends, many fathers felt increasingly called upon to announce their feelings.

By demanding conformity, fathers invited rebellion, and so the volatility of father-daughter relations increased as young women reached marriageable age. Learning that her father thought it "wrong for young ladies to correspond with young men," nineteen-year-old Jessie Phelps of Pontiac, Michigan, promptly broke off correspondence in 1889 with a beau in Ann Arbor, agreeing, however, to her suitor's plea for letters at Christmas, Thanksgiving, and on their birthdays. Phelps's older sister, Mary, was less compliant. Although she, too, knew her father's views, she chose to correspond with impunity with "at least seven or eight" young men.[75] In this and similar instances, fathers navigated a difficult course between strict authority and activist family leadership, on the one hand, and more relaxed views of family governance consistent with child-centered family values, on the other.[76]

Although fathers were consulted about marriage proposals throughout the century, and the ritual of obtaining paternal consent endured, a father's actual authority over such decisions was quite circumscribed. Studies of courtship have shown that, from about the time of the American Revolution, parents exercised limited control over matrimonial decisions. Typically, parents deferred to children's wishes regarding the choice of a spouse and exercised only somewhat more authority over the timing of marriage. This limited control is well illustrated by the response of Eleazer Lindsley to a request for his seventeen-year-old daughter's hand in marriage. An affluent and politically prominent resident of Steuben County, New York, Lindsley wrote to his daughter's suitor in 1806: "It is the wish of Mrs. Lindsley and myself that Maria would not leave us for a year or two to come. Our reasons for the same I shall with freedom mention. We view her as being too young to bear the care and troubles which necessarily attend the married state. . . . I shall, however, lay Maria under no positive restraint. Trusting the event to her own good sense and discretion and to that kind Providence which guides and superintends the words of Universal Nature."[77] Lindsley wrote that letter in February; Maria was married before the year was out.

Marriage prospects were a minefield of potential misunderstanding, and fathers exercised authority in these matters at the peril of being ignored. In the minds of their daughters, fathers walked a fine line between offering use-ful guidance and meddling in matters of the heart. Nonetheless, through-out the century fathers were involved in the marriage transition. Formally at least, "what father would think" was an issue in the minds of both daugh-ters and their suitors, although how much a father's thoughts actually mat-tered is debatable.[78]

Assertions of paternal authority characteristically met with ambiguous re-sponses. Harriet Amelia Johnson was twenty-one years old and working as a schoolteacher in Maumee City, Ohio, in 1853 when she received a proposal of marriage from twenty-seven-year-old Henry Parker Smith. "I have to-night committed myself more fully than before, and honor now calls for some prompt decision," she confided to her diary on June 25, one week after Smith had first broached the subject of marriage. "But be my feelings what they may, I shall not act contrary to the *will* of my parent—my father. I be-lieve that I sincerely *love* H[enry] and could be happy with him, but whether our destinies are to be linked is uncertain."[79] We learn from Henry's diary that he formally asked Harriet's father for his consent on July 17: "Twas a trial I had never undergone and I now wonder that I conducted myself so coolly throughout. He consented that his darling child should be mine, left it entirely to her which moved a great heavy load from my breast. I could hardly realize my success but knew that my prayers had been answered and felt grateful. I then obtained Mrs. Johnson's consent and my cup was full."[80]

That Harriet had discussed the proposal with her parents to pave the way for her father's consent seems likely. Her diary, though, is silent on the mat-ter, perhaps because she and Henry exchanged diaries as part of their court-ship ritual. At the very least, Harriet's June 25 diary entry indicates that she wanted Henry to know that her father's opinion mattered to her and there-fore should matter to him. Hence Henry's trepidation when he formally asked Mr. Johnson for his consent. Johnson's declaration to Henry that the decision was "left entirely" to Harriet raises intriguing questions. Did she in fact have more autonomy in the matter than she believed? Or was the mat-ter "entirely" hers to decide once it was understood that she and her father were of a mind about Henry's prospects and suitability as a spouse? Such ambiguity underscores the extent to which paternal authority was in flux and, accordingly, a source of anxiety for both fathers and their children.

It was not at all clear whether a father's interest in marriage plans would

be taken by daughters as an expression of paternal concern or merely as med-
dlesomeness. Nor was it certain whether paternal pronouncements would
be obeyed. The following exchange between a father and daughter serves
as an example. Eli Regal was an itinerant Baptist minister with the activist
family role we associate with evangelical fathers. When he believed a marriage
proposal was in the offing for his daughter Emma, he reproached her for not
coming to him to discuss the matter. Here is her response, in a letter dated
November 29, 1868:

> I received your letter. I cannot tell you how much I was surprised by
> what you said. I had not anticipated any such thing [a proposal of mar-
> riage] as occurring for a long time yet. If I had, I would not have missed
> the opportunity of speaking to you concerning it and of availing my-
> self of your wise and kind advice, which I know I so much need. It was
> not from any lack of confidence in you, dear father, or from any distrust
> of your ability and desire to aid me that I did not mention the matter
> to you. . . . I should be glad if I should not be asked to decide yet; but
> if I am, I shall try, God helping me, to do what is right. I have not de-
> cided in my own mind what to do.[81]

Emma was uncertain about the proposal because she doubted whether she
truly loved her suitor. "I do not know what I *ought* to do under such circumstances," she told her father in the same letter. "Will you tell me, please,
what you think? I have told you as nearly as I can, what my feelings on the
subject are and I hope you will be able to understand me." Emma, it seems
fair to say, protested too much. Her gratitude for her father's "wise and kind
advice" sugar-coated her underlying determination to be guided more by
her own heart than by her father's opinions, a decision that she hoped he understood.

Indulging Daughters

The ambiguous but real role that fathers played during their daughters'
courtship culminated a series of ongoing involvements that wove together
the lives of fathers and daughters in the nineteenth century. Notwithstanding a father's role as guardian of the sexual double-standard and the considerable service that his daughters owed him, various evidence suggests that
relations with daughters were appreciably warmer than those with sons.

When nineteenth-century childhoods were recalled, grown daughters were more likely than sons to remember their fathers with affection, as parents who provided protection and comfort as well as guidance and discipline. Adult children of either sex cited instances of paternal solicitude, but daughters more frequently evoked the gentler, companionable side of their father's nature, whereas sons' memories highlighted a father's control and emotional distance.

Glowing images of fathers were especially prominent in the recollections of girls from privileged urban households. Susan Leyman, who grew up in Boston during the first half of the century, recalled an indulgent father who was "a great favorite with all who knew him." She continued: "To myself he was particularly kind. I do not remember that he ever refused me anything, more than once or twice in his life, and when I asked anything of him, he was generally ready to grant the request." Similarly, Elizabeth Douglas Hall, who was born into a well-to-do Detroit family in 1862, recalled a father with a "sweet disposition," who was extremely solicitous of her health.[82]

Greater indulgence of daughters seems to have been the rule for middle-class fathers in small towns as well as large cities. Oscar Talcott combined farming with a fire insurance business in Ionia, Michigan, in the second half of the century, and he later organized a number of building and loan associations. His daughter Elta May, who was born in 1863, recalled Talcott as a "kind indulgent man" for whom "no sacrifice was too great to help any of his three girls." When Elta May was old enough to marry, she said, "I wanted my husband to be like my father, and he was, in his affection for me."[83]

While the memoirs of middle- and upper-middle-class daughters are not devoid of tension, they tilt toward acclamation. Descriptions similar to the foregoing examples can be adduced without difficulty.[84] These recollections might simply reflect the fact that female narrators were more adept with the language of affection, accessing a vocabulary to better express aspects of the paternal relationship that their brothers could not describe. The personal documents of fathers themselves, however, refute this interpretation. Letters written to daughters frequently contain explicit statements of affection not often included in correspondence with sons. Now, of course, fathers did not love their sons less and their daughters more. They did, however, consider greater emotional distance necessary for a son's own good and for the sake of his success. Reserve, rather than intimacy, raised manly men, but such restraint could be dispensed with for bringing up daughters. Greater warmth and a distinctive language of sentiment, therefore, ring through nineteenth-century father-daughter correspondence.

From the earliest part of the century, middle-class fathers voiced warm affection for daughters, employing such tender epithets as "my sweet little girl" or "my much loved child." Fathers increasingly spoke to sons as well about being their "companions" and "friends," but the language of parental friendship was employed earliest and most often vis-à-vis daughters. "You are very near my heart, & none but a parent can feel the affection of a parent," Abijah Adams told his fourteen-year-old daughter in 1808. "Young folks are not often fond, I know, of moral lectures but they are necessary sometimes, & must be expected from those who are their *best* friends & who they will sometime rather know to be so—'give me the friend,' said one, 'who will tell me my faults.'"[85] Adams's tone of loving admonition was echoed by fathers time and again in their correspondence.

The extent to which father-daughter relations fit the pattern of a companionate marriage was a result of nineteenth-century culture's ardent celebration of the analogy. The father-daughter bond was considered a prelude to the marital relationship. Fathers, who were enjoined to prepare daughters for marriage by modeling the role of husband for them, were thought to benefit, in turn, from their daughters' improving influence. A daughter's dependency, in particular, had moral consequence, eliciting the maximum in masculine devotion. "If I mistake not, there are some special reasons why the solicitude of a parent should be awakened by contemplating the condition of a *daughter*," said the anonymous author of a book of advice for girls published in 1833. "In addition to all the other circumstances which render her an object of deep interest and in which she shares in common with children of the other sex, she is, in a higher degree than they, dependent on parental aid: there is a sort of natural defenselessness in her condition, independently of the fostering care of those from whom under God she received her being, that makes an appeal to a parent's heart, which if it be not a heart of stone, he will strive in vain to resist."[86] An "amiable and affectionate daughter" was thought capable of leading a father to repentance and spiritual salvation. Accordingly, girls were instructed to be "friends" and "companions" of their fathers, to make his concerns their own and to "enter into his feelings and views."[87]

These injunctions, indistinguishable from those directed at wives, enfolded female subordination in the language of love. Girls were said to occupy an exalted place in the constellation of family affection, analogous to the one occupied by their mothers. Girlhood's "honor and purity, its grace and happiness, constitute the inner sanctuary of every family," said the author and essayist Nathaniel Parker Willis. Daughters, who were uniquely able to reward a father's fondness and devotion, represented his "deepest stake in life's chances for good and evil," Willis said.[88]

Just as fatherly love reinforced female dependency, it inserted into the nineteenth-century family constellation a new member—the trophy daughter. Among the urban middle class, having an educated and accomplished daughter became a point of pride for many fathers, a symbol of their social standing. Fathers who would not think of affording their sons a high school education eagerly enrolled their daughters. By the late nineteenth century, most high school students, and an even larger proportion of high school graduates, were young women. These daughters of the middle class were sent to school not to train for college or a career, but rather to acquire the faculties required of wives and mothers. In the words of one educator, high school teachers sought to instill female pupils with "a well-disciplined mind, high moral aims, refined tastes, gentle and graceful manners, practical views of her own duties and those resources of health, thought, conversation and occupation which bless alike the highest and lowest station of life."[89]

Evidence of the pride that might move a father to invest in a daughter's leisured refinement, rather than her economic usefulness, comes from the diary of a girl named Mary Thomas, whose father's financial status in 1873 was less solvent than it appeared. "If I ever have to work for my living, I think I will give lessons in Calysthenics [sic]," Thomas recorded. "I wonder what Papa would say, if I was to read him this part of my Journal, he would feel like shaking me, he has so much pride, he could never bear to see his daughter teach & right there where he is so well known & everyone thinks he is so well off too."[90]

In the decades after the Civil War, the prevalence of trophy daughters in the upper reaches of American society became a source of cultural anxiety, tempering the earlier celebration of the father-daughter tie. By 1884, William Dean Howells had identified in the character of Silas Lapham the social type of the new-middle-class father whose aspirations for social standing were hitched to the hopes he invested in his daughter's future. Late-century moralists shared Howells's critical assessment, chiding overly indulgent fathers for raising a generation of daughters whose taste for luxury disqualified them for matrimony and motherhood. Behind certain conspicuous displays of wealth in gilded-age America, social observers now found a father whose "fondness for his daughter enters less of affection than of pride."[91]

Like the relationship with sons, then, the father's role with daughters came to absorb a full measure of anxiety about class status in the nineteenth-century American North. The emotional norms of family life encouraged considerably more warmth and tenderness toward daughters. That affection was real, but romanticism's impact on domestic relations never immunized men against the forces in nineteenth-century society commodifying family ties—not when children were young, nor as they grew older. If anxiety about fulfilling the obligations of a father's care became a hallmark of middle-class masculinity in the nineteenth-century American North, so did the notion that children existed as much to reward the family man for his devotion as they did to pursue their own ends.

Conclusion

Beyond Breadwinning

We are told that the nineteenth century was the age of the mother, a time when the controlling patriarch yielded his place as a cultural ideal to the affectionate matriarch—a parent of sensibility, of feeling. As the old patriarchal structure faded, solicitude and emotion took on value in themselves, and friendship (emphasizing equality rather than hierarchy) displaced superiority as the favored child-rearing attitude.[1] This thumbnail account of the modernization of parenting ideology in the last century captures nicely the unity of Victorian culture, which exalted parenthood from beginning to end. The story of motherhood's rise highlights the profound impact that romanticism had on the intimate relations of family life and accounts as well for the emergence of the child-centered private home.

Where, however, amidst the surge of sentiment, did the father reside in this modern, mother-dominated middle-class household? Did the expansion of motherhood crowd fathers to the margins of family life? Or was the father's role somehow reimagined to prevent his falling by the wayside of domestic existence? These are critical questions for the history of the American family, to which there are no easy answers. This study suggests, however, that, rather than let fatherhood lose its meaning, middle-class parents in the nineteenth-century American North sought to modernize the father's role. Alongside the ideal of a "moral mother," parents (and the family advisers constantly tugging at their sleeves) established the "family man," someone who prized marriage, family making, and child rearing no less than did his self-sacrificing wife. In significant ways, the nineteenth century was less the age of the mother than it was an era of the parent. For as surely as nineteenth-century Americans believed in the power of "mother's love," they believed in the need for a "father's care."

This is not to suggest that men and women in the last century were held to the same standard of parental care. More was expected of women, the supposed "natural" parent, and mothers took the lead in bringing up children. Mothers and fathers alike were encouraged, however, to believe that parenting was a social virtue pertinent to both sexes, an activity that benefited not only the rising generation but society at large. From the century's opening decades, men were cautioned not to allow all parenting responsibility to devolve on women. They were told by an indefatigable army of moralists and advisers that it was their Christian responsibility to be engaged parents. When that religious advice began to ring hollow in an increasingly secular society, men were told by scientists and physicians later in the century that assuming paternal responsibility would make them better, more virile specimens of upright masculinity.

This abiding idealization of parenthood for both men and women went hand in glove with the nineteenth century's celebration of childhood. It was, in short, romanticism's tribute to nineteenth-century families. If the Romantic Movement's bouquet to mothers was belief in the transcendent power of their love, its legacy to fathers was affirmation of the transformative power of paternity itself—the belief that fatherhood made men better than they otherwise would be. This conceptualization of fatherhood's moral value was a mixed blessing. On the one hand, it encouraged men to maintain their involvement in family life, even as work commitments drew them away from home and their domestic dominance receded in the face of ever-present mothers. But at the same time, this viewpoint downgraded specifically paternal responsibility, highlighting as it did what fatherhood could do for men, rather than what fathers should do for their children.

Just as the entry of mothers into the paid labor force has been the central catalyst of family life in recent decades, the increasing subjection of fathers to the demands and discipline of an emergent market economy was the material basis of the nineteenth century's parenting revolution. As the century unfolded, the good father came to be seen as a successful economic competitor, someone who worked hard to provide his children with a financially secure home. The "good provider" relied on a nurturing wife to meet his children's daily needs for emotional and physical care and justified his supportive role at home by the need to earn a living. As important as breadwinning became, however, it never accurately captured the full range of fathering behavior. Mounting pressure to provide identified fathers ever more closely with the scramble for success, but one of the great ironies of nineteenth-century family life is that fatherhood was considered a redemptive antidote to the grasping competitiveness required to get ahead. From its inception, modern fatherhood was more than earning a paycheck; it was the vehicle through which men gained access to the idealized domestic circle constituted by women and children.

Although mothers provided children with most of their physical and emotional care, middle-class family men engaged actively in domestic life as their work commitments permitted. They used mealtimes, fireside gatherings in the evening, and, especially, their presence on Sundays to exercise paternal authority and companionship. The family man's main intent in all this was not to manage motherhood but rather to reinforce maternal child rearing whenever necessary, especially during times of family crisis. This periodic, but ongoing and intense, involvement in family life commenced even before men became parents. Many men participated in preparations for childbirth and then helped to bring their children into the world by assisting in the birthing chamber. Active engagement persisted when children were small and continued as they grew older. Indeed, periodic domesticity was such a fixture of men's experience that it became a principle sign of middle-class respectability. Adherence to the precepts of a father's care, especially the willingness to work hard for the sake of a child's education and life chances, became a way that middle-class urban fathers distinguished themselves from bachelors, on the one hand, and working-class fathers, on the other—men who supposedly could not appreciate the sentimental value of children.

Modern fatherhood emerged, in short, as part of the nineteenth-century consolidation of middle-class identity. If this resulted at times in an insufferable sense of moral superiority, we need not be too harsh in our judgment. For while encouraging complacency, the Victorian idealization of fatherhood also brought about a great deal of positive domestic engagement, a development amply documented in the letters, diaries, and reminiscences that nineteenth-century family members have left behind.

I do not mean to suggest that nineteenth-century fathers were paragons of parenthood. Some men have always lacked the playfulness, empathy, and capacity for the loving, consistent discipline needed to raise children well. Those attributes, however, were held out as the ideal toward which a middle-class father's parenting should tend, and I would be less than candid if I did not confess to the reader that I found more fathers to admire than to scorn as I researched and wrote this book.[2]

Even so, a nagging reservation persists. For, if the notion that fatherhood was good for men encouraged positive engagement in family life, it also promoted a therapeutic view of fathering which limited the scope of paternal responsibility. This therapeutic view of fatherhood—what settled domesticity could do for men, rather than what fathers should do for their children—increasingly turned home life into something to be consumed by fathers, a reward for all the hard work they performed elsewhere. The romantic revaluation of fatherhood did nothing to contest traditional presumptions of patriarchal privilege. If fathers no longer presided over their households to the extent that they had in the past, they nonetheless retained a sense of entitlement that colored their ties to children young and old. Men's capacity to enjoy the companionship of young children, for instance, expanded enormously in the nineteenth century. Playful fathers were key to the new premium that nineteenth-century families placed on togetherness. Even so, small children could seem at times like little more than toys for masculine amusement. More to the point, fathers who acted primarily as playmates were, by definition, less responsible for a young child's moral and intellectual upbringing.

A similar dynamic influenced the tie to growing daughters and sons. The father-daughter bond was appreciably warmer than the relations of fathers and sons. The affection that many doting fathers felt for their daughters rested on a foundation of genuine romantic feeling to be sure, but it also reflected the belief that a cultivated daughter was a bright token of a father's success. The affection that an older daughter owed her father was matched by the deference expected of a growing son. Fathers took great pains to guide a son into a useful occupation. They worried about his moral welfare and material prospects in a mobile and rapidly changing society, so much so that anxiety on this score became another hallmark of modern fatherhood. Nonetheless, the anxious father commanded acquiescence. He imposed on sons implicit obedience as a requirement to live in his household, a demand that tended to choke off affection as boys became men.

If the foregoing is true—if family men inhabited the nineteenth century from beginning to end—then fatherhood's salience to manhood should have been apparent during the Civil War, and in fact it was. More than any other event in the last century, the Civil War dramatized the importance both of fathers to their families and of domesticity to fathers. Analogies between the domestic circle and the Union pervaded contemporary political discourse. Lincoln's "house divided" speech in 1858, to cite only the most famous example, described the Union as a family writ large and secession as filial betrayal of the Founding Fathers.[3] Such familial metaphors transcended rhetoric, reflecting the abiding desire of Northerners to extend the "natural affections" of the home circle to the public realm. Conversely, this political discourse garbed parenting with public purpose, since the fate of the republic depended on raising virtuous children.

Familial values also infused the reasons that Northern soldiers fought. Because companies and regiments were raised locally, soldiers fought the war as representatives of their families and their communities. Men experienced military service not as detached individuals or abstract patriots, but rather in terms of their concrete familial roles—that is, as fathers, sons, husbands, and brothers.[4] Servicemen regularly claimed in their letters home that it was only through leaving their families and suffering through army life and the violence of war that they learned domesticity's true value. Separation and the stress of combat heightened men's predisposition to see families as sources of emotional satisfaction. Men also worried that military service would cripple family feeling. "Old soldiers tell me that it always spoils men to go to war," the father of a young daughter wrote to his wife. "They say it makes them cross, ugly to their wives & children & 9 cases out of ten if they are in service 6 months they will go home the wickedest kind of men."[5] The familial sacrifice that military service demanded was trumpeted as well in popular culture, notably in the songs of the Civil War era. Lyrics immortalized, sometimes mawkishly, the ultimate sacrifice of family men. One song representative of the genre recounted the death of a Union volunteer, a devoted husband who fell on the battlefield clutching a photograph of his three children to his breast. In other songs, a soldier's last thoughts turned to loved ones at home.[6]

Since joining the army was an extension of a man's duty to protect his family, Civil War service reinforced traditional notions of paternal responsibility. Not surprisingly, married officers with children tended to think of their command responsibilities in paternal terms. James A. Garfield, who had worked as an educator before the war and later became president, was one such Union officer. In child-rearing advice he sent home to his wife, Garfield likened his command to parenting. Writing of his daughter, he asked: "Have you established such a relation between yourself and her as will lay the basis of both strong control and equally strong affection?" These were his goals as a commander, although, he confessed, "Your task with her is harder than mine with the brigade."[7]

Garfield's preference to act like a father toward his men reflected contemporary ideals of paternal authority. The war's greatest heroes embodied fatherly virtues. Lincoln, a devoted parent himself, became, for many Northerners, the great father figure of the war—"father Abraham," the embodiment of mild paternal authority. Similarly, as historian Phillip Shaw Paludan has observed, Grant's public image was unabashedly that of a family man. Photographs of Grant with his wife, Julia, and their children circulated throughout the North, as did lithographs of the general and his daughter Nellie. If such images softened the edges of a hard-drinking soldier consumed with public purpose, they reflected as well the reality of a loving husband and father. Like other officers, Grant brought his family to camp when he was not campaigning. Throughout his life, he evinced, in the words of one recent biographer, "deep love for and confidence in his children," doting on them when they were small and worrying about their education as they grew up, just as nineteenth-century fathers were supposed to do.[8]

The paternal imagery surrounding Lincoln and his generals echoed in the images of fatherhood inscribed in the letters of ordinary soldiers.[9] Men who fought to maintain a way of life for loved ones at home spoke time and again of their desire to resume fatherly care when the fighting ended. "Oh how I long to be at home once more," a soldier from Michigan confided to his wife in June of 1863. "I feel anxious about Ed [young son] and wish to be with him all the time." Six months earlier he had written: "Should I ever reach home again I feel thankful to think I am spared on Edwin's account as I know he will grow up a bad boy unless some father guides him."[10]

It troubled soldier fathers that they were no longer able to lend parenting support. "The extra duty of caring for May [daughter] will add much to your labors which cannot be shared by me so long as [I] am absent," a company surgeon named George Trowbridge told his wife, Lebbie. "I have added to your cares without rendering aid and comfort." Like other fathers' correspondence, Trowbridge's letters at times brimmed with parenting advice. He provided counsel on: diet ("should think it advisable to let her have her milk the best diet known for children"), dress ("keep Pet in good shoes while cold damp weather continues"), medical care ("consult medical works on all points you are in doubt"), and discipline ("Let love ever be prominent in the correction: that she may see 'tis from a sense of duty that you correct & that her disobedience causes the punishment—when you say no let her understand it to be such"). Men like Trowbridge, in short, wished to remain fathers in fact as well as in name during their years of military service.[11]

After the guns fell silent, what lasting impact did the Civil War have on Northern fatherhood? The war's influence on American society is fiercely contested. Important new scholarship interprets the conflict as a socially conservative, rather than transforming, event.[12] The history of fatherhood lends credence to this argument for the essential continuity of nineteenth-century experience. Nothing in the conduct of the war and little in its reflection in postwar popular memory challenged traditional understandings of the father's role.

By highlighting the importance of men's familial obligations, the Civil War demonstrated the vitality of nineteenth-century fatherhood under extraordinary circumstances. Ultimately, a war that cast the shadow of death over 250 thousand American homes underscored the importance of domestic relations by reminding combatants and civilians alike that life was precious and that families could be destroyed.

After a decade of hibernation in the 1870s, popular interest in the war's impact revived in the 1880s and 1890s. As the sons of 1861 became the fathers of the Gilded Age, they tended to look back at the war as a successful mission to preserve intact their inherited republican social order.[13] As memories faded, men who had suffered through and survived the war tended to glorify their trials as a heroic rite of passage, telling their sons that military experience was crucial to manhood.[14] In this respect, as the nineteenth century drew to a close, the war contributed to changes in the definition of masculinity that emphasized passion and action over self-control and family obligation.

If the Civil War, or more precisely its refracted memory, helped to pave the way for a new passionate masculinity, however, it had a countervailing impact on men's lives as well. Expansion of the Civil War pension system kept men's familial obligations in the forefront of political debate in the post-bellum years. Throughout the post–Civil War period, lawmakers argued that pensions encouraged patriotism and willingness to volunteer in wartime by assuring that a father's responsibility to care for his family would be met, come what may.[15] This sense of a father's necessary family involvement, of the importance of "a father's care," was also the inheritance of a war that highlighted images of paternal authority. This apparent contradiction should come as no surprise, reflecting as it did the paradoxical faces of nineteenth-century fatherhood.

Notes

Introduction: A Father's Care

1. Louisa Hughes Diary transcript, March 29, 1864, Louisa Walter (Bishop) Hughes Papers, Schlesinger Library, Radcliffe College.

2. Nathan M. Thomas, *An Account of His Life Written by Himself* (Cassapolis, Mich., 1925), 22, Michigan Historical Collection, Bentley Historical Library, University of Michigan.

3. This argument, which emphasizes the interdependence of the sexes, accords with recent scholarship that questions the paradigm of "separate spheres" as a model for nineteenth-century gender relations. For more than two decades now, historians of women and the family have described the nineteenth century as a period of increasing differentiation in the social roles of women and men, which established separate male and female spheres. The classic expression of this view is Nancy F. Cott, *The Bonds of Womanhood: "Women's Sphere" in New England, 1780–1835* (New Haven, Conn., 1977). More recent scholarship recognizes that the family operated as a meeting ground of divergent roles within the nineteenth-century gender system. In this view, men's and women's experiences overlapped so substantially that one cannot speak of separate male and female spheres. For an excellent example of this revisionist approach, see Nancy Grey Osterud, *Bonds of Community: The Lives of Farm Women in Nineteenth-Century New York* (Ithaca, N.Y., 1991). Cott herself offers a cogent reassessment of the historiography in her essay "On Men's History and Women's History," in *Meanings for Manhood: Constructions of Masculinity in Victorian America*, ed. Mark C. Carnes and Clyde Griffen (Chicago, 1990).

4. The universe of subjects embodied in the source material for this book is described in the Note on Method and Sources, but a word about the use of personal documents as primary sources is warranted here. Letters and, especially, memoirs tend to be biased in favor of more positive emotions. Members of families in which relations are strained or broken are less likely to correspond than those in which relations are healthy and intact. Reminiscences are particularly prone to the vagaries of memory and the force of nostalgia, which color and frequently distort recollection. This is an issue for all scholars who use such material, and I was careful to bear this in mind when interpreting these sources.

5. For the argument that the primacy of the father began to erode after the mid-seventeenth century, see Gerald F. Moran and Maris A. Vinovskis, *Religion, Family, and the Life Course: Explorations in the Social History of Early America* (Ann Arbor, Mich., 1992). The American Revolution's critique of patriarchal family relations is brilliantly described in Jay Fliegelman, *Prodigals and Pilgrims: The American Revolution against Patriarchal Authority, 1750–1800* (Cambridge, 1982).

6. A growing body of scholarship attributes the changing nature of antebellum society, especially changes in social consciousness, to the impact of commercialization. Historians are divided, however, on how to characterize the changes wrought by this market revolution. Cf. Charles Sellers, *The Market Revolution: Jacksonian America, 1815–1846* (New York, 1991), who describes a fearful age in which dangerous forces were unleashed in American society, and Daniel Feller, *The Jacksonian Promise: America, 1815–1840* (Baltimore, 1995), who portrays an era of optimism. The two views are not mutually exclusive, of course, since hopefulness and anxiety frequently exist side by side. For a valuable historiographic discussion, see Sean Wilentz, "Society, Politics, and the Market Revolution, 1815–1848," in *The New American History*, ed. Eric Foner (Philadelphia, 1990), 51–72.

7. On the emergence of "modern" family values, see, e.g., Carl N. Degler, *At Odds: Women and the Family in America from the Revolution to the Present* (New York, 1980); Cott, *The Bonds of Womanhood*; and Jan Lewis, *The Pursuit of Happiness: Family and Values in Jefferson's Virginia* (New York, 1983). Contrasting views of whether working-class families differed from middle-class families are Daniel J. Walkowitz, "Working-Class Women in the Gilded Age: Factory, Family, and Community Life among Cohoes, New York, Cotton Workers," *Journal of Social History* 5 (1972): 464–90, and Susan E. Hirsch, *Roots of the American Working Class: The Industrialization of Crafts in Newark, 1800–1860* (Philadelphia, 1978).

8. Mary P. Ryan, *Cradle of the Middle Class: The Family in Oneida County, New York, 1790–1865* (Cambridge, 1981); Steven Mintz, *A Prison of Expectations: The Family in Victorian Culture* (New York, 1983); and Richard Sennett, *Families against the City: Middle-Class Homes of Industrial Chicago, 1872–1890* (Cambridge, Mass., 1970). In part, the confusion stems from the paucity of sources consulted to arrive at conclusions about fatherhood specifically. Sennett's otherwise elegant study relies on a handful of reminiscences to make the case for a diminished paternal role. Mintz bases his conclusions on an examination of the family lives of just five literary figures. Ryan consults a wide variety of sources, but not in a focused attempt to describe what fathers did.

9. On the emergence of sentimental views of children, see Viviana Zelizer, *Pricing the Priceless Child: The Changing Social Value of Children* (New York,

1987). On the tension between middle-class and working-class family norms, see Tamara K. Hareven, "The History of the Family and the Complexity of Social Change," *American Historical Review* 96 (1991): 95–124.

10. The discussion of slavery in this paragraph and the next is based on Peter Kolchin, *American Slavery, 1619–1877* (New York, 1993), and Brenda Stevenson, *Life in Black and White: Family and Community in the Slave South* (New York, 1996). See also Eugene Genovese, *Roll, Jordan, Roll: The World the Slaves Made* (New York, 1974); Herbert G. Gutman, *The Black Family in Slavery and Freedom, 1750–1925* (New York, 1977); and Lawrence W. Levine, *Black Culture and Black Consciousness: Afro-American Folk Thought from Slavery to Freedom* (New York, 1977).

11. Robert L. Griswold, *Fatherhood in America: A History* (New York, 1993), 52–56.

12. The territory northwest of the Ohio River was established by Congress in 1787 and was subsequently divided into five states (Ohio, Indiana, Michigan, Illinois, and Wisconsin) and part of a sixth (Minnesota east of the Mississippi River). For a discussion of the area's nineteenth-century settlement, see Thomas J. Schlereth, "The New England Presence on the Midwest Landscape," *The Old Northwest: A Journal of Regional Life and Letters* 9 (Summer 1983): 125–42.

13. Scholarship on this point is by no means conclusive. For instance, Bertram Wyatt-Brown, *Southern Honor: Ethics and Behavior in the Old South* (New York, 1982), argues that child rearing in Southern white families differed substantially from Northern patterns in the antebellum years. Whereas Northern child rearing relied on mother-run childcare and had as its major goal building conscience, primarily through the withdrawal of affection, the Southern white method was father-centered, oriented toward the inculcation of family pride, and used as its major technique honor and shame. In Southern families, the result was an "attitude of bemused indulgence, pride in aggressiveness, and distracted child care" that contrasted sharply with Northern child rearing. See esp. 117–48, quotation at 143.

On the distribution of power between mothers and fathers in planter families, compare Steven M. Stowe, *Intimacy and Power in the Old South: Ritual in the Lives of the Planters* (Baltimore, 1987); Orville Vernon Burton, *In My Father's House Are Many Mansions: Family and Community in Edgefield, South Carolina* (Chapel Hill, N.C., 1985), both of whom portray the seaboard family as patriarchal, with Jane Turner Censer, *North Carolina Planters and Their Children, 1800–1860* (Baton Rouge, La., 1984), who portrays planter families as egalitarian and bourgeois. Daniel Blake Smith, *Inside the Great House: Planter Family Life in Eighteenth-Century Chesapeake Society* (Ithaca, N.Y., 1980), and Jan Lewis, *The*

Pursuit of Happiness: Family and Values in Jefferson's Virginia (Cambridge, 1983), argue that planters became more affectionate with wives and children than they had been in the mid-eighteenth century. For a historiographic summary and the argument that the worst aspects of the patriarchal family were accentuated when seaboard families moved west, see Joan E. Cashin, *A Family Venture: Men and Women on the Southern Frontier* (Baltimore, 1994).

Chapter 1: Fatherhood in Colonial New England and the Early Republic

1. The notion that colonial fathers were vastly more important to the moral and intellectual development of their children than either their nineteenth-century counterparts or fathers today dominates nascent fatherhood historiography. This narrative of "decline"—of the displacement of fathers by mothers as primary parents—originated with John Demos, "The Changing Faces of Fatherhood: A New Exploration in American Family History," in *Father and Child: Developmental and Clinical Perspectives*, ed. Stanley H. Cath, Alan R. Gurwitt, and John Munder Ross (Boston, 1982), 425–45. (This essay is reprinted in Demos, *Past, Present, and Personal: The Family and the Life Course in American History* [New York, 1986], 41–67.) See also E. Anthony Rotundo, "American Fatherhood: A Historical Perspective," *American Behavioral Scientist* 29 (1985): 7–25, and Maris A. Vinovskis, *An "Epidemic" of Adolescent Pregnancy? Some Historical and Policy Considerations* (New York, 1988), chap. 6. For a discussion of twentieth-century developments, see Robert L. Griswold, *Fatherhood in America: A History* (New York, 1993).

2. These points about Protestant beliefs and fatherhood are made in Mary Beth Norton, "The Evolution of White Women's Experience in Early America," *American Historical Review* 89 (June 1984): 606–9.

3. Edmund S. Morgan, *The Puritan Family: Religion and Domestic Relations in Seventeenth-Century New England* (New York, 1966).

4. Horace Mann did more than anyone else to establish the economic usefulness of education. See Maris A. Vinovskis, *Education, Society, and Economic Opportunity* (New Haven, Conn., 1995), chap. 5.

5. For an excellent overview of changing attitudes toward women and maternal care, see Ruth H. Bloch, "American Feminine Ideals in Transition: The Rise of the Moral Mother, 1785–1815," *Feminist Studies* 4 (1978): 101–26.

6. Kenneth Lockridge, *Literacy in Colonial New England: An Enquiry into the Social Context of Literacy in the Early Modern West* (New York, 1974), suggests that the literacy rate for women increased during the colonial period from about 30 percent in the early seventeenth century to at least 60 percent at the end of

the eighteenth century. More recent scholarship suggests that female literacy in New England was higher than Lockridge's estimate of 60 percent by 1800. See, e.g., Gloria L. Main, "An Inquiry into When and Why Women Learned to Write in Colonial New England," *Journal of Social History* 24 (1991): 579–89. Different rates emerge when reading and writing are considered separately.

7. *Massachusetts Laws of 1648*, 11, quoted in Morgan, *The Puritan Family*, 88.

8. Gerald F. Moran and Maris A. Vinovskis, "The Great Care of Godly Parents: Early Childhood in Puritan New England," in *History and Research in Child Development*, ed. Alice B. Smuts and John W. Hagen, Monographs of the Society for Research in Child Development, ser., no. 50, 24–37; David Stannard, *The Puritan Way of Death: A Study in Religion, Culture, and Social Change* (New York, 1977).

9. Rotundo, "American Fatherhood"; Laurel Thatcher Ulrich, *Good Wives: Image and Reality in the Lives of Women in Northern New England, 1650–1750* (New York, 1982), 154–56.

The emotional tenor of patriarchal rule is controversial. Lawrence Stone, *The Family, Sex, and Marriage in England, 1500–1800* (New York, 1977), and Philippe Aries, *Centuries of Childhood: A Social History of Family Life* (New York, 1962), are founding texts for the harsh portrait of patriarchal rule. Revisionist scholars, including Linda Pollock, *Forgotten Children: Parent-Child Relations from 1500 to 1900* (Cambridge, 1983) and Steven Ozment, *When Fathers Ruled: Family Life in Reformation Europe* (Cambridge, Mass., 1983), refute the portrait of harsh treatment of women and children in the family. This revisionist scholarship suggests that family life in the past was characterized by unexpectedly high degrees of mutuality and companionship. Recently, Philip Greven, *Spare the Child: The Religious Roots of Punishment and the Psychological Impact of Physical Abuse* (New York, 1991), suggested that harsh, physically abusive child rearing has been an enduring feature of American family life. Greven, however, bases his conclusions on a handful of extreme cases from evangelical Protestant households.

10. Demos, "Changing Faces of Fatherhood," 429; Peter Laslett, *The World We Have Lost—Further Explored* (London, 1983), 119–20.

11. *Massachusetts Laws of 1648*, 11, quoted in Morgan, *The Puritan Family*, 66.

12. Maris A. Vinovskis, "Family and Schooling in Colonial and Nineteenth-Century America," *Journal of Family History* 12 (1987): 19–37, and Carl F. Kaestle, *Pillars of the Republic: Common Schools and American Society, 1780–1860* (New York, 1983).

13. On mutual decision making, see John Demos, *A Little Commonwealth: Family Life in Plymouth Colony* (New York, 1970), 88. For an overview of apprenticeship, see W. J. Rorabaugh, *The Craft Apprentice: From Franklin to the Machine Age in America* (New York, 1986).

14. Demos, *A Little Commonwealth*, 120; Morgan, *The Puritan Family*, 73–76.

15. Mary Ann Mason, *From Father's Property to Children's Rights: The History of Child Custody in the United States* (New York, 1994), 6–13.

16. Morgan, *The Puritan Family*, 123, 135, 174, 182.

17. Gerald F. Moran, "Religious Renewal, Puritan Tribalism, and the Family in Seventeenth-Century Milford, Connecticut," *William and Mary Quarterly*, 3d ser., 36 (1979), 236–54; Moran, "'Sisters' in Christ: Women and the Church in Seventeenth-Century New England," in *Women in American Religion*, ed. Janet Wilson James (Philadelphia, 1980), 47–65; and Gerald F. Moran and Maris A. Vinovskis, "The Puritan Family and Religion: A Critical Reappraisal," *William and Mary Quarterly*, 3d ser., 39 (1982): 29–63.

18. Daniel Scott Smith, "The Demographic History of Colonial New England," *Journal of Economic History* 1 (1972): 165–83; and Daniel Scott Smith and Michael S. Hindus, "Premarital Pregnancy in America 1640–1971: An Overview and Interpretation," *Journal of Interdisciplinary History* 5 (1975): 537–70.

19. Jay Fliegelman, *Prodigals and Pilgrims: The American Revolution against Patriarchal Authority, 1750–1800* (Cambridge, 1982).

20. Linda K. Kerber, *Women of the Republic: Intellect and Ideology in Revolutionary America* (Chapel Hill, N.C., 1980); Mary Beth Norton, *Liberty's Daughters: The Revolutionary Experience of American Women, 1750–1800* (Boston, 1980); Ruth H. Bloch, "American Feminine Ideals in Transition: The Rise of the Moral Mother, 1785–1815," *Feminist Studies* 4 (1978), 101–26; and Jan Lewis, "The Republican Wife: Virtue and Seduction in the Early Republic," *William and Mary Quarterly*, 3d ser., 44 (1987): 689–721.

21. Bernard Wishy, *The Child and the Republic: The Dawn of Modern American Child Nurture* (Philadelphia, 1968), and Robert Sunley, "Early Nineteenth-Century American Literature on Child Rearing," in *Childhood in Contemporary Cultures*, ed. Margaret Mead and Martha Wolfenstein (Chicago, 1955), 150–67.

22. This demographic identification of fatherhood and male adulthood is a far cry from the situation today, when a variety of trends—including the rising average age at which men and women marry, declining birthrates among married couples, and high rates of divorce and out-of-wedlock births—mean that modern men spend less time than their nineteenth-century counterparts in living arrangements in which they occupy the role of father. See Griswold, *Fatherhood in America*, 229–30.

23. Maris A. Vinovskis, *Fertility in Massachusetts from the Revolution to the Civil War* (New York, 1981), 43–49, 147, and Peter R. Uhlenberg, "A Study of Cohort Life Cycles: Cohorts of Native-Born Massachusetts Women, 1830–1920," *Population Studies* 23 (1969): 407–20.

24. John Demos, "Families in Colonial Bristol, Rhode Island: An Exercise

in Historical Demography," *William and Mary Quarterly*, 3d ser., 25 (1968): 40–57.

25. On the expansion and contraction of households, see Demos, *A Little Commonwealth*, 64–69; on divorce patterns, see Andrew J. Cherlin, *Marriage, Divorce, Remarriage* (Cambridge, Mass., 1981), 21–31.

26. Daniel Scott Smith, "Family Limitation, Sexual Control, and Domestic Feminism in Victorian America," *Feminist Studies* 1 (1973): 44.

27. Steven Ruggles, "The Transformation of American Family Structure," *American Historical Review* 99 (1994): 103–28.

28. For an overview of these and other trends, see Tamara K. Hareven and Maris A. Vinovskis, eds., *Family and Population in Nineteenth-Century America* (Princeton, 1978). Ethnic origins also powerfully influenced fertility. For the argument that second-generation ethnic women had fewer children than either their immigrant parents *or* native-born women because they tended to delay marriage in order to remain home with their parents, see Miriam King and Steven Ruggles, "American Immigration, Fertility, and Race Suicide at the Turn of the Century," *Journal of Interdisciplinary History* 20 (1990): 347–69.

29. Daniel Scott Smith, "Family Limitation, Sexual Control, and Domestic Feminism in Victorian America," *Feminist Studies* 1 (1973): 40–57, and Smith, "'Early' Fertility Decline in America: A Problem in Family History," *Journal of Family History* 12 (1987): 73–84, which revises the earlier essay to stress mutual decision making. On anxieties that men and women shared about the dangers of childbirth, see Chapter 4 of the present study.

30. Richard A. Easterlin, "Population Change and Farm Settlement in the Northern United States: Some Preliminary Research Results," *Journal of American History* 63 (1976): 600–614, and Richard A. Easterlin, George Alter, and Gretchen A. Condran, "Farms and Farm Families in Old and New Areas: The Northern States in 1860," in *Family and Population in Nineteenth Century America*, ed. Tamara K. Haraven and Maris A. Vinovskis (Princeton, 1978), 22–84. See also William A. Sundstrom and Paul A. David, "Old-Age Security Motives, Labor Markets, and Farm Family Fertility in Antebellum America," *Explorations in Economic History* 25 (1988): 164–97. The evidence presented in Chapter 6 of this study offers clear testimony that both sorts of economic concerns, provision for children and old-age security, shaped father relations and family strategies.

31. Maris A. Vinovskis, "Angel Heads and Weeping Willows: Death in Early America," in *Studies in American Historical Demography*, ed. Maris A. Vinovskis (New York, 1979), 181–210; Samuel H. Preston and Michael R. Haines, *Fatal Years: Child Mortality in Late Nineteenth-Century America* (Princeton, 1991), esp. chap. 4.

32. Cf. Pollock, *Forgotten Children*; Stone, *Family, Sex, and Marriage*; and

Edward Shorter, *The Making of the Modern Family* (New York, 1977). Pollock notes that scholars such as Shorter and Stone, who see child mortality as dampening parental affection, posit a substantial improvement in parent-child relations in the eighteenth century, *before* any improvement occurred in child mortality rates.

Chapter 2: "Their Own Proper Task"

1. Laurel Thatcher Ulrich, *Good Wives: Image and Reality in the Lives of Women in Northern New England, 1650–1750* (New York, 1982), notes that the idealization and magnification of motherhood were clearly visible before 1750.

2. On the popularity of parent advice books in the 1840s, see Anne L. Kuhn, *The Mother's Role in Childhood Education: New England Concepts, 1830–1860* (New Haven, Conn., 1947), 41.

3. Within the large body of scholarship on nineteenth-century domesticity, two especially valuable studies of the prescriptive literature are Kuhn, *The Mother's Role in Childhood Education*, and Mary P. Ryan, *The Empire of the Mother: American Writing about Domesticity, 1830–1860* (New York, 1982).

4. See, e.g., Joe L. Dubbert, *A Man's Place: Masculinity in Transition* (Englewood Cliffs, N.J., 1979), 20. In this pioneering study, Dubbert asserts that the topic of fatherhood was missing from nineteenth-century journals and magazines.

5. What I identify as nineteenth-century parentalism was summed up in frequent admonitions to mothers and fathers to display "parental solicitude," a phrase no less pervasive than "mother's love" in much family advice.

6. I use the terms *Christian father* and *Christian fatherhood* throughout because they reflect contemporary usage. The ideal described is a decidedly Protestant invention and cannot be assumed to reflect the thinking in nineteenth-century Catholic homes.

7. E. Anthony Rotundo, *American Manhood: Transformations in Masculinity from the Revolution to the Modern Era* (New York, 1993), 222–46.

8. Margaret Marsh, *Suburban Lives* (New Brunswick, N.J., 1990). Marsh suggests that the ideal of "masculine domesticity" was a distinctive feature of turn-of-the-twentieth-century prescription and behavior. However, late-century norms built upon domestic ideals for men that were clearly visible much earlier.

9. See, e.g., David D. Gilmore, *Manhood in the Making: Cultural Concepts of Masculinity* (New Haven, Conn., 1990).

10. For more than two decades, historians have been nothing if not skeptical of the use of prescriptive literature as primary sources. I do not claim that the normative pronouncements discussed in this chapter reflected actual behavior. Advice literature, however, did find a receptive audience in thousands of Amer-

ican homes, and it would be foolish to discount its significance. The cultural values embodied in this literature served both as a standard to which many men and women held themselves accountable and as a yardstick by which they measured deviance. For a useful but overly cautious perspective on the use of advice literature by historians, see Jay Mechling, "Advice to Historians on Advice to Mothers," *Journal of Social History* 9 (1975): 44–63.

11. On the first wave of British popular writing, see Kirk Jeffrey Jr., "Family History: The Middle-Class American Family in the Urban Context, 1830–1870" (Ph.D. diss., Stanford University, 1972), chap. 1. For a good overview of subsequent developments sketched in the next three paragraphs, see Ryan, *Empire of the Mother*, 1–43.

12. On the distinction between Beecher's advice and that of earlier advisers, see Kathryn Kish Sklar, *Catharine Beecher: A Study in American Domesticity* (New Haven, Conn., 1973), 156.

13. W. J. Rorabaugh, *The Craft Apprentice: From Franklin to the Machine Age in America* (New York, 1986), 158–59.

14. Laura McCall, "Gender in Fiction: The Creations of Literary Men and Women," paper delivered at Social Science History Association annual meeting, November 2, 1991.

15. Joseph F. Kett, *Rites of Passage: Adolescence in America, 1790 to the Present* (New York, 1977), 114–16.

16. Michael Gordon, "The Ideal Husband as Depicted in the Nineteenth-Century Marriage Manual," in *The American Man*, ed. Elizabeth H. Pleck and Joseph H. Pleck (Englewood Cliffs, N.J., 1980), 145–57.

17. Theodore Dwight Jr., *The Father's Book; or Suggestions for the government and instruction of young children, on principles appropriate to a Christian country* (1834; Springfield, Mass., 1835), vii.

18. Rev. John S. C. Abbott, "Paternal Neglect," in *The Parent's Magazine and Young People's Friend* (Concord, N.H.) March 1842, 147–48.

19. Rev. A. B. Muzzey, *The Fireside: An Aid to Parents* (Boston, 1854), vi. The volume went through three editions between 1854 and 1858.

20. S. R. Hall, *Practical Lectures on Parental Responsibility, and the Religious Education of Children* (Boston, 1833), 16–17.

21. Peter Gabriel Filene, *Him/Her/Self: Sex Roles in Modern America* (New York, 1975; reprint ed., Baltimore, 1986), 81.

22. On the ubiquity of the temperance theme in domestic advice, see Kuhn, *The Mother's Role in Childhood Education*, 67. For a discussion of T. S. Arthur's articles in *Godey's Lady's Book*, see Marsh, *Suburban Lives*, 28.

23. Anonymous, "The Father," in *The Parent's Magazine and Young People's Friend* (Concord, N.H.) April 1842, 174–75.

24. William A. Alcott, *The Young Husband, or Duties of Man in the Marriage*

Relation (Boston, 1840), 98–102, 117–32. Jan Lewis, "Mother's Love: The Construction of an Emotion in Nineteenth-Century America," in *Social History and Issues in Human Consciousness*, ed. Andrew E. Barnes and Peter N. Stearns (New York, 1989), 209–29. Cf. Kuhn, *The Mother's Role in Childhood Education*, 74–75.

25. Muzzey, *The Fireside*, 314–17.

26. Dwight, *The Father's Book*, 52–65. For other examples, see Rev. John S.C. Abbott, *The Mother at Home; or, The Principles of Maternal Duty Familiarly Illustrated* (New York, 1833), esp. 184–91, 211–12; Rev. James Bean, *The Christian Minister's Affectionate Advice to a Married Couple* (New York, 1832), 22–28; and Hall, *Practical Lectures on Parental Responsibility*, 141–42.

27. Alcott, *The Young Husband*, 137–38.

28. For a late-century example of such advice, see H. Clay Trumbull, *Hints on Child Training* (Philadelphia, 1891), 109–14.

29. John R. Gillis, *A World of Their Own Making: Myth, Ritual, and the Quest for Family Values* (Cambridge, Mass., 1996), 90–92.

30. Dwight, *The Father's Book*, 34; William P. Dewees, *A Treatise on the Physical and Medical Treatment of Children* (London, 1826), xiii–xiv. For similar advice, see William A. Alcott, *The Young Mother, or Management of Children in Regard to Health* (1836; Boston, 1838), 314–15.

31. Lydia H. Sigourney, *Letters to Mothers* (Hartford, Conn., 1838), 101. This was also the view of such domestic advisers as Catharine Beecher and Sarah J. Hale.

32. For a statement of this viewpoint, see Horace Mann, *Lectures on Education* (Boston, 1855; reprint ed., New York, 1969), 73–74.

33. For examples, see Muzzey, *The Fireside*, 12–13, 61–62; William A. Alcott, M.D., *The Physiology of Marriage* (1855; Boston, 1859), 111; Alcott, *The Young Mother*, 316–17.

34. Dwight, *The Father's Book*, 108–18.

35. See, e.g., Muzzey, *The Fireside*, 94.

36. Ulrich, *Good Wives*, 154.

37. Horace Bushnell, *Christian Nurture* (Edinburgh, 1861; reprint ed., New Haven, Conn., 1967), 292–93. Cf. Bushnell, *Views of Christian Nurture* (Hartford, Conn., 1847). See also Muzzey, *The Fireside*, 158, and Dwight, *The Father's Book*, 97.

38. Muzzey, *The Fireside*, 153–54.

39. Bushnell, *Views of Christian Nurture*, 42–43; Timothy Titcomb [Josiah Gilbert Holland], *Titcomb's Letters to Young People Single and Married* (1858; New York, 1861), 200; Muzzey, *The Fireside*, 273. See also Amariah Brigham, *Remarks on the Influence of Mental Cultivation and Mental Excitement upon Health* (Boston, 1833; reprint ed., Delmar, N.Y., 1973), 90–91.

40. Quoted in Sigourney, *Letters to Mothers*, 19, and Muzzey, *The Fireside*, 20.

41. Dwight, *The Father's Book*, 160.

42. Augustus Woodbury, *Plain Words to Young Men* (Concord, N.H., 1858), 43.

43. Compare, e.g., Edwin H. Chapin, *Duties of Young Men* (Boston, 1840), which is little concerned with fatherhood, to his *Duties of Young Women* (1848; Boston, 1853), which has two chapters on motherhood.

44. William A. Alcott, *The Young Man's Guide* (Boston, 1849), 230.

45. Abbott, *The Mother at Home*, 13, 155–58.

46. Lydia Maria Child, *The Mother's Book* (1830; New York, 1844), 49–51.

47. Alexis de Tocqueville, *Democracy in America*, vol. 2, ed. Phillips Bradley (New York, 1945), 222–25.

48. Kuhn, *The Mother's Role in Childhood Education*, 3.

49. The following analysis is based on Gale Research Publications, comp., *Currier and Ives: A Catalogue Raisonne* (Detroit, Mich., 1983). A note of caution is in order: the analysis relies on the volume's index. The sample of 405 images of parents and children combines the prints listed under the index headings "Domestic Scenes" and "Sentimental Scenes of Children and Family." These headings capture most, though not all, of the prints depicting parents and children. However many prints are omitted, there is no reason to believe that the sample is unrepresentative. Both comical and sentimental prints are included. Too few of the prints were dated (119 of 405 coded) to establish any clear patterns over time. Currier and Ives's output was at its height in the four decades between 1850 and 1890.

50. The figure of 61 percent represents 190 prints of children by themselves, out of a total of 310 for which descriptions were available. There are an additional 95 prints listed by title under the appropriate index headings but not described in the *Catalogue*. Based on the titles, it would seem that 65 percent, or 62 of the prints cataloged without description, represent children by themselves.

51. This observation and the discussion in the next paragraph need to be interpreted with caution. Of the 190 images of children by themselves, 83 represented them in outdoor or rural settings, and only 48 in domestic interiors. However, there were an additional 59 prints for which the setting was not ascertainable based on the descriptions in the *Catalogue*. Of the images of children and their mothers: 33 were set in domestic interiors; 13, outdoors; 7, not ascertainable. Of the images of children and both parents: 10 were set in domestic interiors; 12, outdoors; 1, not ascertainable.

52. Muzzey, *The Fireside*, 8–10. For another statement of the double standard, see Eliza Ware Farrar, *The Young Lady's Friend* (1836; New York, 1838), 3.

53. John Todd, *Todd's Complete Works* (London, [1837?]), 4. For a sketch of Todd's life, see G. J. Barker-Benfield, *The Horrors of the Half-Known Life: Male*

Attitudes toward Women and Sexuality in Nineteenth-Century America (New York, 1976), 135–54.

54. Dewees, *A Treatise on the Physical and Medical Treatment of Children*, 46–48; Sigourney, *Letters to Mothers*, 21.

55. Alcott, *Young Man's Guide*, 270–71; for another example, see Sigourney, *Letters to Mothers*, 48.

56. T. S. Arthur, *Advice to Young Men on Their Duties and Conduct* (Boston, 1850), 103–4. For similar statements about paternal love, see Artemas Bowers Muzzey, *The Young Man's Friend* (Boston, 1836), 85–87, and Augustus Woodbury, *Plain Words to Young Men* (Concord, N.H., 1858), 32–33.

57. Ronald G. Walters, *American Reformers, 1815–1860*, rev. ed. (New York, 1997), 158–65. Phrenological works were quoted by such writers on child rearing as Heman Humphrey and Samuel Goodrich. The education reformer Horace Mann is said to have recommended that if a young man had but one dollar to his name he should spend it "in learning from a Phrenological examination what occupation he should pursue."

58. John D. Davies, *Phrenology Fad and Science: A Nineteenth-Century American Crusade* (New Haven, Conn., 1955), 172.

59. O. S. Fowler, *Creative and Sexual Science: or manhood, womanhood, and their mutual interrelations . . .* (Cincinnati, Ohio, 1875), 323.

60. Ibid., 139, 147. See also Sigourney, *Letters to Mothers*, 48–49, and William Alcott, *The Young Wife* (Boston, 1837; reprint ed., New York, 1972), 269.

61. O. S. Fowler, *Hereditary Descent: Its Laws and Facts Applied to Human Improvement* (New York, 1847), 16–17.

62. O. S. Fowler, *Love and Parentage, Applied to the Improvement of Offspring* (1844; New York, 1850), vi, 19–20, 57–71; see also Fowler, *Creative and Sexual Science*, 304–5. By placing parentage at the heart of marriage and sexuality, phrenological theory departed from a school of thought that considered the primary purpose of marriage to be the mutual perfection of the characters of husband and wife. In this former view, articulated by William Alcott, marriage was first and foremost a "school for the final education of the sexes," and procreation was its "second great design." See Alcott, *Physiology of Marriage*, 13–14.

63. Robert L. Griswold's study of nineteenth-century divorce records found that fatherhood ideals included love, kindness, and affection for children. But whereas mothers' love and affection were thought to be instinctual, these traits in fathers were learned. Griswold found no mention of fatherly instincts in the records, but several references to motherly instincts. See Griswold, *Family and Divorce in California, 1850–1890: Victorian Illusions and Everyday Realities* (Albany, N.Y., 1982), esp. 163–69.

64. O. S. Fowler, *Offspring, and Their Hereditary Endowment* (Boston, 1869),

119–30, and Fowler, *Creative and Sexual Science*, 383–87; see also, Fowler, *Love and Parentage*, 49–50. What Fowler termed the "sexuo-filial" attachment of parents to children of the opposite sex was rooted in the child's "amative," or sexual, nature, which could only find proper expression in the love of someone of the opposite sex. While the amative faculty did not generally become active until a child reached puberty, it did find expression in the love a child felt for his or her parents, and this aided in the child's development. Just as daughters needed to experience sexuo-filial love for their fathers in order to become complete women, so did sons need to experience the attraction for their mothers in order fully to develop their masculine nature.

65. On the importance of the body to late nineteenth-century thinking about manhood, see Rotundo, *American Manhood*, 222–27; for a brief overview of the campaign for social purity, see John C. Burnham, "The Progressive Revolution in America toward Sex," *Journal of American History* 59 (1973); 885–908.

66. For an excellent introduction to hereditarian science, see Charles E. Rosenberg, *No Other Gods: On Science and American Social Thought* (Baltimore, 1976), chap. 1.

67. George H. Napheys, M.D., *The Transmission of Life: Counsels on the Nature and Hygiene of the Masculine Function* (Philadelphia, 1871); Dan Newcomb, M.D., *When and How; or, A collection of the more recent facts and ideas upon raising healthy children* (Chicago, 1871), 70–72.

68. Fowler, *Creative and Sexual Science*, 129–30; Alcott, *Physiology of Marriage*, 143–77.

69. Barker-Benfield, *The Horrors of the Half-Known Life*.

70. Alonzo E. Newton, *The Better Way: An Appeal to Men in Behalf of Human Culture through a Wiser Parentage* (New York, 1875), 41.

71. Fowler, *Offspring and Their Hereditary Endowment*, 132.

72. Ibid., 254–55; Fowler, *Love and Parentage*, 76–77; S. R. Wells, *Wedlock; or, The Right Relation of the Sexes* (1869; New York, 1874), 129.

73. For examples, see Elizabeth Blackwell, *Counsel to Parents on the Moral Education of their Children* (New York, 1879), 101–2; Napheys, *The Transmission of Life*, 68–69. For an interesting discussion of an antecedent debate in Restoration England, see Mark E. Kann, *On the Man Question: Gender and Civic Virtue in America* (Philadelphia, 1991), esp. 65–81. The disparagement of bachelors as "unnatural" had an interesting analogue in the contemporary debate over abortion. Physicians branded women who avoided motherhood as "unnatural." See Carroll Smith-Rosenberg, "The Abortion Movement and the AMA, 1850–1880," in *Disorderly Conduct: Visions of Gender in Victorian America* (New York, 1985), 217–44.

74. For discussions of the recommended age for men to marry, see Dewees,

A Treatise on the Physical and Medical Treatment of Children, 2–4; Fowler, *Hereditary Descent*, 235–39; William Acton, *The Functions and Disorders of the Reproductive Organs in Childhood, Youth, Adult Age, and Advanced Life* (Philadelphia, 1865), 98–102; R. T. Trall, M.D., *Sexual Physiology* (New York, 1866), 283–304; Napheys, *The Transmission of Life*, 134–36; Blackwell, *Counsel to Parents* (1879), 23–29; and E. R. Shepherd, *True Manhood: A Manual for Young Men* (Chicago, 1889).

75. While timing of its emergence is disputed, most historians agree that adolescence became an increasingly distinctive and age-segregated stage of the life course as the nineteenth century progressed. The classic statement that the emergence of a modern concept of adolescence was a creation of late nineteenth-century industrial society is Kett, *Rites of Passage*.

76. See, e.g., Blackwell, *Counsel to Parents*.

77. On Acton's importance, see Filene, *Him/Her/Self*, 102. Acton's views on virility are echoed in the works of George Napheys and Elizabeth Blackwell.

78. Acton, *The Functions and Disorders of the Reproductive Organs*, 98–99.

79. Ibid., 101.

80. Napheys, *The Transmission of Life*, 32.

81. Ibid., 39.

82. Shepherd, *True Manhood*, 62.

83. Ibid., 211.

84. For a fascinating statement that the separation of work and home intensified masculine competitiveness so that men came to define manhood much more exclusively through work, see David Leverenz, *Manhood and the American Renaissance* (Ithaca, N.Y., 1989), esp. 72–90. For an interpretation of fraternalism emphasizing the "familial metaphors" in lodge rituals, see Mary Ann Clawson, *Constructing Brotherhood: Class, Gender, and Fraternalism* (Princeton, 1989), 175.

85. An analogous project was undertaken in the realm of nineteenth-century family law in which, Michael Grossberg argues, the decline of patriarchal authority in the family led to the construction of a new judicial patriarchy in the courts. See Grossberg, *Governing the Hearth: Law and the Family in Nineteenth-Century America* (Chapel Hill, N.C., 1985).

86. Pye Henry Chavasse, *Aphorisms on the Mental Culture and Training of a Child and on Various Other Subjects Relating to Health and Happiness Addressed to Parents* (Philadelphia, 1873), 128–29.

87. Mark Carnes, *Secret Ritual and Manhood in Victorian America* (New Haven, Conn., 1989), 107–16; Marsh, *Suburban Lives*.

88. Rotundo, *American Manhood*, 262–63.

3: Time and Togetherness

1. T. E. Potter, *The Autobiography of Theodore Potter* (Concord, N.H., 1913; reprint ed., Ann Arbor, Mich., 1978), 2, 5.

2. Edna R. Ormsby Diary, December 25, 1895, Schlesinger Library, Radcliffe College, Cambridge, Mass.

3. John Demos, "The Changing Faces of Fatherhood," in Demos, *Past, Present, and Personal: The Family and the Life Course in American History* (New York, 1986), 41–67, and Robert L. Griswold, *Fatherhood in America: A History* (New York, 1993), esp. 10–33.

4. The process of industrialization is conventionally divided into two phases. The first phase, beginning about 1814, when the first integrated textile factory was built in New England, left a rural commercial economy intact. The second phase, which began in the 1870s, transformed the economy into its modern urban industrial form. See Alfred D. Chandler Jr., *The Visible Hand: The Managerial Revolution in American Business* (Cambridge, Mass., 1977). On the far-reaching impact of commercialization, see Charles Sellers, *The Market Revolution: Jacksonian America, 1815–1846* (New York, 1991).

5. Functionalist sociology of the family, pioneered by Talcott Parsons, tends to equate availability and influence. For a cogent critique of the functionalist paradigm underlying the work-separation thesis, see Elizabeth H. Pleck, "Two Worlds in One: Work and Family," *Journal of Social History* 10 (1976): 178–95.

6. Bernard Wishy, *The Child and the Republic: The Dawn of Modern American Child Nurture* (Philadelphia, 1968), and Demos, "Changing Faces of Fatherhood."

7. Asa Sheldon quoted in Joseph F. Kett, *Rites of Passage: Adolescence in America, 1790 to the Present* (New York, 1977), 22, and "Memorial of Leonard Stockwell, 1798–1881" (Privately printed, ca. 1880s), 11–25, American Antiquarian Society, Worcester, Mass.

8. Ann Tompert, ed., *The Way Things Were: An Autobiography of Emily Ward* (Marine City, Mich., 1976), 1–2, 9.

9. For personal accounts documenting these types of absences, see, e.g., Emerson Hutzel, "Memories of Days That Were" (unpublished MS, ca. 1944), 18, Michigan Historical Collection, Bentley Historical Library, University of Michigan (hereafter Mich. Hist. Coll.); George Slayton, "Personal History of George A. Slayton" (handwritten MS, 1927), 1, Box 4, Slayton Family Collection, Mich. Hist. Coll.

10. On this last point, see Michael Anderson, *Family Structure in Nineteenth Century Lancashire* (Cambridge, 1971), 85–87.

11. Alan Pred, *The Spatial Dynamics of U.S. Urban-Industrial Growth, 1800–1914: Interpretative and Theoretical Essays* (Cambridge, Mass., 1966), 208.

12. Sam Bass Warner Jr., *Streetcar Suburbs: The Process of Growth in Boston, 1870–1900* (Cambridge, Mass., 1962), 19, 47–64.

13. Theodore Hershberg, Dale Light Jr., Harold E. Cox, and Richard R. Greenfield, "The 'Journey-to-Work': An Empirical Investigation of Work, Residence, and Transportation, Philadelphia, 1850 and 1880," in *Philadelphia: Work, Space, Family, and Group Experience in the Nineteenth Century: Essays Toward an Interdisciplinary History of the City*, ed. Theodore Hershberg (New York, 1981), 136, 165 (table 2).

14. Elizabeth Gurney Taylor Diary, 1854–59 passim, Box 4, Taylor Family Papers, Mich. Hist. Coll.

15. Walter Curtis Diary, 1887, passim, Walter Curtis Papers, Mich. Hist. Coll.; Amos A. Lawrence Diary, September 22, 1842–June 1855 passim, Box 3, Amos A. Lawrence Papers, Diaries and Account Books, Massachusetts Historical Society, Boston, Mass. (hereafter Mass. Hist. Soc.).

16. William Lawrence, *Life of Amos A. Lawrence, with Extracts from His Diary and Correspondence* (Boston, 1888), 172–73, 222; Amos A. Lawrence Diary, December 31, 1850 (228–29), Box 3, Amos A. Lawrence Papers, Mass. Hist. Soc.

17. Mary-Maud Oliver and Edward Surovell, eds., *The Story of an Ordinary Woman: The Extraordinary Life of Florence Cushman Milner* (Ann Arbor, Mich., 1989), 1–2. For other examples, see Maude Squire Rufus, *Flying Grandma, or Going Like Sixty* (Ypsilanti, Mich., 1942), 9, Mich. Hist. Coll., and Alice Van Atta, "Reflections of a Bygone Era" (Fenton, Mich., 1988), 4, Mich. Hist. Coll.

18. Schools superintendent quoted in Arthur W. Calhoun, *A Social History of American Family Life from Colonial Times to the Present* (New York, 1917), 3:67; Tamara Hareven, *Family Time and Industrial Time: The Relationship Between Family and Work in a New England Industrial Community* (Cambridge, 1982).

19. In 1830 workdays of eleven hours or longer were typical; in succeeding decades the ten-hour day gradually became the norm, as workers demanded more time to spend at leisure. See Roy Rosenzweig, *Eight Hours for What We Will: Workers and Leisure in an Industrial City, 1870–1920* (Cambridge, 1983), 38–39.

20. Carey quoted in Calhoun, *Social History of American Family Life*, 2:177.

21. Sean Wilentz, *Chants Democratic: New York City and the Rise of the American Working Class, 1788–1850* (New York, 1984), 51–52.

22. David J. Rothman, *The Discovery of the Asylum: Social Order and Disorder in the New Republic* (Glenview, Ill., 1971), 261–62.

23. John Howlett to his wife and children, January 27, 1851, Howlett Family Letters, American Antiquarian Society, Worcester, Mass. Howlett's life story was pieced together from the correspondence.

24. Herbert Shapiro and David L. Sterling, eds., *"I Belong to the Working*

Class": The Unfinished Autobiography of Rose Pastor Stokes (Athens, Ga., 1992), esp. 77–81.

25. Steven Ruggles has analyzed census data for 1880 and found that, whereas 72.3 percent of older unmarried women (mostly widows) lived with one of their children, only 54.5 percent of unmarried men did. Ruggles's analysis of nineteenth-century family structure also shows that the poorest elderly were those most likely to live without kin. See Steven Ruggles, "The Transformation of American Family Structure," *American Historical Review* 99 (1994): 103–28, esp. table 4.

26. George A. Slayton Diary, 1888, Box 5, Slayton Family Collection, Mich. Hist. Coll.

27. E. Lakin Brown, *Autobiographical Notes* (Schoolcraft, Mich.: Privately printed, 1906), 15, Mich. Hist. Coll.

28. Ray Stannard Baker, *Native American: The Book of My Youth* (New York, 1941), 34.

29. Charles E. Weller, *Yesterday: A Chronicle of Early Life in the West* (Indianapolis, Ind.:Privately printed, 1921), 40–41, Mich. Hist. Coll.; Oliver and Surovell, *The Story of an Ordinary Woman*, 29.

30. Dolores Hayden, *Redesigning the American Dream: The Future of Housing, Work, and Family Life* (New York, 1984), 22, 34. For a fascinating discussion of the changing social meaning of the household, see Elizabeth Blackmar, *Manhattan for Rent, 1785–1850* (Ithaca, N.Y., 1989), chap. 5. On suburban men's domesticity, see Margaret Marsh, *Suburban Lives* (New Brunswick, N.J., 1990), 74–89.

31. Charles Russell to wife, Persis, February 28, 1836, Charles Russell Papers, General Correspondence, Mass. Hist. Soc.

32. James Valentine Campbell to wife, Cornelia, January 12, 1862, James Valentine Campbell Papers, Mich. Hist. Coll.

33. Alexander Winchell Diary, August 23, 1863, Box 6, Alexander Winchell Papers, Mich. Hist. Coll.

34. Nancy Atwood Sprague, *Pleasant Memories of My Life* (New York: Privately printed, 1916), 82–87, quote at 86, Nancy Ann Atwood Sprague Papers, Schlesinger Library, Radcliffe College.

35. Mary (Tarr) Channing, "Sixty Years Ago" (unpublished MS), 15–16, Grace Ellery (Channing) Stetson Papers, Schlesinger Library, Radcliffe College.

36. Marlene Deahl Merrill, ed., *Growing Up in Boston's Gilded Age: The Journal of Alice Stone Blackwell, 1872–1874* (New Haven, Conn., 1990); Walter Curtis Diary, 1887, Walter Curtis Papers, Mich. Hist. Coll. In her diary for 1872, Alice Stone Blackwell mentions her mother 119 times and her father 84 times. On Sundays, however, she mentions her mother on 16 occasions and her father on 26.

Walter Curtis has 51 references to his mother and 31 to his father in his diary over-all. On Sundays, the count is 13 mentions of his father, 10 of his mother.

37. Baker, *Native American*, 86–87; Merrill, ed. *Growing Up in Boston's Gilded Age*, passim; Curtis Diary, passim.

38. Albert G. Browne to wife, Sarah, 2 December 1838, Browne Family Papers, Box 1, Schlesinger Library, Radcliffe College.

39. Ibid., March 20, 1842.

40. William Appleton, *Selections from the Diaries of William Appleton, 1786–1862* (Boston, 1922), 46–47, Mass. Hist. Soc.

41. George B. Emerson to daughter Lucy, June 4, 1847, Box 6, George B. Emerson Papers, Mass. Hist. Soc.

42. Abijah Bigelow to wife, Hannah, January 9, 1811, Bigelow Family Papers, American Antiquarian Society, Worcester, Mass.

43. Wilentz, *Chants Democratic*, 51–52.

44. The letters of Joseph Curtis, a Maine sea captain, and his wife, Louisa, document a lifelong struggle over his absences from home. Curtis argued that sacrifice involved in providing for his family's wants entitled him to their def-erence, as well as their respect for his wishes in this and other domestic mat-ters. Louisa drew on a religiously inflected version of patriarchal ideology to sug-gest that notwithstanding his provider role, his presence at home was required to exercise family leadership. See Curtis Family Letters, Clements Library, Uni-versity of Michigan. On maritime culture, see Lisa Norling, "Ahab's Wife: Women and the American Whaling Industry, 1820–1870," in *Iron Men, Wooden Women: Gender and Seafaring in the Atlantic World, 1700–1920*, ed. Margaret S. Creighton and Lisa Norling (Baltimore, 1996); and Margaret S. Creighton, "Davy Jones' Locker Room: Gender and the American Whaleman, 1830–1870," ibid., 118–37.

45. See the Bridget and James Birney correspondence in Birney-McLeer-Han-kerd Family Papers, Mich. Hist. Coll. Bridget told James that his children needed "both a father and a mother's care" in a letter dated January 29, 1859.

46. Lucy Stone to Henry Blackwell, April 12, 1858, in Leslie Wheeler, ed., *Lov-ing Warriors: Selected Letters of Lucy Stone and Henry B. Blackwell, 1853 to 1893* (New York, 1981), 178–79.

47. Moores Mirick White to wife, Sophia, July 25, 1841, Box 2, Draper-Rice Family Papers, American Antiquarian Society, Worcester, Mass. For a similar ex-pression of paternal concern, see also Lavius Hyde to father-in-law Asahel I. Bradley, March 9, 1842, Bradley-Hyde Family Papers, Schlesinger Library, Rad-cliffe College.

48. On the persistence of high child mortality rates, see Peter Uhlenberg, "Changing Configurations of the Life Course," in *Transitions: The Family and*

the Life Course in Historical Perspective, ed. Tamara K. Hareven (New York, 1978), 94–95; Samuel H. Preston and Michael R. Haines, *Fatal Years: Child Mortality in Late Nineteenth-Century America* (Princeton, 1991), esp. chap. 4. Preston and Haines find little improvement before 1900. Child mortality varied predictably according to several socioeconomic variables. Literate mothers and fathers had better rates of child survival than did illiterate parents. Working wives, especially African-American and immigrant mothers, had poor child survival, as did fathers who had been out of work in the year preceding the census. Overall, the most important variable was race. On the state of medical science in the late nineteenth century, see Thomas J. Schlereth, *Victorian America: Transformations in Everyday Life, 1876–1915* (New York, 1991), 283–90, and Steven Mintz and Susan Kellog, *Domestic Revolutions* (New York, 1988), 104.

49. Linda Pollock, *Forgotten Children: Parent-Child Relations from 1500 to 1900* (Cambridge, 1983), argues convincingly that more affectionate attitudes toward children had clearly emerged before there was any significant decline in death rates. Cf. Lawrence Stone, *The Family, Sex, and Marriage in England, 1500–1800* (New York, 1977).

50. Amos A. Lawrence Diary, May 12, 1850, Box 3, Amos A. Lawrence Diaries and Account Books, Mass. Hist. Soc. For other examples of fathers who monitored the condition of sick children in their diaries, see William Appleton Diary, February 16, 1838, *Selections from the Diaries of William Appleton, 1786–1862* (Boston, 1922), 60, Mass. Hist. Soc.; Richard S. Edes Commonplace Book and Journal, 50–51, Edes Family Papers, Mass. Hist. Soc.

51. Alexander Winchell, "Tears Over the Tomb" (handwritten MS), 25–27, Box 1, Alexander Winchell Papers, Mich. Hist. Coll.

52. Not surprisingly, when his teenage daughter was mortally ill in 1837, Charles Russell, a shopkeeper from Princeton, Massachusetts, who was serving in the state legislature in Boston, returned home to be with her. Similarly, an itinerant minister from Ohio cut a meeting short in 1852 because a daughter's illness "rendered it necessary" for him to return home. See Charles Russell to nephew Samuel G. Stevenson, May 9, 1837, Charles Russell Papers, Massachusetts Historical Society, Boston, Mass., and Eli Regal to son Abel, August 10, 1852, Regal Family Papers, Mich. Hist. Coll. .

53. Clayton B. Wells, *My Father Benjamin F. Wells* (Ann Arbor, Mich., 1929), 18, Mich. Hist. Coll., and Abel Regal Diary, December 13, 1854, Regal Family Papers, Mich. Hist. Coll. For similar accounts of fathers' care at times of illness, see Nancy Atwood Sprague, *Pleasant Memories of My Life* (New York, 1916), 11–12, Nancy Ann Atwood Sprague Papers, Schlesinger Library, Radcliffe College, and Marjorie Housepaian Dobkin, ed., *The Making of a Feminist: Early Journals and Letters of M. Carey Thomas* (Kent, Ohio, 1979), 34.

54. Ann Douglas, *The Feminization of American Culture* (New York, 1977).

55. Winchell, "Tears over the Tomb," 18. See also Richard S. Edes Commonplace Book and Journal, January 1855, Edes Family Papers, Massachusetts Historical Society; Isaac W. K. Handy, "Little Dilly, or the History of Dilworth Trugen Handy," The Handy Papers, Clements Library, University of Michigan.

56. Lucy Gray to her husband, Joshua Gray, May 6, 1823, Box 1, Hooker Collection, Schlesinger Library, Radcliffe College.

57. It is beyond the scope of this book to take up the issue of how working-class fathers accepted or rejected middle-class norms. Portraits of working-class family life vary widely. Christine Stansell, *City of Women: Sex and Class in New York, 1789–1860* (New York, 1986), esp. 77–78, 207–9, argues that working-class families in the nineteenth century were often disharmonious. She portrays working-class marriages as troubled, with women subject to harsh physical abuse when they failed to keep their households to men's likings. Much of the dysfunction occurred because the role of family breadwinner was so difficult for fathers to fulfill. Episodic employment meant that wives and children, not fathers, sometimes supported families with their earnings, and for most working men a family wage was an elusive ideal. Anger generated by unemployment or loss of status in the workforce and the attempt to recapture other kinds of masculine authority were displaced by fathers onto the family, Stansell maintains.

A more sanguine picture of working-class family life is offered by Susan Hirsch, *Roots of the American Working Class: The Industrialization of Crafts in Newark, 1800–1860* (Philadelphia, 1978). Hirsch portrays working-class households that conformed to bourgeois family ideals. A similar debate informs the literature on British working-class families. In a classic study, *Family and Kinship in East London* (Glencoe, Ill.,1957), Michael Young and Peter Willmott portrayed working-class fathers as harsh, frequently drunk, and brutal. Trevor Lumis refutes this description in "The Historical Dimension of Fatherhood: A Case Study 1890–1914," in *The Father Figure*, ed. Lorna McKee and Margaret O'Brien (London, 1982), 43–56.

58. Penne L. Restad, *Christmas in America: A History* (New York, 1995), 33–34. Restad maintains that the middle class had a twofold agenda: It sought to transcend the legacy of Puritan rejection of the holiday and at the same time control the holiday rowdiness that seemed endemic to the lower classes.

59. Daniel E. Sutherland, *The Expansion of Everyday Life, 1860–1876* (New York, 1989), 236–39. Such heterosocial leisure activities as bicycling, skating, lawn tennis, and archery also enjoyed immense popularity in the 1870s.

60. Mark C. Carnes, *Secret Ritual and Manhood in Victorian America* (New Haven, Conn., 1989). Carnes argues that fraternal ritual offered men an outlet for the psychic pressure of the new familial and economic structures of capital-

ism. See also Carnes, "Middle Class Men and the Solace of Fraternal Ritual," in *Meanings for Manhood: Constructions of Masculinity in Victorian America*, ed. Mark C. Carnes and Clyde Griffen (Chicago, 1990), 37–66. The symbolic meaning of fraternal ritual is controversial. Mary Ann Clawson, *Constructing Brotherhood: Class, Gender, and Fraternalism* (Princeton, 1989), observes that fraternal orders represented an alternative to domesticity based on the same metaphor of family as the domestic model. Carnes, on the other hand, maintains that the lodges symbolically effaced a man's real kin, replacing them with an all-male family.

Chapter 4: Becoming a Parent

1. For a fascinating study of modern relations informed by this perspective, see Carolyn Pape Cowan and Philip A. Cowan, *When Partners Become Parents* (New York, 1992).

2. John Modell, Frank F. Furstenberg Jr., and Douglas Strong, "The Timing of Marriage in the Transition to Adulthood: Continuity and Change, 1860–1975," *American Journal of Sociology* 34, Supplement (1978): S120–50.

3. Daniel J. Levinson, *The Seasons of a Man's Life* (New York, 1978), 219–21.

4. Judith Walzer Leavitt, *Brought to Bed: Childbearing in America, 1750–1950* (New York, 1986).

5. Charles Russell to Joshua Dillingham, July 27, 1815, Charles Russell Papers, General Correspondence, Mass. Hist. Soc. I am grateful to E. Anthony Rotundo for bringing the Russell papers to my attention.

6. Joshua Dillingham to Charles Russell, August 21, 1815, Charles Russell Papers, General Correspondence, Mass. Hist. Soc.

7. Ellen K. Rothman, *Hands and Hearts: A History of Courtship in America* (New York, 1984).

8. For coded references to pregnancy, see Henry Parker Smith Diary, May 10, 1856, Henry Parker Smith Papers, Mich. Hist. Coll. Smith assigned numeric values to letters according to their place in the alphabet. Thus, he wrote of his wife, "I am afraid she is 16–18–5–7–14–1–14–20 [pregnant] again." On the preoccupation with establishing a household, see E. Anthony Rotundo, *American Manhood: Transformations in Masculinity from the Revolution to the Modern Era* (New York, 1993), 17.

9. Elaine Tyler May, *Barren in the Promised Land: Childless Americans and the Pursuit of Happiness* (New York, 1995), chap. 2. See also Margaret Marsh and Wanda Ronner, *The Empty Cradle: Infertility in America from Colonial Times to the Present* (Baltimore, 1996).

10. Richard B. Stott, *Workers in the Metropolis: Class, Ethnicity, and Youth in*

Antebellum New York City (Ithaca, N.Y., 1990), 271–73. The extent to which the working class followed Victorian family norms is controversial. The answer often depends on which segment of the working class is being considered. Susan E. Hirsch, *Roots of the American Working Class: The Industrialization of Crafts in Newark, 1800–1860* (Philadelphia, 1978), has shown that family life for craft workers under industrialization followed bourgeois ideals.

11. Rotundo, *American Manhood*, 87–91.

12. The leading statement is put forth by Karen Lystra, *Searching the Heart: Women, Men, and Romantic Love in Nineteenth-Century America* (New York, 1989).

13. Rothman, *Hands and Hearts*, 69.

14. Natty Bumpo, James Fenimore Cooper's mythic frontiersman, was the prototype for a long line of literary heroes whose freedom was grounded in a repudiation of sex, marriage, and domestic responsibility. For a useful discussion of the bachelor heroes of nineteenth-century American fiction, see G. J. Barker-Benfield, *The Horrors of the Half-Known Life: Male Attitudes toward Women and Sexuality in Nineteenth-Century America* (New York, 1976), 8–22.

15. The topic of bachelorhood demands more attention than it has received to date. For an early discussion, see Arthur W. Calhoun, *A Social History of the American Family from Colonial Times to the Present* (New York, 1917), esp. 2:200–208 and 3:199–206. The American debate about bachelorhood was prefigured by a similar debate in Restoration England. See Mark E. Kann, *On the Man Question: Gender and Civic Virtue in America* (Philadelphia, 1991), 71–72.

16. Harriet Martineau, *Society in America* (London, 1837) 3:127, quoted in Calhoun, *Social History of the American Family* 2:208.

17. Quoted in May, *Barren in the Promised Land*, 45.

18. Catharine Beecher, *Woman Suffrage and Woman's Profession* (Hartford, Conn., 1871), quoted in Calhoun, *Social History of the American Family* 3:204–5.

19. *Harper's Weekly*, December 30, 1871. For late nineteenth-century marriage rates, see John Modell et al., "The Timing of Marriage in the Transition to Adulthood: Continuity and Change, 1860–1975," *American Journal of Sociology* 84, Supplement (1978): S123. Fears of "race suicide" prompted by massive immigration in the late nineteenth century also lent fuel to cultural critics who cast suspicion on Anglo-Saxon childlessness. See May, *Barren in the Promised Land*, 12–18. I am grateful to Peter Laipson for his insights into changing attitudes toward bachelorhood.

20. William Lloyd Garrison to George Benson, September 12, 1834, quoted in Rothman, *Hands and Hearts*, 83.

21. R. R. Richards to Barton S. Taylor, November 15, 1849, Taylor Family Papers, Mich. Hist. Coll.

22. The extent to which actual marriages conformed to companionate ideals is disputed. Timing of the change in ideology is less controversial; a growing consensus suggests that the ideal was in place by 1830. Carl N. Degler, *At Odds: Women and the Family in America from the Revolution to the Present* (New York, 1980), argues that the "modern" American family, characterized by more companionate relations between husband and wife, emerged between the American Revolution and 1830. Other historians as well point to the years from roughly 1780 to 1830 as a period of decisive change in family relations. See, e.g., Nancy F. Cott, *The Bonds of Womanhood: "Woman's Sphere" in New England, 1780–1835* (New Haven, Conn., 1977), and Jan Lewis, *The Pursuit of Happiness: Family and Values in Jefferson's Virginia* (New York, 1983).

23. See, e.g, Kirk Jeffrey, "The Family as Utopian Retreat from the City," *Soundings* 55 (1972): 21–41; Lewis, *The Pursuit of Happiness*, 51.

24. Mary W. H. Bird to Alexander Winchell, February 10, 1850, Box 1, Alexander Winchell Papers, Mich. Hist. Coll.

25. See, e.g., Peter N. Stearns, "Girls, Boys, and Emotions: Redefinitions and Historical Change," *Journal of American History* 80 (1993): 36–74.

26. Martha Felton to son Gilbert, June 23 [n.d., but between 1825 and 1844], Box 4, Nathaniel Stacy Papers, Clements Library, University of Michigan.

27. Henry Parker Smith Diary, June 8, 1850, Henry Parker Smith Papers, Mich. Hist. Coll.

28. Ibid.

29. Ibid., November 23, 1851; April 7, 1852.

30. Ibid., May 15, 1852.

31. Ibid., May 15 and July 3, 1853.

32. Ibid., November 30, 1853.

33. Ibid., May 15, 1854.

34. Ibid., June 5, 1854.

35. For a forceful statement of this position, see Rotundo, *American Manhood*.

36. Joseph Kett, *Rites of Passage: Adolescence in America, 1790 to the Present* (New York, 1977).

37. Lystra, *Searching the Heart*, 121–56.

38. Louisa Park to husband, John Park, January 5, 1800, Park Family Papers, American Antiquarian Society, Worcester, Mass.

39. Louisa J. Curtis to husband, Joseph Curtis, August 16, 1851, Curtis Family Letters, Clements Library, University of Michigan.

40. For an overview of changing childbirth practices, see Leavitt, *Brought to Bed*.

41. See, e.g., Ephraim Russell to Charles Russell, September 29, 1816, Charles Russell Papers, General Correspondence, Mass. Hist. Soc.; Jane Tuckerman to

Elizabeth Salisbury, April 1, 1835, Box 26, Salisbury Family Papers, American Antiquarian Society, Worcester, Mass.; and Alexander Winchell, "Tears Over the Tomb" (handwritten MS), 1, Box 1, Alexander Winchell Papers, Mich. Hist. Coll.

42. Leavitt, *Brought to Bed*, 17–35.

43. Henry Blackwell to wife, Lucy Stone, February 11, 1857, in Leslie Wheeler, ed., *Loving Warriors: Selected Letters of Lucy Stone and Henry B. Blackwell, 1853 to 1893* (New York, 1981), 166–67.

44. Henry Blackwell to wife, Lucy Stone, September 8, 1857, ibid., 171–72.

45. Henry Parker Smith Diary, August 8, 1854. Henry Parker Smith Papers, Mich. Hist. Coll.

46. Ibid., February 24, March 7, and March 10, 1855.

47. Ibid., December 14, 1854.

48. Maria M. Churchill Diary, September 24 and 26, 1845, Clements Library, University of Michigan.

49. William Alcott, *Physiology of Marriage* (1855; Boston, 1859), 143–77. See also Orson S. Fowler, *Creative and Sexual Science* (Cincinnati, Ohio, 1875), 124–25.

50. John R. Gillis, *A World of Their Own Making: Myth, Ritual, and the Quest for Family Values* (Cambridge, Mass., 1996), 158–71.

51. The participation of nineteenth-century fathers in childbirth has not received due attention, but is corroborated by at least two other studies. Nancy Grey Osterud, *Bonds of Community: The Lives of Farm Women in Nineteenth-Century New York* (Ithaca, N.Y., 1991), esp. 114–22, discovered that most husbands in New York state's Nanticoke Valley, a dairy-farming region, participated in childbirth during the second half of the century. J. Jill Suitor, "Husbands' Participation in Childbirth: A Nineteenth-Century Phenomenon," *Journal of Family History* 6 (1981): 273–93, concludes that during the nineteenth century many husbands attended the birth of their children to provide emotional support for their wives. Suitor argued that the presence of husbands coincided with the trend toward marital companionship and was probably related to fertility decline.

52. Lavius Hyde to Asahel I. Bradley, April 12, 1831, Box 1, Bradley-Hyde Family Papers, Schlesinger Library, Radcliffe College. For another example, see Clifford Hiram Nowlin, *My First Ninety Years* (Kansas City, Mo., 1957), 7.

53. Differences in men's and women's abilities to write had little, if any, effect. While measuring literacy is problematical, an upsurge of female literacy in pre-Revolutionary America already had narrowed substantially the gap in male and female literacy rates. Gloria L. Main, "An Inquiry into When and Why Women Learned to Write in Colonial New England," *Journal of Social History* 24 (1991): 579–89.

54. Ephraim Russell to brother Charles Russell, August 23, 1818, Charles Russell Papers, General Correspondence, Mass. Hist. Soc.

55. Charles Fisher to father-in-law Oliver Boizard, October 8, 1870, "The Boizard Letters," *Traverse* (August 1993): 64–65.

56. See, e.g., Emory Rider to James Draper, June 6, 1840, Box 1, Draper-Rice Family Papers, American Antiquarian Society, Worcester, Mass.; Samuel Salisbury to brother Stephen Salisbury, March 4, 1798, Box 9, Salisbury Family Papers, American Antiquarian Society; Anson J. Sperry to father-in-law, Samuel W. Peet, November 28, 1807, Peet Family Papers, Clements Library, University of Michigan; Abbott Lawrence to father-in-law, Timothy Bigelow, April 18, 1820, Box 1, Rotch-Lawrence Family Papers, Mass. Hist. Soc.; Nathaniel S. Porter to father, Huntington Porter, April 10, 1826, Huntington Porter Papers, Mass. Hist. Soc.; Lavius Hyde to father-in-law, Asahel I. Bradley, August 28, 1828, Bradley-Hyde Papers, Schlesinger Library, Radcliffe College; Charles Fay to Katharine Stone, July 21, 1886, Stone-Jackson Family Papers, Mass. Hist. Soc.

57. Henry Parker Smith Diary, March 19, 1855. Henry Parker Smith Papers, Mich. Hist. Coll.

58. Ibid., June 5, 1859.

59. Elizabeth Taylor Diary, Box 4, Taylor Family Papers, Mich. Hist. Coll.

60. Alexander Winchell Diary, September 17, 1867, Box 6, Alexander Winchell Papers, Mich. Hist. Coll. For other examples, see Richard Edes Diary, February 27, 1859, Mass. Hist. Soc.; and Amos A. Lawrence Diary, June 3, 1850, Amos A. Lawrence Journals and Account Books, Mass. Hist. Soc.

61. Charles Russell to brother Ephraim, January 17, 1816, Charles Russell Papers, General Correspondence, Mass. Hist. Soc.

62. Degler, *At Odds*, 66–85.

63. Henry Parker Smith Diary, April 24, 1855. Henry Parker Smith Papers, Mich. Hist. Coll.

64. Abijah Bigelow to wife, Hannah, March 29, 1812, Bigelow Family Papers, American Antiquarian Society, Worcester, Mass.

65. Henry Parker Smith Diary, April 25, 1855, Henry Parker Smith Papers, Mich. Hist. Coll.

66. Maria M. Churchill Diary, October 18, 1845, Clements Library, University of Michigan.

67. Ibid. October 4, 1845, emphasis in original.

68. Henry Parker Smith Diary, March 19 and 24, 1855. Henry Parker Smith Papers, Mich. Hist. Coll.

69. Ibid., July 21 and 22, 1861.

70. Caroline White Diary, September 12, 1858, Caroline Barrett White Papers, American Antiquarian Society, Worcester, Mass.

71. George A. Slayton, "Personal History of George A. Slayton, Written from Memory in 1927, for the Use of His Children," (handwritten MS), Box 4, Slayton Family Collection, Mich. Hist. Coll.

72. Elizabeth Taylor Diary, January 1867-August 1870, Box 4, Taylor Family Papers, Mich. Hist. Coll.

73. See Lucy Stone to Henry Blackwell, April 25, 1858, in Wheeler, ed., *Loving Warriors*, 178–79.

74. Henry Blackwell to Lucy Stone, March 25, 1858, ibid., 177.

75. Richard Holmes, *Communities in Transition* (Ann Arbor, Mich., 1980), 176.

76. W. J. Rorabaugh, *The Craft Apprentice: From Franklin to the Machine Age in America* (New York, 1986), 24.

77. The foregoing observations are based on a sample of thirteen accounts between 1800 and 1892.

78. Louisa Park to husband, John Park, May 21, 1800, Park Family Papers, American Antiquarian Society, Worcester, Mass.

79. Lucy Gray to husband, Joshua Gray, March 13, 1817, Box 1, Hooker Collection, Schlesinger Library, Radcliffe College.

80. John Evarts Tracy, *Autobiography* (Privately printed, 1957), 8, Mich. Hist. Coll.

81. Josiah Loomis Littlefield, *Autobiography* (Privately printed, 1932), 69, Mich. Hist. Coll. For other examples of family consultation after midcentury, see Richard Edes Journal, September 1850, Edes Family Papers, Mass. Hist. Soc.; Alexander Winchell Diary, September 21, 1862, Box 6, Alexander Winchell Papers, Mich. Hist. Coll.; and Edna Ormsby Diary, February 7, 1892, Schlesinger Library, Radcliffe College.

Chapter 5: A Frolic with Father

Epigraphs: The first quoted in William G. McLoughlin, "Evangelical Child-rearing in the Age of Jackson: Francis Wayland's Views on When and How to Subdue the Willfulness of Children," *Journal of Social History* 9 (1975): 35. The second is from Eunice Tripler, *Some Notes of Her Personal Recollections* (New York, 1910), 80, Mich. Hist. Coll.

1. McLoughlin, "Evangelical Childrearing," 28.

2. On the response to Wayland's article, see ibid., 29.

3. In the discussion that follows, "young children" are defined as those about age seven and younger. While age gradations for most of the nineteenth century were less distinct than they are today, a period of "youth" was bracketed between the end of infancy and early childhood, at ages five to seven, and final home-leaving, which could occur anywhere between fifteen and twenty-five. The clas-

sic discussion of the stages of nineteenth-century childhood is Joseph Kett, *Rites of Passage: Adolescence in America, 1790 to the Present* (New York, 1977).

4. For a recent statement of this position, see Ross D. Parke and Peter N. Stearns, "Fathers and Child Rearing," in *Children in Time and Place: Developmental and Historical Insights*, ed. Glen H. Elder et al. (New York, 1993), 147–70.

5. On changing conceptualizations of childhood, see Joseph M. Hawes and N. Ray Hiner, eds., *American Childhood: A Research Guide and Historical Handbook* (Westport, Conn., 1985).

6. On growing demands of conformity, see Barbara Finkelstein, "The Reconstruction of Childhood in the United States, 1790–1870," ibid., 111–52.

7. Two cogent discussions of antebellum parenting ideals are Mary P. Ryan, *Cradle of the Middle Class: The Family in Oneida County, New York, 1790–1865* (Cambridge, 1981), 160–62, and David J. Rothman, *The Discovery of the Asylum: Social order and Disorder in the New Republic* (Boston, 1971), 218–21.

8. Joseph F. Kett, *Rites of Passage: Adolescence in America, 1790 to the Present* (New York, 1977), 173.

9. Abijah Bigelow to wife, Hannah, February 10, 1811, Bigelow Family Papers, American Antiquarian Society, Worcester, Mass.

10. Unfortunately, only Abijah's letters to Hannah have been preserved. But her critique of his family role is clearly reflected in his correspondence. See especially a letter dated December 14, 1811, in which he responds to her accusations.

11. William L. Hudson to wife, Lise, October 1, 1850, William L. Hudson Letterbook, Clements Library, University of Michigan.

12. Louisa Walter Hughes Diary, January 15, 1865, Louisa Walter Hughes Papers, Schlesinger Library, Radcliffe College.

13. Albert G. Browne to wife, Sarah, March 1, 1842, Box 1, Browne Family Papers, Schlesinger Library, Radcliffe College.

14. Barbara M. Cross, ed., *The Autobiography of Lyman Beecher* (Cambridge, Mass., 1961), 1:104. The title of this revealing work is somewhat misleading. The text is in fact a collaborative effort undertaken by Beecher and his children; it reads more like a collective family self-portrait than the autobiography of an individual.

15. Philip Greven, *Spare the Child: The Religious Roots of Punishment and the Psychological Impact of Physical Abuse* (New York, 1991), argues that harsh physical treatment of children has been common throughout American history. While Greven acknowledges that disciplinary practices exist on a continuum, he asserts that a biblically based commitment to corporal punishment has tilted practice toward the harsh end of the scale. Greven's evidence is drawn largely from fundamentalists and extreme evangelicals, and it is unclear whether the cases he cites

are representative. Moreover, he offers little proof that his cases reflect the experience of the majority of more moderate and mainstream Protestants. Indeed, he remarks at one point that moderates tend to use physical punishment only as a "last resort" (94), contradicting the overall impression of an unrelenting reign of terror. The paucity of documentation for corporal punishment, of course, is not conclusive proof that such abuse did not take place. As Greven points out, such memories are likely to be repressed. However, the lack of evidence does at least call into question the tenor of his argument.

16. On the exaltation of childhood innocence, see T. J. Jackson Lears, *No Place of Grace: Antimodernism and the Transformation of American Culture, 1880–1920* (New York, 1981), 144–49.

17. Kirk Jeffrey, "The Family as Utopian Retreat from the City," *Soundings* 55 (1972): 21–41.

18. For an example of such an idealized image of the father's return from work to be greeted by loving wife and the "sweet voices" of his children, see Jesse T. Peck, *The True Woman; or, Life and Happiness at Home and Abroad* (New York, 1857), 243–44.

19. Samuel Moody, quoted in Bernard Mergen, *Play and Playthings: A Reference Guide* (Westport, Conn., 1982), 6.

20. Ibid., 14.

21. Jacob Abbott, *Stories Told to Rollo's Cousin Lucy, When She Was a Little Girl* (Boston, 1845), 168.

22. Mary Elliott, "My Father: A Poem" (New York, printed and sold by Mahlon Day at the New Juvenile Book-store No. 376 Pearl Street [between 1825 and 1833?]), American Antiquarian Society, Worcester, Mass.

23. Horace Bushnell, *Christian Nurture* (Edinburgh, 1861; reprint ed., New Haven, Conn., 1967), 292–93. Cf. idem, *Views of Christian Nurture* (Hartford, Conn., 1847).

24. For a fuller discussion of this trend, see chapter 2 of this study. A good example of such advice is Artemas Muzzey, *The Fireside: An Aid to Parents* (Boston, 1854), 153–54.

25. For an instance of a father acting as play partner with a young child at the turn of the nineteenth century, see Louisa Adams Park Diary, January 18, 1801, Park Family Papers, American Antiquarian Society, Worcester, Mass.

26. The first usage illustration in the *Oxford English Dictionary* associating "frolic" with children is dated 1740. *OED* (Oxford, 1989), 6:210.

27. John Davis to wife, Eliza, December 29, 1825, John Davis Papers, American Antiquarian Society, Worcester, Mass.

28. John Davis to wife, Eliza, January 26, 1826, Davis Papers.

29. Eliza Davis to husband, John, February 6, 1832, Davis Papers.

30. Samuel Emerson to son George, September 25, 1836, Box 5, George B. Emerson Papers, Mass. Hist. Soc.

31. On the construction of the pastoral ideal of suburban life, see Margaret Marsh, *Suburban Lives* (New Brunswick, N.J., 1990), esp. chap. 1.

32. M. J. Channing, "Sixty Years Ago" (unpublished MS), Grace Ellery (Channing) Stetson Papers, Schlesinger Library, Radcliffe College. Mary (Tarr) Channing, who grew up in a devout Universalist household, left this extremely revealing memoir of her youth in various New England factory villages in the 1830s and 1840s. She notes that "indulgence of the *youngest* was no uncommon thing in the very strictest households" (8).

33. Sarah Bigelow Adams to sister, Anne, January 31, 1840, Box 2, Bigelow Family Papers, American Antiquarian Society, Worcester, Mass.

34. Theodore Roosevelt, *An Autobiography* (New York, 1913), pp. 364.

35. Nancy Atwood Sprague, *Pleasant Memories of My Life* (New York, 1916), 30, Nancy Atwood Sprague Papers, Schlesinger Library, Radcliffe College.

36. McLoughlin, "Evangelical Childrearing," 32. The quote is from Francis Wayland and H. L. Wayland, *A Memoir of the Life and Labours of Francis Wayland D.D., L.L.D.* (New York, 1867), 1:23.

37. Cross, ed., *The Autobiography of Lyman Beecher*, 1:104.

38. Ibid. See also ibid., 2:88 for a vivid recollection by Harriet Beecher Stowe of her father's tenderness toward his youngest children. She recalled that when her father was pastoring in Boston during the period 1826–31, the youngest child in the house was assigned the task of waking him up in the morning:

> The reigning baby . . . was solemnly instructed by [father] that it was necessary to take him by the nose, and kiss him many times before the heaviness in his head would go off so that he could lift it. Oftentimes he would lie in bed after his little monitor had called him professing fears that there was a lion under the bed who would catch his foot if he put it out, and requiring repeated and earnest assurance from the curly head that he should be defended from being eaten up if he rose; and often the breadkfast-bell would ring before he could be induced to launch forth. Great would be the pride of the little monitor, who led him at last gravely into the breakfast-room, and related in baby phrase the labors of getting up.

39. James Valentine Campbell to son Harry, June 7, 1857, James Valentine Campbell Papers, Mich. Hist. Coll.

40. James Valentine Campbell to wife, Cornelia, August 10, 1856.

41. James Valentine Campbell to wife, Cornelia, June 17, 1866.

42. For a fascinating discussion of "boy culture," see E. Anthony Rotundo, *American Manhood: Transformations in Masculinity from the Revolution to the Modern Era* (New York, 1993), 31–55.

43. Sophia Amelia Draper White to husband, Moores, June 13, 1841, Box 2, Draper-Rice Family Papers, American Antiquarian Society, Worcester, Mass.

44. William Sever Lincoln to wife, Elizabeth, October 25, 1841, Box 8, Lincoln Family Papers, American Antiquarian Society, Worcester, Mass.

45. Brown Thurston to his daughter, letter dated May 10, 1858, copied in Brown Thurston Journal, February 21, 1877, American Antiquarian Society, Worcester, Mass.

46. Among the more famous reflections on the salutary effect of association with children is the following statement from the 1830s by the educator Bronson Alcott, father of Louisa May Alcott: "Verily had I not been called to associate with children, had I not devoted myself to the study of human nature, in its period of infancy and childhood, I should never have found the tranquil repose, the steady faith, the vivid hope, that now shed a glory and a dignity around the humble path of my life. Childhood hath *Saved* me!" Quoted in Charles Strickland, "A Transcendentalist Father: The Child Rearing Practices of Bronson Alcott," *History of Childhood Quarterly* 1 (1973): 45.

47. On the social history of play, see Kathryn Grover, ed., *Hard at Play: Leisure in America, 1840–1940* (Amherst, Mass., 1992).

48. Leland S. Person Jr., "Inscribing Paternity: Nathaniel Hawthorne as a Nineteenth-Century Father," in *Studies in the American Renaissance*, ed. Joel Myerson (Charlottesville, Va., 1991), 231.

49. Sarah M. Foster to Asa E. Foster, November 19, 1850, Sara Maria (Foster) St. John Papers, Schlesinger Library, Radcliffe College.

50. Edna R. Ormsby Diary, September 22, 1895, Schlesinger Library, Radcliffe College.

51. Ibid., July 23, 1893.

52. The following personal narratives, available in the Mich. Hist. Coll., document this trend:

For the 1800s, see Joseph Bates, *The Early Life and Later Experience and Labors of Elder Joseph Bates* (Battle Creek, Mich., 1878), 18; John Ball, *The Autobiography of John Ball, Compiled by His Daughters* (Grand Rapids, Mich., 1925), 14. For 1810–20, see John B. Gough, *Autobiography and Personal Recollections of John B. Gough* (Springfield, Mass., 1869), 21–22; Laura S. Haviland, *A Woman's Life-Work: Labors and Experiences* (Cincinnati, Ohio, 1881), 9. For the 1820s, see David Ward, *The Autobiography of David Ward* (New York, 1912), 15–18; Giles Stebbins, *Upward Steps of Seventy Years* (New York, 1890), 21–22. For the 1830s, see T. S. Andrews, *Ira Andrews and Ann Hopkinson, Their Ancestors and Posterity, Including the Autobiography of the Author* (Toledo, Ohio, 1879), 2; D. B. Kellogg, *Autobiography of Dr. D. B. Kellogg* (Ann Arbor, Mich., 1869), 6–12. For the 1840s, see T. E. Potter, *The Autobiography of Theodore Edgar Potter* (Concord, N.H.;

reprint ed., Ann Arbor, Mich., 1978), 2; James D. Rowe, "Early Memories of J. D. Rowe" (typescript, 1925), 5. For the 1850s, see Horatio S. Earle, *The Autobiography of "By Gum" Earle* (Lansing, Mich., 1929), 11–12. For the 1860s, see Abraham Leenhouts, *From the Crest of the Hill: The Life and Philosophy of a Dune-Country Doctor* (1948), 33. For the 1870s, see Ray Stannard Baker, *Native American: The Book of My Youth* (New York, 1941), 219. For the 1880s, see James Agnes Stewart, *I Have Recalled: A Pen-Panorama of a Life* (Toledo, Ohio, 1938), 20. For the 1890s, see Herbert R. Simonds, *Reminiscences* (Privately printed, 1968), passim.

53. Leenhouts, *From the Crest of the Hill*, 18.

54. Earle, *Autobiography*, 11–12.

55. Walter Curtis Diary, February 17, 1887, Walter Curtis Papers, Mich. Hist. Coll.; Marlene Deahl Merrill, ed., *Growing Up in Boston's Gilded Age: The Journal of Alice Stone Blackwell, 1872–1874* (New Haven, Conn., 1990), passim.

56. Jeanne Boydston, *Home and Work: Housework, Wages, and the Ideology of Labor in the Early Republic* (New York, 1990).

57. Mergen, *Play and Playthings*, 64–65.

58. Robert L. Griswold, "'Ties That Bind and Bonds That Break': Children's Attitudes toward Fathers, 1900–1930," in *Small Worlds: Children and Adolescents in America, 1850–1950*, ed. Elliott West and Paula Petrik (Lawrence, Kans., 1991), 265–66, observes that in this period leisure time became increasingly segmented. While parents and children in the middle class had a considerable amount of lesiure time each day, they rarely spent it together.

59. Ross D. Parke and Barbara R. Tinsley, "The Father's Role in Infancy: Determinants of Involvement in Caregiving and Play," in *The Role of the Father in Child Development*, 2d ed., ed. Michael E. Lamb (New York, 1981), 429–57; and Michael E. Lamb, "The Development of Father-Infant Relationships," ibid., 459–88. The evidence adduced in this chapter does not speak clearly to differences in parental play styles in the past. However, images of frolic in the last century accord with the low priority placed on conscious instruction in present-day father's play.

60. For a valuable discussion of the ironies inherent in emphasizing the playful interactions of fathers and children, see Parke and Stearns, "Fathers and Child Rearing," 147–70.

Chapter 6: Patrimony's Yardstick

1. On the emergence of a market economy, see Charles Sellers, *The Market Revolution: Jacksonian America, 1815–1846* (New York, 1991). The rise and fall of the apprenticeship system is explored in William Rorabaugh, *The Craft Apprentice:*

From Franklin to the Machine Age in America (New York, 1986). On the decline of small businesses, see note 42 below.

2. Levi Lincoln to grandson William Lincoln, October 13, 1844, Box 8, Lincoln Family Papers, American Antiquarian Society, Worcester, Mass.

3. The following narratives document the progressive nature of a boy's work: Roswell H. Wells, *The Reminiscences of Roswell Henry Wells, 1853–1942* (Kalamazoo, Mich., n.d.), 6–7, Mich. Hist. Coll.; Clifford H. Nowlin, *My First Ninety Years: A Schoolmaster's Story of His Life and Times* (Kansas City, Mo., 1955, 16–17); and Horatio Sawyer Earle, *The Autobiography of "By Gum" Earle* (Lansing, Mich., 1929), 20–40.

4. Abraham Leenhouts, *From the Crest of the Hill: The Life and Philosophy of a Dune-Country Doctor* (1948), 16. For other examples, see Emerson E. Hutzel, "Memories of Days That Were" (unpublished MS, ca. 1944), 5; Wells, *Reminiscences*, 8-9. The foregoing narratives are available in the Mich. Hist. Coll.

5. Clement Smith Diary, 1860, Mich. Hist. Coll.

6. Cf., Walter Curtis Diary, 1887, Walter Curtis Papers, Mich. Hist. Coll. Curtis was born in 1874 and grew up in Detroit. A content analysis of the diary he kept for 1887, the year he turned fourteen, documented fifty-one references to his mother, thirty-one to his father, and seven simply to his "parents."

7. See, e.g., David Ward, *The Autobiography of David Ward* (New York, 1912), and Joseph Bates, *The Early Life and Later Experiences and Labors of Elder Joseph Bates* (Battle Creek, Mich., 1878). Both narratives are available in the Mich. Hist. Coll.

8. See chapter 1 of the present study; see also Mary Ann Mason, *From Father's Property to Children's Rights: The History of Child Custody in the United States* (New York, 1994).

9. The quasi-contractual relation of fathers and sons was first noticed by Joseph Kett, *Rites of Passage: Adolescence in America, 1790 to the Present* (New York, 1977), 29. This classic study, highlighting the "semidependent" status of youth, accurately captures the flux of youthful experience and status, but it underestimates the extent to which chronological milestones conditioned parent-child relationships.

10. The salience of age twenty-one in father-son relations owed as well, of course, to the fact that this was the age of political majority. A youth of twenty-one was now his father's political equal as a voter, if still his social inferior.

11. Edmund Morgan, *The Puritan Family: Religion and Domestic Relations in Seventeenth-Century New England* (New York, 1966); John Demos, *A Little Commonwealth: Family Life in Plymouth Colony* (New York, 1970); Rorabaugh, *The Craft Apprentice*.

12. Charles R. Harding, *Autobiography* (handwritten MS, ca. 1868), chap. 1, American Antiquarian Society, Worcester, Mass.

13. John Ball, *Autobiography of John Ball, Compiled by His Daughters* (Grand Rapids, Mich., 1925), 13; Nathaniel Stacy, *Memoirs of the Life of Nathaniel Stacy* (Columbus, Pa., 1849), 43–46. Both narratives are available in the Mich. Hist. Coll.

14. This account is drawn from Samuel W. Durant, comp., *History of Kalamazoo County, Michigan, with Illustrations and Biographical Sketches of Its Prominent Men and Pioneers* (Philadelphia, 1880), 477. The sketches in this and other county histories were based on personal interviews with the subjects. Accordingly, the references to "owing time" probably came from Morgan himself. If it did not, the author of the sketch assumed that the practice was common enough to be readily recognizable to an audience of readers in 1880.

15. William G. Grow, *Eighty-five Years of Life and Labor* (Carbondale, Pa., 1902), 15–16, Mich. Hist. Coll.

16. Ibid., 17.

17. For examples of such conflict, see T. E. Potter, *The Autobiography of Theodore Edgar Potter* (Concord, N.H., 1913; reprint ed., Ann Arbor, Mich., 1978), 21–23; Nels Anderson, "Sociology Has Many Faces: Part I," *Journal of the History of Sociology* 3 (1980–81): 14; and Herbert R. Simonds, *Reminiscences* (unpublished MS, 1968), Mich. Hist. Coll.

18. The tendency of personal documents to reflect more positive than negative emotions has been frequently remarked by historians. Correspondents did not necessarily share hostile feelings, and when family members were completely alienated they did not write. Furthermore, existing collections of family documents may reflect editing by family members who might have chosen to eliminate material that revealed skeletons in the family closet. For a recent discussion of this problem, see Linda W. Rosenzweig, *The Anchor of My Life: Middle-Class American Mothers and Daughters, 1880–1920* (New York, 1993), xi.

19. Julia Fish to brother Carlton, December 8, 1862, and Dan Fish to sister Julia, January 25, 1867, Fish Family Papers, uncataloged collection, Clements Library, University of Michigan.

20. Nancy Grey Osterud, *Bonds of Community: The Lives of Farm Women in Nineteenth-Century New York* (Ithaca, N.Y., 1991), 62–71. Osterud found that children generally received the bulk of their patrimony while parents were still alive. Sons were given land, but daughters received household furnishings when they married. Children who were not already provided for when their parents died would be compensated by the inheriting son. Alternatively, the farm was bequeathed to all children and one son would buy the others out.

21. Marcus Lee Hansen, *The Immigrant in American History* (Cambridge, Mass., 1940), 61–62.

22. Nathaniel Stacy to Stephen Rennselaer Smith, draft letter, January 17, 1830, Box 2, Nathaniel Stacy Papers, Clements Library, University of Michigan. For

an insightful discussion of rural inheritance practices, see Hal S. Baron, "Staying Down on the Farm: Social Processes of Settled Rural Life in the Nineteenth-Century North," in *The Countryside in the Age of Capitalist Transformation: Essays in the Social History of Rural America*, ed. Steven Hahn and Jonathan Prude (Chapel Hill, N.C., 1985), 335–38.

23. Ball, *Autobiography*, 13.

24. William Stedman to wife, Almy, November 5, 1804, William Stedman Letters, Mass. Hist. Soc.; E. Lakin Brown, *Autobiographical Notes* (Schoolcraft, Mich., 1906), 27; and Royal W. Danforth to Sister Richardson, April 19, 1863, Folder 35, Boynton Family Letters, Clements Library, University of Michigan.

25. Rorabaugh, *The Craft Apprentice*.

26. See Christopher Clark, "The Diary of an Apprentice Cabinetmaker: Edward Jenner Carpenter's 'Journal,' 1844–45," *Proceedings of the American Antiquarian Society* 98 (1989): 305–94.

27. On the collar-line and class formation, see Stuart M. Blumin, *The Emergence of the Middle Class: Social Experience in the American City, 1760–1900* (Cambridge, 1989).

28. On the family safety first mentality, see John Modell, "Changing Risks, Changing Adaptations: American Families in the Nineteenth and Twentieth Centuries," in *Kin and Communities*, ed. Allan J. Lichtman and John R. Challinor (Washington, D.C., 1979), 128.

29. For a summary of these trends, see Maris A. Vinovskis, *Education, Society, and Economic Opportunity: Some Historical Perspectives* (New Haven, Conn., 1995), chap. 1.

30. In a sample of seventy autobiographies, supplemented by the letters and diaries of an additional twenty-four writers, I counted eight families in which a father's attitude toward schooling was at odds with the views of his wife and children. Given the higher-than-average educational achievement of the narrators, there is probably a bias in the evidence toward fathers who supported their children's educational aspirations.

31. Quoted in Ray Stannard Baker, *Native American: The Book of My Youth* (New York, 1941), 99.

32. Stacy, *Memoirs*, 32; Maxwell P. Gaddis, *Foot-Prints of an Itinerant* (Cincinnati, Ohio, 1855), 40–41. For other examples, see Ball, *Autobiography*, 8; Brown, *Autobiographical Notes*, 27; Laura S. Haviland, *A Woman's Life-Work: Labors and Experiences* (Cincinnati, Ohio, 1881), 13; James Inglis, *A Sketch of My Life* (unpublished MS), 4, Mich. Hist. Coll.; Leslie Dick, ed., *A Michigan Childhood: The Journals of Madelon Louisa Stockwell* (Albion, Mich., 1988), 131; and Mary-Maud Oliver and Edward Surovell, eds., *The Story of an Ordinary Woman: The Extraordinary Life of Florence Cushman Milner* (Ann Arbor, Mich., 1989), 2–4.

33. James Oliver Curwood, *Son of the Forests* (Garden City, N.Y., 1930), passim; for another example, see Leenhouts, *From the Crest of the Hill*, 46.

34. Nels Anderson, "Sociology Has Many Faces," 4–20; quotes at 4 and 19.

35. For examples, see Baker, *Native American*, 26; Barton S. Taylor to his grandfather, Daniel Reed, August 30, [1827?], Box 1, Taylor Family Papers, Mich. Hist. Coll.; Daniel Abrey, *Reminiscences* (Corunna, Mich., 1903), 11; Charles T. Selkirk Diary, October 25, 1852, Mich. Hist. Coll.; "The Life of Rev. James (Selkirg) Selkirk" (typescript), 1, Mich. Hist. Coll.; Eugene Chapin, *By-Gone Days or the Experiences of an American* (Privately printed, Boston, Mass., 1898), 42, Mich. Hist. Coll.; and Elizabeth Taylor, to son Hartley, April 4, 1883, Taylor Family Papers, Mich. Hist. Coll.

36. On the attitudes of urban and rural parents toward schooling and social mobility, see Barbara Finkelstein, "In Fear of Childhood: Relationships Between Parents and Teachers in Popular Primary Schools in the Nineteenth Century," *History of Childhood Quarterly* 3 (1976), 321–36.

37. James B. Angell, *The Reminiscences of James Burrill Angell* (New York, 1912), 16–17. Angell accepted his father's offer and eventually became president of the University of Michigan.

38. Elias Nason to his parents, October 29, 1833, Box 1, Elias Nason Papers, American Antiquarian Society, Worcester, Mass. For more evidence that keeping children in school was a marker of class boundaries, see George B. Emerson Diary, [August 2, 1832], Box 4, George B. Emerson Papers, Mass. Hist. Soc.

39. John Davis to wife, Eliza, April 2, 1830, John Davis Papers, American Antiquarian Society, Worcester, Mass.

40. Economic historians estimate that in 1860 fathers of male children in farming households would not "break even" on their investment in their first-born son until he reached age twenty-six. The cost of raising daughters was even greater because most of their labor was devoted to household services rather than the production of cash crops. Consequently, parents who had fewer children tended to have larger estates than did their counterparts with large families. See Robert W. Fogel et al., "The Economics of Mortality in North America, 1650–1910: A Description of a Research Project," *Historical Methods* 11 (1978): 92.

41. John Davis to wife, Eliza, March 23, 1832, John Davis Papers, American Antiquarian Society, Worcester, Mass.

42. Mary P. Ryan, *Cradle of the Middle Class: The Family in Oneida County, New York, 1790–1865* (Cambridge, 1981), 152, 255; Michael B. Katz, *The People of Hamilton, Canada West: Family and Class in a Mid-Nineteenth-Century City* (Cambridge, 1975), 167–71.

43. For examples, see Anson J. Sperry to Samuel W. Peet, September 20, 1813,

Peet Family Papers, Clements Library, University of Michigan; William Richmond to his sister, Mrs. Charles Tillinghast, March 20, 1825, Box 1, Hooker Collection, Schlesinger Library, Radcliffe College; Isaac Stephenson, *Recollections of a Long Life, 1829–1915* (Privately printed: Chicago, 1915), 54, Mich. Hist. Coll.; Brown, *Autobiographical Notes*, 15–24; Giles B. Stebbins, *Upward Steps of Seventy Years* (New York, 1890), 33; and Baker, *Native American*, 157–219.

44. Charles Russell to son Theodore, September 13, 1832, Charles Russell Papers, General Correspondence, Mass. Hist. Soc.

45. Albert G. Browne to daughter Nellie, December 7, 1857, Box 1, Browne Family Papers, Schlesinger Library, Radcliffe College. For similar statements emphasizing parental sacrifice for a child's education, see Rev. J. W. Hough, D.D., "Fifty Years of My Life; A Sermon Preached to the First Congregational Church of Jackson, Mich., on the Fiftieth Anniversary of His Birth, November 26, 1882," (Jackson, Mich., 1882), Mich. Hist. Coll.; Amos A. Lawrence Diary, July 31, 1857, Box 3, Amos A. Lawrence Diaries and Account Books, Mass. Hist. Soc.; Daniel Abrey, *Reminiscences* (Corunna, Mich., 1903), 17, Mich. Hist. Coll.; and *Leibman Adler: His Life through his Letters* (Privately printed, 1975), ix–x, Mich. Hist. Coll.

46. Jan Lewis, "Mother's Love: The Construction of an Emotion in Nineteenth-Century America," in *Social History and Issues in Human Consciousness*, ed. Andrew E. Barnes and Peter N. Stearns (New York, 1989), 209–29.

47. On the Christian fatherhood ideal, see chapter 2 of this study.

48. On the shift from patriarchy to paternalism, see Jay Fliegelman, *Prodigals and Pilgrims: The American Revolution against Patriarchal Authority* (Cambridge, 1982).

49. James Barnard Blake Diary, January 1, 1851, American Antiquarian Society, Worcester, Mass.

50. Ibid., June 27, 1851.

51. Ibid., June 28, 1851.

52. This dynamic is accurately described by Steven Mintz in *A Prison of Expectations: The Family in Victorian Culture* (New York, 1983), 27–39.

53. Charles Russell to son Theodore, September 27, 1834, Charles Russell Papers, General Correspondence, Mass. Hist. Soc.

54. Giles Stebbins, *Upward Steps*, 121. On the importance of the middle-class father's role as career adviser and teacher of business ethics to his sons, see E. Anthony Rotundo, *American Manhood: Transformations in Masculinity from the Revolution to the Modern Era* (New York, 1993), 25–30, and Rotundo, "Learning about Manhood: Gender Ideals and the Middle-Class Family in Nineteenth-Century America," in *Manliness and Morality: Middle-Class Masculinity in Britain and America, 1800–1940*, ed. J. A. Mangan and James Walvin (New York, 1987), 35–51.

55. The classic statement of a separate female domestic sphere is Carroll Smith-Rosenberg, "The Female World of Love and Ritual: Relations Between Women in Nineteenth-Century America," *Signs* 1 (1975): 1–29. Smith-Rosenberg's thesis is a misleading guide for assessing the extent and nature of father-daughter relations in the nineteenth century. While this thesis informs Robert L. Griswold's discussion of the topic, Griswold acknowledges that men's participation in the female domestic world is now open to debate. See Robert L. Griswold, *Fatherhood in America: A History* (New York, 1993), 17.

56. Smith-Rosenberg, "The Female World of Love and Ritual."

57. Anna Howard Shaw, *The Story of A Pioneer* (New York, 1915), 11; Ward, *Autobiography*, 18.

58. Elliott West, *Growing Up with the Country: Childhood on the Far Western Frontier* (Albuquerque, N.Mex., 1989), 74–75.

59. Bertha Van Hoosen, *Petticoat Surgeon* (Chicago, 1947), 16–17.

60. Florence Hartsuff, "My Education" (unpublished MS, n.d.), Hartsuff Family Papers, Mich. Hist. Coll.

61. Leslie Wheeler, ed., *Loving Warriors: Selected Letters of Lucy Stone and Henry B. Blackwell, 1853 to 1893* (New York, 1981), 7–8.

62. Stephen B. Oates, *A Woman of Valor: Clara Barton and the Civil War* (New York, 1994), 41.

63. Sarah Partridge Diary, March 17, 1881, Mich. Hist. Coll.

64. Jessie Phelps Journal, March 2, 1888, Jessie Phelps Papers, Mich. Hist. Coll.; Elizabeth Gurney Taylor Diary, May 31, 1857, Box 4 Taylor Family Papers, Mich. Hist. Coll.

65. Ellen Regal Diary, March, 23, 1857, Regal Family Papers, Mich. Hist. Coll.

66. When Emerson Hutzel's mother died from complications of childbirth in 1892, leaving six children, the eldest daughter, thirteen, filled her mother's role for two years. Emerson Hutzel, "Memories of Days That Were" (unpublished MS, ca. 1944), 1, Mich. Hist. Coll.

67. Emily Ward, *The Way Things Were: An Autobiography of Emily Ward*, ed. Ann Tompert (Marine City, Mich., 1976), 16–17, 28. For other examples, see Maude Rufus, *Flying Grandma or Going Like Sixty* (Privately printed, 1942), 11; A. L. Mayhew, "Sixty Years of Life" (unpublished MS, 1937). Rufus and Mayhew are available in the Mich. Hist. Coll.

68. See, for example, Mayhew, "Sixty Years," and Grow, *Eighty-five Years*.

69. Joseph Curtis to wife, Louisa, September 1866, Curtis Family Letters, Clements Library, University of Michigan.

70. Asa Emerson Foster to daughter Sarah, March 25, 1862, Sarah Maria Foster St. John Papers, Schlesinger Library, Radcliffe College.

71. For an interesting case study of an eighteenth-century father who advised

his daughter on topics one would expect a "republican mother" to have taken up, including pregnancy and childbirth, see David W. Robson, "The Republican Father: The Family Letters of Charles Nisbet," in *The American Family: Historical Perspectives*, ed. Jeane E. Hunter and Paul T. Mason (Pittsburgh, Pa., 1991), 90–99.

72. Abijah Adams to daughter Maryanne, September 19, 1808, Abijah Adams letter, Schlesinger Library, Radcliffe College.

73. Eleazer Lindsley to daughter Jerusha, October 3 and 6, 1806, Lindsley Family Papers, Clements Library, University of Michigan; Joseph Burt Holt to daughter Emily, February 25, 1868, Box 3, Holt-Messer Family Papers, Schlesinger Library, Radcliffe College; Stephen Foster to daughter Alla, January 1, 1864, Box 2, Abigail Kelley Foster Papers, American Antiquarian Society, Worcester, Mass.

74. Joseph Curtis to daughter Josephine, September 4, 1864, Curtis Family Letters, Clements Library, University of Michigan. For other examples of fathers' advice to daughters see, Lavius Hyde to daughter Sarah, September 1, 1851, October, 21, 1851, Bradley-Hyde Family Papers, Schlesinger Library, Radcliffe College; John Glen King to daughter Augusta, December 1837, Box 2, Ellis Gray Loring Collection, Schlesinger Library, Radcliffe College; Abbott Lawrence to daughter Anna, April 18, 1841, Box 1, Rotch-Lawrence Family Papers, Mass. Hist. Soc.

75. Jessie Phelps Journal, October 27, 1889, Jessie Phelps Papers, Mich. Hist. Coll.

76. For other examples, see Elizabeth Gurney Taylor Diary, December 29, 1856, Box 4, Taylor Family Papers, Mich. Hist. Coll.; Jane Agnes Stewart, *I Have Recalled: A Pen-Panorama of a Life* (Toledo, Ohio, 1938), 16.

77. Eleazer Lindsley to James Ford, February 8, 1806, Lindsley Family Papers, Clements Library, University of Michigan. For a good overview of American courtship, see Ellen K. Rothman, *Hands and Hearts: A History of Courtship in America* (New York, 1984).

78. The meaning of a mother's advice was also ambiguous. In her survey of the history of American courtship, Ellen K. Rothman argues that during the first two-thirds of the nineteenth century, young women did not share the details of their relations with men with their mothers. Rothman suggests that this situation changed in the decades after the Civil War, but that the tendency to seek maternal advice about love and marriage was confined to a brief period at the end of the century. See Rothman, *Hands and Hearts*, 218–19, 221–23.

79. Harriet Amelia Johnson Diary, 1853, Henry Parker Smith Papers, Mich. Hist. Coll.

80. Henry Parker Smith Diary, July 17, 1853, Henry Parker Smith Papers, Mich. Hist. Coll.

81. Emma Regal to father Eli Regal, November 29, 1868, Regal Family Papers, Mich. Hist. Coll.

82. Susan B. (Coolidge) Leyman, "My Early Home" (unpublished MS, 1893), 21–22, Mass. Hist. Soc.; Elizabeth Douglas Hall, "Reminiscences of Elizabeth Douglas Hall as told to Ethel H. Bonner" (unpublished MS, 1959), 1–2, Mich. Hist. Coll.

83. Elta May Talcott Luther, "My Memoirs" (unpublished MS, 1949), 19–20, Mich. Hist. Coll.

84. For other examples of such recollections, see Ward, *The Way Things Were*, 12–13; Eunice Tripler, *Some Notes on Her Personal Recollections* (New York, 1910), 70–71; Helen Dunn Gates, *A Consecrated Life: A Sketch of the Life and Labors of Rev. Ransom Dunn, D.D., 1818–1900* (Boston, 1901), passim; Mary L. Ninde, *William Xavier Ninde: A Memorial by His Daughter* (New York, 1902), passim; Uldene Rudd Leroy, *Six on an Island: Childhood Memories From Lake Huron* (New York, 1956), passim. The foregoing narratives are available in the Mich. Hist. Coll.

85. Abijah Adams to daughter Maryanne, September 19, 1808, Abijah Adams letter, Schlesinger Library, Radcliffe College. For other examples, see Eleazer Lindsley to daughter Jerusha Lindsley, August 23–31, 1807, Lindlsey Family Papers, Clements Library, University of Michigan; James Draper to daughter Sophia, May 31, 1840, Box 1, Draper-Rice Family Papers, American Antiquarian Society, Worcester, Mass.; Abbott Lawrence to daughter Anna, April 18, 1841, Box 1, Rotch-Lawrence Family Papers, Massachusetts Historical Society, Boston, Mass.; Ellis Gray Loring to daughter Anna, April 13, 1852, Box 1, Ellis Gray Loring Collection, Schlesinger Library, Radcliffe College.

86. *The Daughter's Own Book; or, Practical Hints from a Father to His Daughter* (Boston, 1833), 9–10.

87. See E. Douglas Branch, *The Sentimental Years, 1836–1860* (New York, 1934), 207.

88. Quoted ibid., 205–6.

89. On daughters as middle-class status symbols, see Kett, *Rites of Passage*, 138. On the reasons for female high school attendance, see Maris A. Vinovskis and Richard M. Bernard, "Beyond Catharine Beecher: Female Education in the Antebellum Period," *Signs* 3 (1978): 865.

90. Mary Thomas Diary, June 27, 1873, quoted in Jane H. Hunter, "Inscribing the Self in the Heart of the Family: Diaries and Girlhood in Late Victorian America," *American Quarterly* 44 (March 1992): 61.

91. William Dean Howells, *The Rise of Silas Lapham* (Boston, 1885; reprint ed., New York, 1991). See also Herbert Santley, "Marriage," *Lippincott's Magazine* (Philadelphia) 8 (October 1871): 401; Paul C. J. Bourget, *Outre-mer* (London,

1895), Bourget quoted in Arthur W. Calhoun, *A Social History of American Family Life from Colonial Times to the Present* (New York, 1917), 3:158.

Conclusion: Beyond Breadwinning

1. The theme of paternal displacement by mothers dominates the discussion of nineteenth-century parenthood. For a recent statement, see John R. Gillis, *A World of Their Own Making: Myth, Ritual, and the Quest for Family Values* (New York, 1996).

2. I recognize that many family documents, especially letters, are biased toward expressions of positive emotion. For a discussion of this problem, see Chapter 6, n18.

3. On the pervasive application of domestic rhetoric in politics, see George B. Forgie, *Patricide in the House Divided: A Psychological Interpretation of Lincoln and His Age* (New York, 1979). One need not accept Forgie's Freudian thesis that a loosely defined "post-heroic" generation of sons was historically fated to work out Oedipal conflicts with the "fathers" of the Revolution to recognize the truth of his claims about the political salience of domestic rhetoric in the Civil War era.

4. Reid Mitchell, *The Vacant Chair: The Northern Soldier Leaves Home* (New York, 1993), 31. Why soldiers fought has been an abiding concern of Civil War historians for more than four decades, beginning with the work of Bell Irvin Wiley. The most recent treatment is James M. McPherson, *For Cause and Comrades* (New York, 1997).

5. Judson L. Austin to his wife, undated fragment, probably written in spring 1863, Austin Papers, Box 1, Folder 9, Ness Collection, Bentley Historical Library, University of Michigan.

6. J. G. Clark, *The Children of the Battle Field* (Philadelphia, 1864). Many Civil War songs, with such titles as "Dear Mother I've Come Home to Die" and "Just Before the Battle Mother," sentimentalize maternal affection.

7. Cited in Mitchell, *Vacant Chair*, 51–52.

8. Phillip Shaw Paludan, *A People's Contest: The Union and Civil War, 1861–1865* (New York, 1988), 295; William S. McFeely, *Grant: A Biography* (New York, 1981), 400–403, 491, quote at 63.

9. For an in-depth discussion of this topic, see Stephen M. Frank, "'Rendering Aid and Comfort': Images of Fatherhood in the Letters of Civil War Soldiers from Massachusetts and Michigan," *Journal of Social History* 26 (fall 1992): 5–31.

10. Eli A. Griffin to his wife, June 30, 1863 and January 29, 1863, Griffin Papers, Mich. Hist. Coll.

11. George Trowbridge to his wife, Lebbie, January 3, 1864, December 27, 1863, and September 13, 1864, Trowbridge Papers, Boxes 25 and 26, Schoff Collection,

Clements Library, University of Michigan. See also Trowbridge to his wife, Lebbie, November 27, 1863, January 3, 1864, January 12, 1864, January 28, 1864, February 11, 1864, February 13, 1864, April 30, 1864, and April 15, 1864.

12. A useful synthesis of this revisionist trend is J. Matthew Gallman, *The North Fights the Civil War: The Home Front* (Chicago, 1994).

13. See Stuart McConnell, *Glorious Contentment: The Grand Army of the Republic, 1865–1900* (Chapel Hill, N.C., 1992).

14. On the reconceptualization of the war, see Gerald F. Linderman, *Embattled Courage: The Experience of Combat in the American Civil War* (New York, 1987), 266–97.

15. Megan J. McClintock, "Civil War Pensions and the Reconstruction of Union Families," *Journal of American History* 83 (1996): 456–80.

Note on Method and Sources

To treat the large subject of nineteenth-century fatherhood in as few pages as I have done suggests that I have used sources selectively, which I take this opportunity to acknowledge. The personal documents of 192 fathers and their families constitute the empirical core of this study. I cannot say that this compilation of primary source material represents a scientific sample of households in the nineteenth-century American North, or even of families in the burgeoning middle ranks of society, with whose experience I was chiefly concerned. The documents do, however, shed light on the father's role in a varied universe of white, middle-class families. The time encompassed by the documents spans the nineteenth century, but is concentrated in the years between 1800 and 1879. The birth dates of the study's principal subjects were:

1760–1779 (11)
1780–1799 (28)
1800–1819 (44)
1820–1839 (46)
1840–1859 (27)
1860–1879 (25)
1880–1899 (11)

Nearly half the subjects (47%) were born in the four decades between 1800 and 1840. A man born in 1800 who became a father at age 30, would, if he lived to age 65, have experienced the unfolding meaning of fatherhood through the time of the Civil War. A man born in 1840 could have occupied the social role of father to the end of the century.

In terms of religion and ethnicity, the families studied were overwhelmingly white, Protestant, and native-born. In terms of place of residence, the vast majority of subjects (169) lived in New England and the Midwest, with the rest scattered across the map from New Jersey to Oregon. The states with the largest number of families represented are Michigan, with 62 families, and Massachusetts, with 61. Other states with more than 10 families represented include New York and Vermont, both with 11, and Ohio, with 12. Most of the families studied lived in predominantly rural areas, towns, and small cities—places like Princeton, Massachusetts, and Schoolcraft, Michigan. Only 36 families lived in the major metropolitan areas of Boston, Chicago, Detroit, New York City, or Philadelphia, reflecting the fact that the United States had not yet become an urban society.

Household heads in these families made their living predominantly as farmers (54), shopkeepers (24), ministers (17), lawyers (14), and physicians (10). The sample includes men with a wide range of callings, however, from peddler and day laborer to a state Supreme Court judge and a university professor. Occupations in which at least 10 household heads are represented include, besides those mentioned above: businessman (11), educator (10), and laborer (10). Other occupations represented include: architect, banker, blacksmith, civil engineer, cobbler, fisherman, grist mill operator, innkeeper, journalist, military officer, miner, politician, printer, railroad engineer, sea captain, ship chandler, stonemason, surveyor, tailor, and teamster.

Reviewing biographical data that I collected on these families, and weighing such rough measures of wealth as a father's occupation, home ownership, and amount of children's education, I judged that half the families (97 of 192) were "middle class." This is an admittedly elastic and somewhat impressionistic category. It contains some families whose economic position seemed secure and others in which fathers struggled under a large burden of debt to maintain a home (usually a farm) and their family's middle-class respectability. Another 78 families (40.6%) I considered upper middle class, and a few of these were among the elite.

I have cited in the text all the primary sources from which I quote, as well as those that offer corroboration for a particular line of argument. The notes also include references to many of the secondary sources on which I have relied, but I wish to name here a few of those works I have found most useful, together with some in which the reader will find viewpoints that differ from my own.

The study of fatherhood remains a nascent field in the historical profession. What we know about its history owes largely to the pioneering work of a handful of scholars. The first book-length study of American fatherhood and the starting point for all future historical investigation is Robert L. Griswold, *Fatherhood in America: A History* (New York, 1993). Griswold's work, which concentrates on twentieth-century experience, was preceded by a number of path-breaking essays, which sketched the overall trajectory of American fatherhood from colonial times to the present and established the prevailing interpretive paradigm—that of decline in the father's role over time. This interpretation, which highlights the displacement of fathers by mothers as primary parents, was first developed in John Demos's seminal essay, "The Changing Faces of Fatherhood: A New Exploration in American Family History," in *Father and Child: Developmental and Clinical Perspectives*, ed. Stanley H. Cath, Alan R. Gurwitt, and John Munder Ross (Boston, 1982); reprinted in Demos, *Past, Present, and Personal: The Family and the Life Course in American History* (New York, 1986). Demos's view received confirmation in E. Anthony Rotundo, "American Fatherhood: A Historical Perspective," *American Behavioral Scientist* 29 (1985).

The future of nineteenth-century fatherhood historiography hinges, in part, on the outcome of a lively debate about the meaning of the "separate spheres" model and the extent to which heightened sex-role stereotyping in the nineteenth century permitted, or prevented, interaction across the gender divide. Carroll Smith-Rosenberg, "The Female World of Love and Ritual: Relations Between Women in Nineteenth-Century America," *Signs* 1 (1975), and Nancy F. Cott, *The Bonds of Womanhood: "Woman's Sphere" in New England, 1780–1835* (New Haven, Conn., 1977), are classic statements of the older view that the nineteenth-century gender system sharply circumscribed the interaction of men and women. A revised interpretation, emphasizing interdependence, is convincingly advanced in Nancy Grey Osterud, *Bonds of Community: The Lives of Farm Women in Nineteenth-Century New York* (Ithaca, N.Y., 1991). A fascinating study of the common ground afforded by courtship and romance is Karen Lystra, *Searching the Heart: Women, Men, and Romantic Love in Nineteenth-Century America* (New York, 1989). Ellen K. Rothman, *Hands and Hearts: A History of Courtship in America* (New York, 1984), also offers insight into this topic.

A vast literature on women and the family contains much useful interpretation of the father's role. While it seems dubious to highlight a single volume, Carl N. Degler's *At Odds: Women and the Family in America from the Revolution to the Present* (New York, 1980) is a magisterial work, full of pertinent insights. For a valuable overview of scholarship through the mid-1980s on women and the family in colonial America and the early republic, see Mary Beth Norton, "The Evolution of White Women's Experience in Early America," *American Historical Review* 89 (June 1984).

We have no single study of the domestic experience of colonial fathers, but the large amount of literature on colonial family life can be gleaned for valuable insights. Particularly useful for the New England experience are: Edmund S. Morgan, *The Puritan Family: Religion and Domestic Relations in Seventeenth-Century New England* (New York, 1944; rev. ed. 1966); John Demos, *A Little Commonwealth: Family Life in Plymouth Colony* (New York, 1970); and Laurel Thatcher Ulrich, *Good Wives: Image and Reality in the Lives of Women in Northern New England, 1650–1750* (New York, 1982). Philip G. Greven's *Four Generations: Population, Land, and Family in Colonial Andover, Massachusetts* (Ithaca, N.Y., 1970) advances a controversial thesis on the impact of growing land scarcity on patriarchal power. Greven's *The Protestant Temperament: Patterns of Child-Rearing, Religious Experience, and the Self in Early America* (New York, 1977) offers a masterly if somewhat static interpretation of the impact of religion on parenting. His more recent work, *Spare the Child: The Religious Roots of Punishment and the Psychological Impact of Physical Abuse* (New York, 1991), paints an unduly harsh picture of child-rearing practices in the past and present. For an intriguing argument that the father's primacy began to erode as early as the mid–seventeenth century, see Gerald F. Moran and Maris A. Vinovskis, *Religion, Family, and the Life Course: Explorations in the Social History of Early America* (Ann Arbor, Mich., 1992).

The meaning of, and reasons for, changes in household size and family composition—demographic variables with important implications for fatherhood—are fiercely debated by historical demographers. For a recent authoritative statement on this topic, see Steven Ruggles, "The Transformation of American Family Structure," *American Historical Review* 99 (February 1994). The impact of divorce on family life in the late nineteenth and early twentieth centuries has attracted considerable scholarly attention as well. Two especially valuable monographs are Robert L. Griswold, *Family and Divorce in California, 1850–1890: Victorian Illusions and Everyday Realities* (Albany, N.Y., 1982), and Elaine Tyler May, *Great Expectations: Marriage and Divorce in Post-Victorian America* (Chicago, 1980). Changing custody practices and other legal constructions of the father's role are treated in a growing body of work on the history of family law. Two especially valuable studies are Michael Grossberg, *Governing the Hearth: Law and the Family in Nineteenth-Century America* (Chapel Hill, N.C., 1985), and Mary Ann Mason, *From Father's Property to Children's Rights: The History of Child Custody in the United States* (New York, 1994).

Another demographic variable relevant to parenting is the prevalence of child morbidity and mortality. On this subject, see Samuel H. Preston and Michael R. Haines, *Fatal Years: Child Mortality in Late Nineteenth-Century America* (Princeton, 1991). For a convincing study examining the impact of high infant mortality rates on parents' willingness to bond with their children, see Linda A. Pollock, *Forgotten Children: Parent-Child Relations from 1500 to 1900* (Cambridge, 1983).

A large body of scholarship analyzes Victorian advice literature. Anne L. Kuhn, *The Mother's Role in Childhood Education: New England Concepts, 1830–1860* (New Haven, Conn., 1947), remains a reliable, and in many ways the best, introduction to antebellum parenting ideology. Ruth H. Bloch's seminal essay, "American Feminine Ideals in Transition: The Rise of the Moral Mother, 1785–1815," *Feminist Studies* 4 (1978), offers a perceptive overview of changing attitudes toward women and maternal care. Other valuable studies on this topic include: Jan Lewis, "Mother's Love: The Construction of an Emotion in Nineteenth-Century America," in *Social History and Issues in Human Consciousness*, ed. Andrew E. Barnes and Peter N. Stearns (New York, 1989); Mary P. Ryan, *The Empire of the Mother: American Writing about Domesticity, 1830–1860* (New York, 1982); and Bernard Wishy, *The Child and the Republic: The Dawn of Modern American Child Nurture* (Philadelphia, 1968).

The history of childhood, no less than changing attitudes toward mothers, has obvious relevance to the study of fatherhood. A useful introduction to this extensive literature is Joseph M. Hawes and N. Ray Hiner, *American Childhood: A Research Guide and Historical Handbook* (Westport, Conn., 1985). Joseph F. Kett's classic study of adolescence, *Rites of Passage: Adolescence in America, 1790 to the Present* (New York, 1977), is full of fascinating insight. More specialized studies of the experience of childhood in particular times and places are too numerous to mention, but a useful sampling of recent work can be found in *Small Worlds: Children and Adolescents in America*, ed. Elliott West and Paula Petrik (Lawrence, Kans., 1992). West's *Growing Up with the Country: Childhood on the Far Western Frontier* (Albuquerque, N.Mex., 1989) is a model of lucid historical scholarship. A fascinating, if controversial, account of American childhood history by a sociologist is Viviana Zelizer, *Pricing the Priceless Child: The Changing Social Value of Children* (New York, 1985).

A lively debate over the origins and rise of the common-school system has obvious pertinence to the history of parent-child relations in the nineteenth century. For a reliable introduction to this literature, see Maris A. Vinovskis, *Education, Society, and Economic Opportunity: Some Historical Perspectives* (New Haven, Conn., 1995). See also Carl F. Kaestle, *Pillars of the Republic: Common Schools and American Society, 1780–1860* (New York, 1983).

The impact of the so-called market revolution on nineteenth-century society and, by implication, on family life, is a topic of controversy. For a useful historiographic discussion, see Sean Wilentz, "Society, Politics, and the Market Revolution, 1815–1848," in *The New American History*, ed. Eric Foner (Philadelphia, 1990). Contrasting interpretations of the impact of capitalist transformation on American society are offered by Charles Sellers, *The Market Revolution: Jacksonian America, 1815–1846* (New York, 1991) and Daniel Feller, *The Jacksonian Promise: America, 1815–1840* (Baltimore, 1995). A fascinating study of the cultural anxiety inspired by the expansion of the marketplace is Karen Halttunen, *Confidence Men and Painted Women: A Study of Middle-Class Culture in America, 1830–1870* (New Haven, Conn., 1982).

Nineteenth-century masculinity, the topic of a rapidly expanding literature, is being investigated from a number of interesting angles. The required introduction to the study of middle-class manhood is E. Anthony Rotundo, *American Manhood: Transformations in Masculinity from the Revolution to the Modern Era* (New York, 1993). Rotundo was inspired by Charles E. Rosenberg's influential essay, "Sexuality, Class, and Role in 19th-Century America," *American Quarterly* 25 (1973). Other pioneering texts with continued relevance are Peter N. Stearns, *Be a Man! Males in Modern Society* (2d ed., New York, 1990) and Peter Gabriel Filene, *Him/Her/Self: Sex Roles in Modern America* (2d ed., Baltimore, 1986). Rotundo's essay "Learning About

Manhood: Gender Ideals and the Middle-Class Family in Nineteenth-Century America," in *Middle-Class Masculinity in Britain and America, 1800–1940,* ed. J. A. Mangan and James Walvin (New York, 1987), is a useful supplement to his full-length work.

Path-breaking essays by Rotundo and other leading scholars in the field are also collected in *Meanings for Manhood: Constructions of Masculinity in Victorian America,* ed. Mark C. Carnes and Clyde Griffen (Chicago, 1990). Particularly salient to fatherhood's history is Margaret Marsh's essay in this collection, "Suburban Men and Masculine Domesticity, 1870–1915," which foreshadows the argument in her book *Suburban Lives* (Rutgers, N.J., 1990). Carnes's own volume on fraternal ritual, *Secret Ritual and Manhood in Victorian America* (New Haven, Conn., 1989) should be read alongside Mary Ann Clawson, *Constructing Brotherhood: Class, Gender, and Fraternalism* (Princeton, 1989). Other assessments of nineteenth-century manhood that offer valuable insight into how men behaved when they left their homes and families to work or play include: David Leverenz, *Manhood and the American Renaissance* (Ithaca, N.Y., 1989); Elliott J. Gorn, *The Manly Art: Bare-Knuckle Prize Fighting in America* (Ithaca, N.Y., 1986), and Ted Ownby, *Subduing Satan: Religion, Recreation, and Manhood in the Rural South, 1865–1920* (Chapel Hill, N.C., 1990).

An extensive social science literature affords valuable theoretical perspectives on masculinity and fatherhood. Two works by anthropologists that I found particularly thought provoking are David D. Gilmore, *Manhood in the Making: Cultural Concepts of Masculinity* (New Haven, Conn., 1990), and David Schneider, *American Kinship* (2d ed., Chicago, 1980). A fascinating ethnography of family life among Midwestern farmers is Sonya Salamon, *Prairie Patrimony: Family, Farming, and Community in the Midwest* (Chapel Hill, N.C., 1992). Insight into the social psychology of fatherhood can be gained from John Snarey's careful longitudinal study, *How Fathers Care for the Next Generation: A Four-Decade Study* (Cambridge, Mass., 1993). Other works by social scientists that merit study are: Ross D. Parke, *Fathers* (Cambridge, Mass., 1981), and essays by Michael E. Lamb and others collected in *The Role of the Father in Child Development,* ed. Michael E. Lamb, 2d ed. (New York, 1981). A wonderfully perceptive discussion of masculine psychology, with keen insight into fatherhood, is Daniel J. Levinson, *The Sea-*

sons of a Man's Life (New York, 1978). Eventually, any historical investigator with an interest in social theory must come to terms with Talcott Parsons's functionalist family sociology, elaborated in his classic text *Family, Socialization, and Interaction Process* (Glencoe, Ill., 1955).

A more comprehensive bibliography of works consulted in the preparation of this book can be found in Stephen M. Frank, "Life with Father: Parenthood and Masculinity in the Nineteenth-Century American North" (Ph.D. diss., University of Michigan, 1995).

Index

Library of Congress Cataloging-in-Publication Data

Frank, Stephen M., 1951—
    Life with father : parenthood and masculinity in the nineteenth-century
American North / Stephen M. Frank.
        p.   cm. — (Gender relations in the American experience)
    Includes bibliographical references (p.   ) and index.
    ISBN 0-8018-5855-0
    1. Father and child—United States—History—19th century. 2. Fathers—
United States—History—19th century. 3. Family—United States—History—
19th century. 4. Fatherhood—Religious aspects. I. Title. II. Series.
HQ756.F7   1998
306.874'2—dc21   97-50105
                                                              CIP